NANNY WOOD
From Washington Belle to Portland's Grande Dame

Nanny Wood in 1872 when she was 17 years old.
Courtesy of J. Kirkham and Patricia Corbin Johns.

NANNY WOOD

*From Washington Belle to
Portland's Grande Dame*

Philip W. Leon

HERITAGE BOOKS
2007

HERITAGE BOOKS
AN IMPRINT OF HERITAGE BOOKS, INC.

Books, CDs, and more – Worldwide

For our listing of thousands of titles see our website
at
www.HeritageBooks.com

Published 2007 by
HERITAGE BOOKS, INC.
Publishing Division
65 East Main Street
Westminster, Maryland 21157-5026

Copyright © 2003 Philip W. Leon

Other books by the author:
Sir William Osler; Medical Humanist

Designed by Dianna Rich and set in Classic Garamond type

Cover: Edmund C. Tarbell, *Portrait of a Woman in White*, ca. 1885-90
Courtesy of the Spanierman Galleries, LLC, New York City

This book was made possible by a grant from The Citadel Foundation.

All rights reserved. No part of this book may be reproduced or transmitted in any form or by any means, electronic or mechanical, including photocopying, recording or by any information storage and retrieval system without written permission from the author, except for the inclusion of brief quotations in a review.

International Standard Book Number: 978-0-7884-2440-8

"Always there hung about her an impalpable but imperishable dignity. She was and will remain our only grande dame."

—Barbara Bartlett Hartwell
Portland, 1942

*To John Gibbon Wood
and
John Gray Foster Moale*

CONTENTS

Illustrations	xi
Preface	xiii
Acknowledgments	xvii

PART ONE: HER LIFE

CHAPTER I	WAR	3
CHAPTER II	ADOLESCENCE	25
CHAPTER III	LOVE	33
CHAPTER IV	NEWLYWEDS	57
CHAPTER V	WEST POINT	85
CHAPTER VI	PORTLAND	101
CHAPTER VII	INFIDELITY	129

PART TWO: HER TIMES

CHAPTER VIII	PATRIOTS	159
CHAPTER IX	PHYSICIANS	183
CHAPTER X	PAINTERS AND SCULPTORS	193
APPENDIX I	THE WOOD HOUSEHOLD	215
APPENDIX II	NANNY'S PORTLAND GARDEN	225
WORKS CITED		235
INDEX		249

ILLUSTRATIONS

Edmund C. Tarbell, *Portrait of a Woman in White*   cover

1.	Nanny Wood in 1872, age 17	*frontispiece*
2.	The Officers' Quarters at Fort Sumter	8
3.	Good-By to Fort Sumter	10
4.	A Secessionist Showing Her Colors	16
5.	Nanny in 1874, age 19	29
6.	C.E.S. Wood as a West Point cadet	35
7.	Nanny visiting West Point, 1874	38
8.	Union Pacific train, 1878	63
9.	Chief Joseph	109
10.	Nanny about 1904, Portland's grande dame	131
11.	Nanny and C.E.S. Wood in 1917	138

PREFACE

Nanny Moale Smith Wood (1855-1933) led an exciting life of social privilege, adventure, and controversy. Although she wrote no memorable literature, championed neither social nor political causes, created no enduring works of art, she stood in the center of all these fields of endeavor in the late nineteenth and early twentieth centuries. Her life is emblematic of the status of most women of that time who often had little choice but to stand by silently, while the men in their lives were free to make fulfilling and noteworthy contributions to American history in literature, medicine, law, politics, finance, art, and the military.

Part one, Her Life, relates her story as a child who witnessed combat during the Civil War, as a headstrong adolescent, as a flirtatious Washington belle, and as wife and mother in Portland, Oregon. Literally on her deathbed, Nanny talked discursively about her life, recalling memorable events in no order. Her nurse and family friend, Dean Fischer, wrote down these disjointed recollections, often guessing at the spelling of proper names. Nanny's children and grandchildren preserved these memories, and some years later Nanny's grandson John Gibbon Wood attempted to put them in some semblance of order, an impossible task because they do not form a seamless narrative; her recollections are fraught with errors, inconsistencies, and large gaps in chronology.

My task as Nanny's biographer was to untangle and clarify what she reveals about herself in her memoirs and to discover additional material to supply dimension to this interesting woman's life. From disparate sources there emerged the picture of a woman of substance and character, a complex mix of her heritage as a member of one of America's most distinguished families and her own inner pluck and self-possession developed through adversity. While Nanny refused to discuss her husband's frequent infidelities and his final flight from their marriage with his mistress, much is known of their marital situation from other sources. Any details of Nanny's life not otherwise attributed come from her incomplete memoirs.

Part two, Her Times, explores her relationship with influential and powerful leaders of American society. Her ancestors on both sides participated in the establishment of America. Her uncles played significant roles in the American Civil War. Extending just a step or two laterally to her cousins, one finds relatives of equal prominence in the settlement of the West following the Civil War.

Together, the two parts of this book seek to reveal her links to history and the place of women in her time. Her history contains some remarkable events:

One of Nanny's great-grandfathers owned the land upon which the city of Baltimore was built. He was also a personal friend of George Washington and served valiantly in the Revolutionary War and the War of 1812.

Her other great-grandfather influenced medical education in America by founding the medical colleges at Dartmouth, Yale, Bowdoin, and the University of Vermont.

Two of her relatives who were physicians treated two Presidents of the United States.

During the Civil War two of her relatives were at Fort Sumter when the Civil War began, and three were at Appomattox when the war ended. Two of her uncles became general officers on the Union side, while two others became officers in the Confederacy. One of her uncles drafted the terms of surrender signed by Grant and Lee at Appomattox.

Three of her relatives had United States Navy ships named after them.

Several uncles were United States Representatives to Congress, Senators, and cabinet officers.

Her father-in-law was the first surgeon general of the United States Navy.

A cousin died riding next to George Armstrong Custer as they swept into Chief Black Kettle's camp in the Plains Indians wars. This cousin was the grandson of Alexander Hamilton, George Washington's trusted aide and first Secretary of the Treasury.

A cousin became president of the Wells Fargo Company and United States ambassador to the Court of St. James's.

Nanny was closely related to Elizabeth Ann Seton, the first American-born saint.

She was a cousin of the designer Louis Comfort Tiffany.

In Portland, Nanny and her husband formed friendships with many famous people of the day, and together they entertained many notable late nineteenth and early twentieth-century figures: sculptors Olin Warner and Phimister Proctor; painters Childe Hassam, Albert Pinkham Ryder, George de Forest Brush, and J. Alden Weir; and writer Mark Twain. Later Wood developed close friendships with John Steinbeck; poets Robinson Jeffers and William Rose Benét; flamboyant lawyer Clarence Darrow; champion of women's rights Emma Goldman; writer and social activist Lincoln Steffens; Socialist John Reed (who lies buried next to Lenin in the Kremlin); and photographer Ansel Adams.

One of Nanny's daughters, Nan Wood Honeyman, became the first woman elected to Congress from the state of Oregon, an indication of the changes that took place in society during Nanny's lifetime.

Nanny Moale Smith Wood lived in the most exciting years of the American experience. When she was born, slavery was legal in the United States. When she was a married woman and a mother, she could not vote. When she died in 1933, Adolf Hitler was consolidating his power. Against the backdrop of history, her personal story shows a woman dealing stoically with her husband's frequent infidelities, facing the deaths of two children, making civic and social contributions to Portland, and finding contentment at the end of a rich and full life.

ACKNOWLEDGMENTS

IN WRITING THIS LIFE of Nanny Moale Smith Wood (1855–1933), I have had the advantage of the repository of memory of her relatives as well as archival records from many public and university libraries, galleries, museums, churches, and other institutions.

To John Gibbon Wood and his wife Betty of San Mateo, California, I am most indebted. After reading about the friendship of his grandfather Charles Erskine Scott Wood and Mark Twain in my book *Mark Twain and West Point* (1996), he wrote to me to say that while much had been written about his grandfather, his grandmother had not received the same attention and that she was a "pretty spunky gal in her own right." John Wood was correct on both points, and it is he who began the chain of events leading to this book.

Other descendants with whom I corresponded and received both information and encouragement are Nanny's grandchildren Marian Wood Kolisch and Katherine "Tash" Smith Livingston of Portland where Nanny and Wood lived most of their married life. Marian Wood Kolisch took me on a tour of places in Portland where Nanny used to live; she granted permission to quote portions of an important letter from her grandfather to her father Berwick Bruce Wood; and she furnished several photographs. Great-grandchildren who contributed to this book are Robert Bruce Livingston and Diana Wood, both of Portland, and Nancy Wood Robinson von Gimbut of Danville, California. Nancy von Gimbut sent me items not available in public sources: Nanny's favorite recipes and menus, prescriptions of medications for Nanny and her family from around 1900, and unpublished letters from artist Childe Hassam. Nanny's great-great-grandson, Christopher R. Kosel of Faribault, Minnesota, sent copies of entries in

Nanny's Bible, written by her, recording births and deaths of her famous relatives. Nanny's great-grandson Kirk Johns and his wife Patty of Bainbridge Island, Washington, became faithful correspondents, furnishing me with genealogical information, family lore from one of Nanny's private journals, and other items that I would not otherwise have seen.

Lt. Col. (Ret.) John Gray Foster Moale of Melbourne, Florida, and his son John Gray Foster Moale III of Duluth, Georgia, generously granted interviews, and John Moale III and his wife Jean Ann provided photographs, genealogies, and family records. Robert and Eileen Bird of Manlius, New York, also provided information about the Moale family; Eileen Bird is a direct descendant of Brig. Gen. Edward Moale, Nanny's uncle.

Interestingly, cousins John Gibbon Wood and John Gray Foster Moale were named for two of Nanny's uncles—each married to sisters of Nanny's mother—who were famous major generals in the United States Army both during and after the Civil War. My correspondents, the current John Wood and John Moale, at the time of this writing both eighty-two years old, born within three months of each other, living on opposite coasts, have never met; ironically, they both attended the New Mexico Military Institute as young men. Now, thanks to this project that allowed me to serve as intermediary, they have written, talked, and exchanged family photographs and other memorabilia. Such is the joy of research.

Every academician knows the value of reference librarians, and my thanks are due to the following on the east coast: Lee Lears, of the Enoch Pratt Free Library in Baltimore for assistance with city directories and histories of the Moales of Baltimore; Ruth Sweet, of the Troy (New York) Public Library for information relating to the Gould family who, by marrying into Nanny's family, caused her much misery; Sarah Palmer, of the Hyattsville (Maryland) Public Library for historical records about the Pattersons, Nanny's wealthy relatives in the Washington–Baltimore region; Jerry McCoy, of the Washingtoniana Collection, Martin Luther King Jr. Memorial Library,

ACKNOWLEDGMENTS

Washington, DC, for city directories and histories of residences in nineteenth-century Washington; and Debbe Causey of the interlibrary loan department of the Daniel Library at The Citadel.

On the west coast, I am grateful to Mitzi Kanbara, of the San Francisco Public Library for information about Nanny's influential banking relatives, the McLane family; Kathryn Samuelson of River View Cemetery in Portland for escorting me to Nanny's grave site and making a rubbing of her marker; Bruce Guenther and Debra Royer of the Portland Art Museum, founded by C.E.S. Wood, for granting permission to publish archival material, and Steve Conover for showing me the museum's paintings by Wood, Childe Hassam, J. Alden Weir, and Albert Pinkham Ryder. I also want to thank Robert Craddock of the Pacific Northwest College of Art for information about the influence of these artists in the Portland area. Shawna Gandy, manuscripts associate at the Oregon History Center, home of the Oregon Historical Society, led me to many newspaper articles concerning Nanny and her family. I am also grateful to the reference staff of the Central Library, Multnomah County Library system. At the Oregon Episcopal School in Portland, Lynn Regelin provided material concerning St. Helen's Hall school for girls. Mary Kline Rose of Vancouver, Washington, a Northwest maritime and military historian, furnished materials from her files dealing with young Erskine's time he spent with Chief Joseph of the Nez Perce. Also in Portland, Dr. J. Dudley Weaver and his wife Mary, and Tom and Pauline Reimers extended their hospitality during my research trip there.

In Poulsbo, Washington, near Seattle, Phimister Proctor "Sandy" Church, grandson of the Woods' sculptor friend Alexander Phimister Proctor, supplied me with information about his famous grandfather. Church is the curator of the A. Phimister Proctor Museum. Nancy Aldrich of Dublin, New Hampshire, furnished material dealing with her grandfather, Impressionist artist George de Forest Brush; Jim Vadeboncoeur, graphic art dealer of Palo Alto, California, also provided material on Brush.

Nanny's widowed mother married Nathan Smith Lincoln, M.D., a cousin of her first husband. During and after the Civil War, Dr. Lincoln was an important surgeon on the staff of Providence Hospital, in Washington, founded by the Daughters of Charity, led by Saint Elizabeth Ann Seton, to whom Nanny was related. For information about his service there I wish to thank Sister Kathleen Shannon, DC, the archivist for Providence Hospital.

At the Huntington Library in San Marino, California, Romaine Ahlstrom, Peter Blodgett, Susi Krasnoo, Mona Noureldin, Anne Mar, and Robert Ritchie narrowed my search for material in the vast C.E.S. Wood collection and granted permission to quote from correspondence between Nanny and Wood during their courtship as well as during their later separation.

I received much kindness and help when I visited the Green Spring Valley, west of Baltimore, where the Moale family owned several vast estates in the eighteenth and nineteenth centuries. Searching tombstones and grave markers in the old cemetery at St. Thomas' Church in the Garrison Forest of Green Spring Valley yielded information that clarified relationships and dates. At St. Thomas' Church, my special thanks are due to the Rev. William P. Baxter, Jr., rector, for relating to me the story of the stained glass window designed and executed by Nanny's relative Louis Comfort Tiffany; Stuart Stewart, former chief warden, for giving me a copy of the church's history; and Ann A. Shutt, parish secretary, for allowing me to roam freely about the grounds and take many photographs and for answering correspondence subsequent to my visit. Albert L. Cummings, current owner of Nanny's family estate Atamasco in the Green Spring Valley, hospitably gave me a tour of the buildings and grounds.

I also want to thank the Rev. Thomas L. Culbertson, Ph.D., rector of Emmanuel Episcopal Church in Baltimore for kindly obtaining the marriage records of Nanny Moale Smith and Charles Erskine Scott Wood.

ACKNOWLEDGMENTS

When Nanny was ten years old, her mother Ann Moale Smith Lincoln was suffering from tuberculosis, so the two of them relocated from Washington, DC, to the more salubrious climate at Aiken, South Carolina. For information about the colony of healing hotels popular there in the nineteenth century, I am indebted to my colleague Tony N. Redd, Ph.D.; Melisa Hann, chief desk editor of the Aiken *Standard*; and Allen Riddick of the Aiken County Historical Society.

For information concerning the exciting cross-country journey by railroad of the newly married Nanny and Wood, I want to thank Mark Davis, a regional director of public relations with the Union Pacific Railroad, and Don Snoddy, the historian for the Union Pacific in Omaha, Nebraska. From them I obtained information about routes, typical lengths of journeys on sections of the railroad and availability of food for travelers. The Union Pacific Railroad also provided a photograph of the type train that Nanny and Wood took on their honeymoon.

Shortly after Nanny's eldest son Erskine graduated from Harvard, he contracted tuberculosis, so Nanny accompanied him to a famous sanitarium in Nordrach, Germany, in the Black Forest. Research is often a collaborative effort, and I am indebted to all those who helped piece together the story of Nanny's trip to Germany. My good friend and fellow member of the American Osler Society, Claus Pierach, M.D., and his wife Rosemarie of St. Paul, Minnesota, enthusiastically became partners in my quest for information about this clinic. They translated my queries and sent them to Frau Tanja Zimmermann of the legal department of Stadt Gengenbach, the largest municipality near the parish of Nordrach. Frau Zimmermann kindly forwarded the request to Herr Herbert Vollmer, Bürgermeister of Nordrach, who supplied me, through Dr. and Mrs. Pierach, exactly the information I was seeking. I want to thank my colleague Albert E. Gurganus, Ph.D., of the modern language department at The Citadel for translating the documents sent by Herr Vollmer.

When I chanced upon the painting *Portrait of a Woman*

in White (ca. 1885–90), an oil on canvas by the important American Impressionist Edmund C. Tarbell (1862–1938), I realized that this painting of a woman in her garden captured Nanny's beauty and grace. Not only did Lisa Peters, Ph.D., director of research for the Spanierman Gallery, LLC, New York City, grant permission to use Tarbell's painting as cover art, but also she supplied a professional transparency and information about the painting and the artist. I am deeply appreciative of the generosity of the Spanierman Gallery.

I wish to thank the Citadel Foundation for granting me a sabbatical leave and for providing funds for my research trips to Baltimore, Washington, San Francisco, Portland, Seattle, and San Marino. I want to acknowledge the enthusiastic support of faculty research by Major General John S. Grinalds, president of The Citadel, and Harrison S. Carter, Ph.D., provost and dean of the college. My department head James S. Leonard, Ph.D., and our departmental administrative assistant Libby Walker provided valuable computer support and advice.

Finally, my sincerest gratitude is due to my wife Joan for her steadfast encouragement and helpful suggestions for textual revision.

PART ONE:
Her Life

CHAPTER ONE

WAR

I
CHARLESTON

Late at night on December 26, 1860, five-year-old Nanny Smith awakened to her mother's soft but urgent plea for obedience. Her uncle, Captain John Gray Foster, United States Army, carried her the short distance from their home to the federal garrison at Fort Moultrie, South Carolina. All about them blue-clad soldiers moved with alacrity and a sense of purpose that Nanny had never seen before. Officers issued orders in strained whispers, and the men complied silently.

Assisted by soldiers, Nanny and her mother Ann, widow of Dr. Berwick Bruce Smith, joined other families making their way through the dark winter night across the narrow stretch of sand separating Fort Moultrie from Charleston harbor. Native Baltimoreans, they had recently joined the extended family of Captain Foster; his wife Mary was Mrs. Smith's sister, and the Fosters' only child Annie, three years older than Nanny, was her playmate. Another member of the family was a twenty-one year old civilian, Edward Moale, Nanny's mother's brother. Uncle Ned, as Nanny called him, was an aide to his brother-in-law Foster.

The Fosters lived in quarters in Moultrieville outside the walls of the small fort, so when the order came to evacuate

Fort Moultrie and move to relatively safer Fort Sumter, they left behind and lost all their possessions. Only 1820 yards away in Charleston harbor, Fort Sumter also lay within cannon range of the southern batteries being fortified on nearby Morris Island and Charleston's Battery.

So secretive had Major Robert Anderson been about his plan to evacuate the fort, he had attended a Christmas Day party at Captain Foster's home without a hint to his key staff officers of the next day's exciting relocation. A federal lieutenant with the improbable name of Jefferson C. Davis flirted with Nanny's mother, and she presented him with a pocket flask of brandy.[1] Their inchoate romance would be terminated by the dramatic circumstances of the next few hours. During the Civil War, Jefferson C. Davis would become one of General William T. Sherman's ablest officers.[2]

Nanny was allowed to keep one doll, and she and Annie watched in anger and confusion as their Christmas gifts received only the morning before were distributed to the children of their Negro servants, hired from their owners as cooks, washerwomen, chambermaids, gardeners, and nurses for the Union families.

Nanny's mother rushed to the garden to remove as many clothes from the line as would be practicable to take with them. One of the stories from family lore holds that Mrs. Smith, in her haste, inadvertently gathered a chicken into the clothesbasket and did not discover the stowaway until the party reached Fort Sumter.

Once inside Fort Moultrie, Nanny and her family joined Mary Doubleday, wife of Captain Abner Doubleday, credited by some with inventing baseball; she was the only wife living within the walls of the fort at that time.

The women and children were rushed toward the teams of soldiers waiting in craft obtained earlier that day by the quartermaster officer for the secret evacuation. Even at five years of age Nanny sensed her mother's urgency as they hurried toward their boat, but she was too young to understand that she was about to be an eyewitness to the start of the most dramatic event in the history of the United States.

Major Robert Anderson of the United States Army, a

Southerner by birth and former slave owner, commanded the federal installations around Charleston harbor. From his vantage point atop the fortification walls, he watched families of his officers and soldiers struggle in controlled confusion, wishing that he could conduct military business without the encumbrances of dependent family members, including his own wife who was also present. But the federal military, even in those days, went to considerable expense to ensure that the wives could accompany their husbands whenever feasible, even into dangerous assignments such as the untamed West or the politically volatile South, lest men of substance would choose not to enter career military service.

The presence of the women and children also made a clear Union propaganda statement that the North did not seriously believe the South would resort to open warfare. But the signs that hostilities would occur had been becoming more evident in the passing weeks, and the chain of events that began with the tempestuous April 1860 convention of the National Democratic Party in Charleston had, at year's end, reached the point of violence. South Carolina and six other pro-slavery Southern states walked out of the convention in defiance of the anti-slavery faction, vowing secession if the Republicans elected Abraham Lincoln.[3]

On 6 November 1860, the day of the election, the South Carolina legislature unanimously passed an Ordinance of Secession, formally signed on 20 December 1860, less than one week before Nanny and the others evacuated the fort. Charlestonians took to the streets in jubilation, anticipating that the other Southern states would follow their lead and break away from the Union. For months prominent citizens of Charleston had organized new militia units and reinvigorated existing units that had evolved into little more than social and political debate clubs. Armed citizens in a variety of independently designed gaudy uniforms added a festive atmosphere to the streets of the old city.

The citizens of Charleston and Sullivan's Island felt enormous pride in the role the fort had played in American history. Designed as a coastal artillery base to protect Charleston harbor, Fort Moultrie first saw action on 26 June

1776, during the Revolutionary War. This fort was the third structure built on the same location. Charlestonians took a proprietary attitude toward the fort; the secession vote made the presence of Union forces an insufferable affront to their pride, but the locals did not want to rush an eviction because the fort was being repaired with federal dollars. They could act when it pleased them.[4]

Fort Moultrie was accessible to any civilian who took the time to stroll casually over the high sand dunes of Sullivan's Island, some of which actually looked down on the twelve-foot high walls of the fort. For weeks the local citizenry had been taunting the nervous federal soldiers about the easy time they would have in taking the fort at their leisure.

When he arrived to take command, Anderson realized that his position was indefensible, and he began to formulate a plan to prevent the capture of his troops by the newly organized Confederate forces, an untrained, randomly equipped mix of a few veterans of the Mexican War who had actually seen combat and anyone who could be recruited by the prospect of wearing a uniform and performing glorious deeds on the field of battle.

Fort Sumter, sitting atop a man-made island in the middle of Charleston harbor, was under construction and not occupied when the events of 1860 occurred. Major Anderson's successful evacuation disappointed the local citizenry because the opportunity for heroics in combat had been denied them, but, at the same time, they felt smug satisfaction because the federal troops had sneaked away under the cover of darkness, an indicator, they felt, of how easily this secession would be accomplished and independence established.

Anderson must have felt many emotions that night, for he was abandoning the same Fort Moultrie where his father had served in the American army against the British in 1780; the elder Major Anderson was taken prisoner and held for nine months when Charleston surrendered to the redcoats.

Following standard military procedure, Anderson ordered the cannons "spiked"—forcing nails and other material down the fuse touch-hole to render them inoperable—and burning the carriages, the wooden substructure upon which the guns swivel.[5] One of Anderson's last acts as commander of Fort Moultrie before his troops evacuated was to have the flagstaff sawn down so that the Southern forces would at least have some inconvenience and delay in hoisting their own standard when they took possession.[6] A Charleston woman recorded in her diary the indignation of the locals who were "startled and almost stunned by the intelligence that Anderson had evacuated Fort Moultrie. . . . The evacuation took place during the night of the 26th, [Anderson] stealing away in the darkness like a thief after cutting the flagstaff [and] to add insult to injury, spiking the guns and burning the carriages."[7]

As the flotilla cast off, cold rain began to pour down, but Nanny, wrapped in a blanket and nestled beside her mother, felt safe. Even their departure and journey across Charleston harbor formed part of Anderson's elaborate ruse to avoid arousing the suspicions of the locals. Lieutenant Norman J. Hall, the quartermaster officer who had obtained the schooners and barges for the evacuation, took the women and children to a site near Fort Johnson, dilapidated federal property on the opposite side of the harbor, where they remained in the boats.[8]

Anderson's primary mission was to relocate his soldiers; secondarily, he wanted to move the dependents into the new fort as well. Had the dependents been detected, no harm would have come to them, but spies would have alerted the local militia about the evacuation, so the timing of the movements of both groups, military and civilian, had to be precise.

The women and children waited in the boats until the soldiers had successfully debarked at Fort Sumter. Then, seeing the fire from a pre-arranged signal gun, Lieutenant Hall steered his charges to their new location.[9]

Captain Foster and his civilian brother-in-law Edward Moale volunteered to stay behind to cover the last boats out. They planned to fire cannon shot on the Confederate guard boats if the local militia detected and pursued the federal forces en route to Fort Sumter.[10]

The next day, 27 December, the lone overseer who remained, an engineer sergeant, surrendered Fort Moultrie without a shot being fired by either side. Since no formal state of war yet existed, the sergeant could not be taken prisoner, so the local militia allowed him to rejoin his unit.[11]

When the boats landed safely, the long night continued for the federal soldiers who had to begin preparing the fort against immediate attack, a task that would take months, not days. There being little point in trying to maintain the secrecy of their whereabouts, Anderson ordered large bonfires built so that the men and the civilians could dry themselves and announce Fort Sumter's new occupants to any Charlestonians who looked across the harbor. As soon as she arrived, Mrs. Smith made the first of several large pots of coffee for the exhausted soldiers who would continue to work through the night.

The Officers' Quarters at Fort Sumter. This engraving depicts Nanny's uncle John Foster in his rooms where Nanny stayed in the months leading up to the bombardment of Fort Sumter in 1861. SOURCE: *Harper's Weekly.*

Nanny and her cousin Annie, feeling warm, dry, and safe in the presence of their mothers and the familiar soldiers from whom they received constant coddling, were tucked in for the night. Major Anderson could not share their comfort. Not knowing whether the clandestine removal of his troops would anger the local forces so much that they might open fire on his new location, he worried about the danger to the women and children as well as to his men.

The next morning, while Charlestonians discovered the evacuation, Nanny awoke to a brilliantly sunny day. No one had time to attend to the two girls, so they took advantage of their freedom to make their way to the top parapet of the fort, a tremendous height with no guard rail to prevent an inattentive sentry—or two little girls—from falling directly into the sea. These walls were sixty feet high and from eight to twelve feet in thickness.[12] As the girls played a game of catch, Nanny's mother spotted them and sent a soldier scrambling up the parapet to retrieve them.

By her own admission Nanny had been a spoiled child, taking advantage of the tenderness which her adult relatives showered on the "poor little fatherless girl," as she later described herself. But taking a soldier away from his important business of readying the fort in the face of genuine danger to rescue two young miscreants could not be tolerated. Uncle John Foster, a strict disciplinarian by nature and profession, spanked both girls—the first spanking Nanny had ever received.

The officers' families went over to Charleston on 4 January 1861 and installed themselves in the Mills House with orders not to leave their rooms. Many of the officers' wives, however, had already established friendships with Charleston society women through churches, literary discussion groups, and benevolent organizations, so the women and children chafed under the order not to go about the city until they could be taken north.[13]

While the Union soldiers dared not venture to the city, the wives could obtain passes and cross the harbor to visit their husbands who worked frantically to equip the fort for defense against artillery fire. The women could take no food, candles, or similar contraband that would make life more comfortable for the occupants of the fort. Later the Charleston authorities relented and allowed cooks to go into the city markets to buy food and other essentials.

On 8 January Nanny and the officers' families departed in a group for the North. The enlisted men's wives and children had to wait until 30 January to leave the fort, steaming for New York on 3 February.[14] The delay in departure of the enlisted wives did not constitute insensitive class distinction as might first appear; an enlisted soldier's wife often supplemented her husband's pay by performing such functions as cooking, cleaning, doing laundry, and other domestic tasks for the entire garrison, chores an officer's lady customarily would not do. These enlisted soldiers' wives freed their husbands for the physically demanding work necessary to prepare the fort for defense against an attack.[15]

Good-By to Fort Sumter. Nanny and her mother say goodbye as they depart Fort Sumter. A cannon signals a salute to the women and children. SOURCE: *Harper's Weekly.*

Nanny would miss by one day witnessing the first shots fired in the Civil War. In a little-known episode occurring on the morning of 9 January 1861, later overshadowed by the more dramatic shelling of Fort Sumter in April 1861, a federal steamer named the *Star of the West* attempted to re-supply Anderson with troop reinforcements, food, and ammunition. The *Star of the West*, a merchant ship, not a war vessel, had no guns of any sort. General Winfield Scott, commander of the Union army, had taken her out of civilian service for this mission precisely because she offered no threat as an actual warship would have done. Her mission was well known, leaked to the newspapers that published the intentions of the ship three days before she arrived in the channel.[16]

Politicians and military commanders in both the North and the South watched the voyage of the *Star of the West* with intense interest. Southerners viewed the ship's mission to Charleston as an attempt by Abraham Lincoln to goad the South into either hostile action or submission. If the South fired on the ship, Southerners would bear the burden of starting the war. If they allowed the ship to pass undeterred, the North could surmise that Southern opposition was all talk and no action.

Cadets from The Citadel, the Charleston military college, manned the artillery battery on nearby Morris Island that fired the unofficial first shots of the Civil War. Major P. F. Stevens, a professor at the college, had received orders from Francis W. Pickens, the governor of South Carolina, to fire on any vessels attempting to go up the channel toward Fort Sumter. Stevens sighted a gun on the *Star of the West*, then turned the piece over to Cadet G. W. Haynesworth who pulled the lanyard at 7:15 a.m. Two cannon balls struck the ship, but no one was injured and no significant damage resulted.[17] The first shots of the Civil War had been fired.

Captain Charles J. Woods, commander of the reinforcements aboard the ship, his men exposed to artillery shells with no means of returning fire, ordered the ship's captain to turn about, and she steamed away as spectators on shore cheered.

When the first shots were fired, Major Anderson and his two ranking captains, Foster and Doubleday, could hardly believe what they were seeing. They suspected, but did not know, that this was their resupply ship, but this was clearly no warship. The *Star of the West* flew a huge, garrison-size Stars and Stripes, much larger than a standard ship's ensign. The action by the Southerners could not have been a mistake; they knew they were firing on an unarmed ship bearing the flag of the United States.

Edward Moale took his two sisters and nieces back to Nanny's maternal grandmother's home in Baltimore, but her stay at Grandmother Moale's house turned out to be a brief respite from the war for young Nanny. She would soon return to the South, and this time she would experience combat.

II
BALTIMORE

Before Nanny left Baltimore for Charleston in 1860, she and her parents had lived with her paternal grandparents, Dr. and Mrs. Nathan Ryno Smith. The Smiths were a distinguished family of medical doctors whose roots were in the North— New Hampshire, Vermont, Connecticut, and Pennsylvania. Yet Nanny's Uncle Walter Smith broke with the family and joined the Confederacy; he died in 1863 at age twenty-one from an infection in Danville, Virginia, while serving in gray.[18]

The other side of Nanny's family, the Moales, emphatically sympathized with the South, yet her uncle Edward joined the Union army, eventually rising to the rank of brigadier general. Edward's sister Mary, as we have seen, married Union officer John Gray Foster, and another sister, Frances (Fanny) North Moale, married Captain John Gibbon who became a major general in the Union army while his three brothers fought for the Confederacy. Although these two sisters married Union officers, another sister, Augusta (Gussie), married Wilson Cary Nicholas II who, as a captain in the earliest days of the war, led a rebel force to seize the federal arsenal at Pikesville, Maryland, near his home in the Green Spring Valley west of Baltimore.

Nanny's Uncle Ned Moale was the son of Anne Green White Moale whose sister was the mother of John White Scott, Ned's first cousin. As boys in Baltimore the two were inseparable. When the war broke out, they remained friends although John Scott joined the Maryland company in the Twenty-first Virginia Regiment. When Scott was captured in 1863 and confined to the old Capitol prison in Washington, Ned visited him there, taking him gifts from the family. After the war they resumed their friendship. Three weeks before Ned's death in 1913, he returned to the Green Spring Valley where he and Scott reminisced about their days together as boys and about the war that temporarily separated them.

Nanny's family was not unique in its divided loyalty. Three brothers of Abraham Lincoln's wife died fighting for the Confederacy. Major General T. L. Crittenden, United States Army, and Major General G. B. Crittenden, Confederate States Army, chose different sides despite being brothers. Samuel P. Lee, Robert E. Lee's nephew, commanded Union naval forces on the James River in their home state of Virginia.[19]

Nanny's Grandmother Moale continued to support the South, even though her daughters Fanny Gibbon and Mary Foster married Union officers. A new law required every home in Baltimore to display a flag of the United States. From the window of her front room on the third floor of the house, Fanny hung a huge Union flag, but Grandmother Moale begrudgingly obeyed the law by sticking a tiny Union flag in the front door keyhole. Nanny inherited her spunk and independence from the women in her family.

The death of Nanny's father, Dr. Berwick Bruce Smith (1826-60), resulting from an infection received in the dissecting room, caused Nanny and her mother to leave the Smith household with Edward and join the Fosters in Charleston. They had been away from Baltimore only about one year, but the changes in the family were profound.

In the time before the war, the Smiths enjoyed the cheerful

chaos of a huge extended family accustomed to wealth and comfort. Nanny enjoyed the attention lavished on her by several aunts and their families who had returned home because of the threat of war: Sarah Francis Smith Theobald, the widow of Elisha Warfield Theobald, a young physician from Kentucky, with her five children; Mary Smith Lanier and her daughter, her United States Navy officer husband Captain Edmund Lanier being on a voyage to China; and Ellen Montgomery, a divorcee. Aunt Ellen became the official housekeeper. Although not living in the house, another aunt, Adelia, wife of George Hall, lived nearby with her two daughters and one son. Nanny was one of sixteen grandchildren of Dr. and Mrs. Nathan R. Smith.[20]

The Smith household before the war and the Moale household during the war consistently showered love and security on Nanny, even amidst the disagreements over loyalty and secession. The social and political climate outside the home changed dramatically once the war began, the split in loyalty inside both the Smith and Moale families simply mirroring the civil discontent occurring in Baltimore.

Few cities suffered as much division of loyalties as Baltimore. Not the Deep South, but not quite North, Baltimoreans keenly felt the intensity of arguments over secession, slavery, and states' rights, with most people favoring the Southern cause.

While Nanny was still at Fort Moultrie, Captain Foster, as chief engineer officer with the responsibility of repairing the fort, arranged for about 150 brick masons and other civilian workers to come down from Baltimore to assist in the effort. When Anderson took command, he asked the workers if he could count on them to join the fight if the local militia attacked. To a man the Baltimoreans said they would not fight the Southerners (although some that remained for the bombardment of Fort Sumter did fire off a few Union cannon shots as a lark).[21]

In Baltimore on 19 April 1861, one week after the bombardment of Union forces at Fort Sumter, a secessionist mob threw stones and fired weapons at young southbound soldiers of the Sixth Massachusetts Volunteers as they changed trains, killing four and wounding thirty. President Lincoln suspended the writ of habeas corpus—meaning citizens could be arrested without evidence of a crime—and sent General Benjamin Butler to Baltimore to subdue the populace. So strong were the Southern sympathies in Maryland that Butler arrested and jailed the mayor of Baltimore and nineteen members of the state legislature.[22]

On 6 July 1861, *Harper's Weekly* reported that federal authorities, now under the command of General Banks, continued to suppress a perceived conspiracy on the part of the Baltimore police against the United States government. Banks arrested on 1 July the entire board of Police Commissioners and sent them to Fort McHenry. Infantry and artillery units were positioned at strategic locations in Baltimore to quell "any rioters who may show themselves."[23]

In the social context, Nanny remembered that before the war many of Baltimore's society girls welcomed as suitors young officers stationed in Washington, but after the war began the same girls shunned all Union men. On 7 September 1861 *Harper's Weekly* ran a front page illustration of an attractive young woman walking the streets of Baltimore wearing a dress that artfully incorporated one of the early versions of the Confederate flag. The drawing is titled "A Female Secessionist Flaunting Her Colors," and the accompanying article says, "This has been an everyday incident at Baltimore ever since the 19th April. The men dare not insult the troops, but the women of Baltimore presume upon their sex and wear secession colors, and salute our boys with — 'Hurrah for Jeff Davis!' 'How about Bull Run?' 'Why don't you go home?'"[24] Such was the volatility in Baltimore when Uncle Ned took Nanny, her mother, aunt, and cousin to live in Grandmother Moale's house.

The conflicting sympathies between Grandmother Moale and her children was but one part of the complex social structure of the house. Edward Moale, despite his mother's wishes, entered the Union army when he returned to Baltimore but almost immediately contracted typhoid fever and had to

A Secessionist Showing Her Colors. A southern-sympathizing young woman walks defiantly about the streets of Baltimore having artfully incorporated the Confederate flag into her dress. Nanny's family, as were many in Baltimore, was divided during the Civil War. SOURCE: *Harper's Weekly.*

come home on extended medical leave. As his condition improved, the young officer, still in his early twenties, discovered alcohol and often returned to the house at night inebriated. He had a friend in the home, Grandmother Moale's cook, a tall, black woman named Henny. She terrified Nanny and her cousin Fanny Gibbon with her imperious ways. Too young to understand that Henny had never been to Africa, they fantasized that she must certainly have been a princess in her tribe because of her airs and graces. Yet for all her fierceness, she lovingly protected Ned and would watch patiently for him to return from his evenings of overindulging and surreptitiously admit him to the house through the kitchen gate and assist him up the stairs to his room.

III
NEW BERN

Nanny remained at Grandmother Moale's for more than a year, but, incredibly, in 1862, she and her mother along with Aunt Mary and Cousin Annie, rejoined Foster in the South. By this time, Foster had been promoted from captain to brigadier general and had displayed heroic action, especially with the taking of Washington, North Carolina, and the more important nearby coastal city of New Bern.

As implausible as it might seem that northern women and children would venture into the South during the war, eastern North Carolina was fairly safe. North Carolina in general escaped much of the intense combat that Virginia, Tennessee, and other states experienced. Eastern North Carolina did not share the passion for secession of its neighboring state to the south for several reasons: the soil in that region was not conducive to the growth of cotton and so required a smaller slave labor force; coastal communities on isolated barrier islands traditionally felt little connection to the interior; and the predominant fishing industry there set them apart from the largely agrarian culture found elsewhere in the state. In pockets of eastern North Carolina, the locals were decidedly Unionist.

In relatively safe eastern North Carolina, John Foster had been promoted to brigadier general under a complex rank system of that time. Regular army officers held rank apart from that of "Volunteers," but regular officers such as Foster could simultaneously hold a higher Volunteer rank. Officers could also receive brevet promotions, temporary promotions above their regular rank. For example, although George A. Custer had been a general in the Civil War, he held the regular army rank of lieutenant colonel when he died at Little Bighorn in 1876. When the war began, regular army officers received elevated rank based on combat experience, years of service, and political influence; they formed a cadre to train and lead the swelling ranks of citizen-soldiers. Foster was appointed brigadier general of Volunteers on 23 October 1861, then major general of Volunteers on 18 July 1862. He was brevetted major general in the regular army 13 March 1865, but as late as 7 March 1867 he still held the rank of lieutenant colonel in the regular army corps of engineers.

Inexperienced officers often led troops on both sides in the Civil War. The volunteer units often elected their officers, or a wealthy man might recruit, organize, and equip his own command. As a West Pointer and regular army officer with combat experience from the Mexican War, Foster deserved his accelerated promotion. His Fort Sumter comrade Abner Doubleday described Foster as "one of the most fearless and reliable men in the service."[25]

The battle of New Bern, a brief but vicious fight, began on 13 March 1862 with Foster commanding a regiment under General Ambrose Burnside. On 14 March Foster led his troops against the Confederates' left. Brigadier General Jesse L. Reno, moved his regiment against the right, and the third regimental commander Brigadier General John G. Parke attacked the center. Foster met stiff resistance for several hours. Reno was able to make a penetration of the line, and attacked the militia units to their right. When they discovered they had been flanked, the Confederate militia units retreated in confusion, and other units followed them. The Confederate side lost 64 killed, 101 wounded, and 413 taken prisoner. The Union side suffered 90 killed and 380 wounded.[26] The Confederates abandoned New Bern and shifted their forces to Goldsboro in the interior of the state.

Because New Bern was the major town in that area, when

it fell federal troops soon occupied other population centers. Carolina City, Morehead City, Beaufort, and Newport all came under Union sway with little or no resistance. On 6 July, the area was so secure that Burnside could depart with a force of seven thousand troops to reinforce General George McClellan in the Peninsula campaign around Norfolk, Virginia. General Foster kept nine thousand soldiers and became commander of the Department of North Carolina. He set as his highest priority the strengthening of the fortifications in New Bern and elsewhere in the vicinity. As an engineer, Foster knew how to make the key town defensible and ensure the stability of the area. As word spread to farms in the interior that Union forces occupied New Bern, slaves deserted their homes and flocked to freedom in the town. Foster put the men to work on the entrenchments, earthworks, and breastworks. He made his sector even safer by sending out on daily patrol a fearsome armored train with a large contingent of soldiers.

Nanny, her mother, Aunt Mary Foster, and Cousin Annie could travel by sea from Baltimore to New Bern with ease and safety, particularly aboard a warship carrying plenty of armaments. With reinforcements and supplies coming regularly into New Bern from the northern cities, General Foster could easily arrange for his family's passage.

Nanny's house in New Bern was opulent. When the secessionist citizens of New Bern fled the city, they left behind silver, linens, and other possessions, including slaves who were joined by the refugees from the interior. Thus the officers, particularly the commander, enjoyed both comfortable quarters and an available labor force from which they could obtain a large staff of household servants.

In order to control the area, General Foster regularly sent out various kinds of patrols: the aforementioned armored train, infantry and cavalry, and, most importantly, boat patrols up the many rivers leading to the interior, especially the Neuse River. Equipped with small cannon, these steam-powered boats could carry an armed contingent of several dozens of soldiers whose firing positions on deck would be protected by sandbags and bales of hay. If they encountered serious gunfire from shore, they could usually steam out of sight in just moments. Still, the danger was real.

On one occasion, Foster was aboard the steamboat *Escort* conducting a similar patrol when the boat was hit forty times by gunfire. The boat was able to steam away from the hostile fire. Foster suspected that the civilian captain of the boat had rebel sympathies and that he might have arranged to have the vessel captured, so he pulled out his revolver and kept it trained on the captain as they passed through another section of the river where a rebel ambush might likely occur. When they passed the last obstacle in the river, the captain turned to Foster and said, "I reckon we're all right now." At that moment a rebel bullet fired from shore struck the boat's captain, killing him on the spot.[27]

One day Foster received a field report that some Confederate soldiers, size and organization unknown, were hiding in an area up the Neuse River. Foster frequently went on these patrols—a commander cannot remain safely behind the walls all the time. He proposed that his wife accompany him on a boat to seek out this group of rebels. He regarded the mission as little more than a pleasure excursion. Mary declined her husband's invitation.

General Foster then invited his sister-in-law, Nanny's mother, who accepted. She took Nanny, then seven years old, and her Negro maid. No other women were aboard. Nanny missed the firing on the *Star of the West* and the shelling of Fort Sumter in Charleston harbor, but on this day she would see combat at close range.

The pleasure excursion suddenly turned deadly when they received fire from the riverbank. Foster ordered Nanny and the women below deck, and Mrs. Smith and her maid obeyed the order without protest, but in the confusion Nanny slipped away from her mother and took a position on the upper deck to see the fight.

Bullets ripped into the hay bales, and several hapless soldiers were killed and wounded. Nanny heard the cries of pain and fear mingled with shouted commands of officers and non-commissioned officers. She smelled the burning powder as some soldiers fired rifles against unseen targets on shore.

In ambushes such as this, the first action is to return heavy fire to the source of the attack, either through massing small arms fire or, preferably, through cannon fire. Incredibly, none of the men on deck knew how to fire the cannon—perhaps another indication of General Foster's failure to take the patrol seriously. If he had expected to encounter opposition, not only would he not have had women aboard, but also he or one of his subordinates would surely have drilled and rehearsed a gun crew on how to fire the deck cannon.

Foster himself took charge of the cannon and returned fire. When she was elderly Nanny said that she could still see the flash of flame, hear the awful roar, and smell the acrid gunpowder. The general's shot silenced the ambushers, and the boat steamed back to New Bern with dead and wounded soldiers. Incongruously, a beautiful moonlit evening revealed the dead bodies lying beneath sheets on the upper deck near the flagpole.

Just as Nanny's mother had acted calmly in the evacuation from Fort Moultrie and as she had gone into action preparing coffee and cheering the soldiers on their arrival at Fort Sumter, now, after seeing that Nanny had survived the attack, she turned her attention to the wounded. Nanny looked down a stairway to the lower cabin and watched her mother wash the blood from the back of a soldier.

From her mother, Nanny learned that women did not have to fall to pieces or swoon or otherwise become a disruptive presence in a crisis as writers of romantic novels of that time usually depicted them. These lessons in courage learned during the Civil War would serve Nanny well in her adolescence and adulthood where further challenges and adventures awaited her.

NOTES

[1] W. A. Swanberg, *First Blood: The Story of Fort Sumter* (New York: Charles Scribner's Sons, 1957), 95–96.

[2] Robert M. Utley, *Frontier Regulars: The United States Army and the Indian, 1866-1891* (New York: Macmillan Publishing Company, 1973), 187.

[3] Arthur M. Wilcox and Warren Ripley, *The Civil War at Charleston* (Charleston, SC: The Post and Courier, 2000), 2.

[4] Abner Doubleday, *Reminiscences of Forts Sumter and Moultrie in 1860-61* (New York: Harper & Brothers, 1876), 14.

[5] "Fort Sumter." *Harper's Weekly* 26 January 1861: 53.

[6] *Frank Leslie's Illustrated Newspaper* 19 January 1861: 1.

[7] John F. Marszalek, ed.," *The Diary of Miss Emma Holmes, 1861–1866* (Baton Rouge: Louisiana State University Press, 1979), 2.

[8] First Lieutenant Hall, from the state of Michigan, graduated from West Point in 1859. He received four rapid brevet promotions, going from lieutenant to colonel in one year. With the 7th Michigan Volunteers he was wounded at Antietam and retired on disability pay in 1865. He never recovered from his wounds and died in New York state 26 May 1867 [*Register of Graduates* (West Point, NY: United States Military Academy, 1990), 282].

[9] Roy Meredith, *Storm Over Sumter* (New York: Simon and Schuster, 1957), 60. Lieutenant Hall achieved a place in the history books for his participation in the evacuation. A few months earlier, when Governor Francis Pickens ordered Fort Sumter blockaded, Hall crossed Charleston Harbor to meet with Pickens. When the governor wanted to keep Hall waiting, the lieutenant demanded, and got, an immediate audience.

[10] Meredith, 60.

[11] Wilcox, 5.

[12] "Fort Sumter." *Harper's Weekly* 26 January 1861: 1.

[13] Doubleday, 100.

[14] *Harper's Weekly* 10 February 1861: 6.

[15] Michele J. Nacy, *Members of the Regiment: Army Officers' Wives on the Western Frontier, 1865–1890* (Westport, CT: Greenwood Press, 2000), 58.

[16] Robert Hendrickson, *Sumter: The First Day of the Civil War* (New York: Promontory Press, 1990), 103.

[17] Wilcox, 11.

[18] William H. Child, *History of the Town of Cornish, New Hampshire,* vol. 2 (Concord, NH: The Rumford Press, 1911), 336.

[19] Samuel Eliot Morison and Henry Steele Commager, *The Growth of the American Republic*, vol. 1 (New York: Oxford University Press, 1962), 681.
[20] "Death of Mrs. Julietta Smith," *Baltimore Sun* 12 April 1883: 1.
[21] Doubleday, 152–53.
[22] Kevin H. Siepel, *Rebel: The Life and Times of John Singleton Mosby* (New York: St. Martin's Press, 1983), 12–13.
[23] "More Arrests at Baltimore," *Harper's Weekly* 6 July 1861: 435.
[24] "A Female Secessionist Flaunting Her Colors." *Harper's Weekly* 7 September 1861: 1.
[25] Doubleday, 22.
[26] Clement A. Evans, ed., *Confederate Military History*, vol. 4 (Atlanta: Confederate Publishing Company, 1899), 40–41.
[27] John G. Barrett, *The Civil War in North Carolina* (Chapel Hill: University of North Carolina Press, 1963), 161.

CHAPTER TWO

ADOLESCENCE

IN 1866 NANNY'S MOTHER married her late husband's first cousin, Dr. Nathan Smith Lincoln (1828–98) of Washington, DC. His mother, Gracia Eliza Smith Lincoln, was Dr. Berwick Bruce Smith's sister. The Lincoln family had roots in New England. Dr. Lincoln's father was the Reverend Increase Sumner Lincoln of Massachusetts. His brother, Sumner H. Lincoln joined the Union army as a private in 1861 and retired as a brigadier general forty years later.[1]

The patriarch of his mother's family, Nathan Smith (1762–1829), was the distinguished physician who influenced the world of medicine in New England by taking his Bachelor of Medicine degree from Harvard and founding the medical schools at Dartmouth, Yale, Bowdoin, and Vermont.[2] Nanny's father was a grandson of Nathan Smith.

Whether Nanny's mother's marriage to Dr. Lincoln was the result of passion or practicality can never be fully known, but Nanny remembered that her mother felt dependent on either her father-in-law Dr. Nathan Ryno Smith (1797–1877), or on the extended Moale family. Unprepared, as were so many women of that time, to make her way in the world, she agreed to marry Dr. Lincoln, a sober, kind, and respectable member of Washington's medical profession. In 1861 he was appointed surgeon-in-chief of the army hospitals in Washington, a position he held for the duration of the war. After the war he was associated for many years with the Providence Hospital, founded in 1861 by the Sisters of Charity to treat wounded soldiers in the Civil War.

Dr. Lincoln's status in Washington may be inferred from an incident occurring during the early days of the war when Lincoln was a professor at Columbian College[3] and maintained a private practice. In the chaotic political situation in Washington with its divided sympathies, someone accused one of his patients, James Chesney, a clerk in the Pension Office, of being a Confederate spy. Dr. Lincoln went directly to the White House, asked for and received an immediate audience with President Lincoln (no relation), and vouched for his patient's loyalty. On the strength of Dr. Lincoln's intercession, the President ordered Chesney released from prison.[4]

The wedding occurred at Nanny's Grandmother Smith's home in Baltimore, and she remained there while her mother and new stepfather went on a short wedding trip. Dr. Lincoln had thoughtfully given Nanny a gold necklace to wear at the wedding. She soon discovered that he would be indulgently generous. When they moved to Washington, she found that she had a bedroom of her own—the largest in the house—a luxury not possible in her crowded Smith and Moale households. When she hinted to Dr. Lincoln that her room needed a shelf and a collection of books of fairy tales, he promptly supplied them for her.

Nanny always called Dr. Lincoln "Cousin Nathan" because she had known him all her life and grew up calling him that. Her mother never asked Nanny to call him "Father," a way of honoring the memory of her first husband.

Nanny was fourteen years old when her mother became ill with tuberculosis; her doctor advised her to go south for the warmer climate, so Ann Smith and Nanny went to one of the "healing hotels" in Aiken, South Carolina, across the border from Augusta, Georgia. Dr. Lincoln had to remain in Washington to conduct his medical practice at Providence Hospital.

They arrived in Aiken on the daily train from Charleston,

135 miles away, the scene of their adventures at the outbreak of the Civil War. Even by the late 1860s Aiken had an established reputation as a health resort. Known as the "Queen of Winter Resorts," Aiken's dry, mild climate attracted victims of tuberculosis. In a district known as the Winter Colony, the wealthy could rest and convalesce in healing hotels, also known as "cottages," some containing as many as ninety rooms.[5] Years later, herself then a mother, Nanny would accompany her son Erskine to Germany for treatment at a similar sanitarium for tubercular patients.

Nanny and Mrs. Lincoln stayed in a healing hotel and hoped that the calmer life outside Baltimore and Washington and the temperate climate would ameliorate her condition, but she did not improve; she died 6 June 1869. Fortunately for Nanny, Dr. Lincoln arrived in Aiken before his wife died, so they could spend her last days together. Nanny and her stepfather accompanied her mother's body back to Washington where she was buried in Oak Hill Cemetery.

One might suppose that Nanny would have returned to the Baltimore area to the household of either the Moale, Smith, Foster, or Gibbon families, with whom she had already lived, rather than remain with her stepfather, but Nanny had established a social life among friends from the best families in Washington. She attended a private school located at 391 H Street North[6] run by Madam Burr, an elderly French woman, wife of Henry A. Burr.

Although Nanny's family in Baltimore belonged to a social order composed of physicians and military officers, in Washington she ascended to a higher social level to which she soon became accustomed. Her classmates, daughters of high government officials, invited the intelligent, charming Nanny to join their circle, and she became a frequent guest in the homes of Secretary of State Hamilton Fish, Secretary of War Edwin Stanton, and Secretary of the Navy George M. Robeson. Many of these classmates from her youth in Washington remained her friends throughout their lives. They entertained each other with wonderfully quaint nineteenth-century pastimes: making taffy, gossiping, going for walks to gather flowers, strolling where boys—beaux, as they called them—could see them. She and many of her friends came out in society together, their debutante balls signaling their eligibility for serious courtship and marriage.

    Dr. Lincoln loved Nanny and indulged every whim. He placed few restrictions on her and never spoke to her in a cross manner. She, in turn, genuinely loved her stepfather but took advantage of his easygoing way to stay in the middle of the Washington social world as she matured into a beauty. More than just physically attractive, Nanny possessed a bold personality and a sly sense of humor that made her one of Washington's most desirable young women.

    In addition to his sending Nanny to a superb private school where she would develop future social prospects, Dr. Lincoln gave her a horse and phaeton or small carriage. No modern day teenager could be more excited about getting a personal car than Nanny was about getting this means of conveyance. Her pleasure in driving the horse and phaeton about the streets of Washington shows that Nanny was developing an awareness of the power of material display, soon to become known as "conspicuous consumption."

    Dr. Lincoln provided her also with the services of a young Negro named Theodore, the son of the household cook. In an upper class colonial British style, she called him her "tiger," or personal servant, such as government officials in India or Africa were accustomed to having. When she would go to her grandfather Smith's estate, Wilton, near Baltimore to spend the summer, she sent Theodore ahead in the phaeton with her saddle and her two greyhound dogs.

    She dressed Theodore in livery: a tailcoat adorned with silver buttons and fancy breeches. While she drove the carriage herself, she made him sit on a seat outside the rear of the carriage with his arms folded, coachman style. When they rode through the streets of Washington, other young Negro boys would hoot in derision at Theodore who burned in shame. Whenever he would protest to her that he felt foolish and

Nanny in 1874, age 19, a Washington belle.
SOURCE: Private collection of Marian Wood Kolisch.

humiliated in his costume, Nanny would mollify him by telling him that the other boys were simply jealous of his fine clothes.

Nanny was also beginning to be daring. She drove fearlessly on streets that were not yet paved. Mud holes and bumps demanded caution, but she would have none of that. One day, driving too fast, she hit a bump in the street and, looking around, saw that Theodore was not in his seat. Several blocks away she could see the hapless Theodore dragging his lap robe behind him struggling to keep up. When he finally did catch up, Nanny teased him for falling off the carriage, but the proud young man fixed her with a glare and said, "You bump me out!"

Nanny recalled that story and told it often with glee; she seems not to have appreciated Theodore's faithful patience in honoring her desire to costume him out of all proportion to their economic station. Dr. Lincoln's income certainly provided Nanny with a comfortable life, far better than average, but they by no means enjoyed the wealth of the robber baron class, and Theodore's ostentatious costume reveals her adolescent interest in material possessions.

In addition to giving her status symbols, Dr. Lincoln provided Nanny with singing, dancing, and music lessons. All young women of a certain class in that time were expected to have some musical accomplishment, usually playing the piano and singing. They might also learn how to sketch and do needlework of various types. Nanny did not take advantage of these opportunities and soon lost interest; she preferred to visit the homes of her girlfriends where older teenage brothers and cousins would somehow always be about and available for teasing and flirting. When she was older, Nanny regretted these lost opportunities for self-development. In later life she did learn to sew splendid garments for herself and her family; she became a first-rate cook; and her gardening skills were unequalled in her adopted home in Portland, Oregon.

When she was sixteen, men began to notice her. In 1871, she visited relatives, the Pleasants family, in Richmond, Virginia. Her Aunt Elizabeth Moale Poultney married Richard Hall Pleasants; the Pleasants, Moale, and Poultney families had intermarried in Baltimore in the late eighteenth and early nineteenth centuries. While she was in Richmond, a young physician friend of the Pleasants family who was chief surgeon for the local penitentiary became devoted to her. Apparently the young doctor had not had much experience courting because he took Nanny on a tour of the penitentiary—the best he could do to entertain her. She discouraged any further attentions from this unimaginative fellow.

In that same year, her uncle, General John Foster with whom she had stayed in Charleston and New Bern, reversed the living arrangements of Nanny's youth and came to live with her and Dr. Lincoln. Foster's wife, Mary Moale Foster, died 6 June 1871, two years to the day after the death of her sister, Nanny's mother. The Fosters' only child, Annie, Nanny's old playmate from Fort Sumter, had married an army officer, Henry Seton, who was stationed out West, so General Foster, recently widowed, was glad to find companionship of family at Dr. Lincoln's hearth.

General Foster served at that time as deputy chief of the army engineer corps in Washington. Nanny was delighted to have her uncle live with them. Handsome and full of fun, General Foster soon became a favorite in Washington society, and the women there considered him quite a catch.

When Nanny was seventeen years old, one of her school chums, Nannie Davis, came for a visit to Dr. Lincoln's house. Foster noticed her and asked Nanny to introduce them. They fell in love, he proposed, and plans ensued for a quick wedding. The night before the wedding Nanny went to her uncle's room and helped him burn a stoveful of love letters he had received from dozens of women in his bachelor days.

The wedding took place in the evening on 9 January 1872, scarcely six months after the death of his first wife. The Moale side of the family, scandalized and disapproving of the marriage, blamed Nanny for introducing them. Further, she seemed a willing conspirator in this unseemly union by assisting him before the wedding ceremony in getting all the accouterments on his dress uniform and winding his sash around his waist, pulling it tight as she circled him.

Their wedding was a formal military affair with groomsmen, all young engineer officers who worked for General Foster, forming an archway of swords for the happy couple. The bridesmaids—who enjoyed flirting with the groomsmen—were all teenage friends of Nanny and the bride. Among the guests, the contrast between the bride's young friends and Foster's contemporaries was striking; the bridesmaids wondered who all the grandfathers were.

NOTES

[1] "Sumner H. Lincoln." *Who Was Who in America*, vol. 1 (Chicago: A. N. Marquis Co., 1942), 730.
[2] Oliver S. Hayward and Constance E. Putnam, *Improve, Perfect, and Perpetuate: Dr. Nathan Smith and Early American Medical Education* (Hanover, NH: University Press of New England, 1998), 271–72.
[3] W. H. Boyd, *City Directory* (Washington: W. H. Boyd, 1860), n. p.
[4] *Providence Centennial Book, 1861-1961* (Washington, DC: Providence Hospital, 1961), n.p.
[5] Gasper Loren Toole II, *Ninety Years in Aiken County* (Charleston, SC: Walker, Evans, and Cogswell, 1958), 110.
[6] W. H. Boyd, *Boyd's Washington and Georgetown Directory* (Washington, DC: Boyd & Waite Brothers, 1866), 180.

CHAPTER THREE

LOVE

SIX MONTHS after the wedding of her Uncle John Foster, in the summer of 1872 when Nanny was seventeen, she met the man who would become her husband, Charles Erskine Scott Wood (20 February 1852–22 January 1944). By any measure, he was the great love of her life, selected from among many attractive suitors and potential husbands who actively courted her.

Wood was known by several first names over the course of his life, perhaps an indicator of his lifelong search for his own identity. He was never called Charles; in his boyhood his family called him Ern, and Nanny called him that for most of their time as a married couple; as a West Point cadet and young army officer, he was called Erskine; his young law colleagues and friends in Portland called him "Ces"; as he matured, he was known in Portland as "Colonel" Wood, an honorific title; after he and Nanny separated, she wrote letters to him addressed to "my dearest Scotty"; when he remarried at age 86, five years after Nanny's death, he reverted to the name "Erskine" in his marriage vows. For consistency and simplicity, I call him Wood.

Nanny missed her first opportunity to meet Wood when he came to her home in Washington where her cousin Fanny Gibbon was visiting her. One night while the two girls lolled on Nanny's bed in their undergarments because of the intense summer heat, drinking raspberry vinegar, a servant brought up a card bearing the name of Cadet Charles Erskine Scott Wood. He had brought a note from Fanny's mother asking that she return to the Moale family home, Atamasco, in Green Spring Valley near Baltimore. Nanny's Aunt Augusta Moale Nicholas, or Gussie, ruled Atamasco, which remained for many years the Moale family gathering place for special events and holidays.

Wood's father, Dr. William Maxwell Wood, retired as Fleet Surgeon for the United States Navy and moved the family from its native Pennsylvania to the Green Spring Valley near Atamasco.[1] Unlike most of the residents of the Valley, he did not have a longstanding membership in the exclusive society found there. However, he became an accepted member of the community because of his former high rank in the navy and because he actively participated in St. Thomas' Episcopal Church which all the best families attended. Dr. Wood served one term as warden and two terms as vestryman.[2] He named his estate Rosewood Glen after Wood's mother Rose. Atamasco exists at the time of this writing relatively unchanged, but the Wood estate is now the Rosewood Center, a treatment facility for mentally retarded adults.

When Nanny saw by his card that the caller was merely a West Point cadet, she haughtily dismissed the thought of getting dressed to meet one so young. She had been escorted by older men and thought a cadet would be too immature for her. Fanny got dressed, descended alone to meet Wood, and returned with him to Atamasco; Nanny and Wood did not see each other.

Later that summer, when she visited Atamasco, she met the handsome, confident Wood and began to grow close to him. They went for long horseback rides together, sharing picnic lunches in the shade of the large oaks along the Jones Falls. Initially, Nanny regarded Wood as a summer flirtation, nothing more, but Wood soon fell in love with her as other young men had when they discovered that a liveliness and ready laughter complemented her physical beauty. She enjoyed the attention of this earnest young man who pursued her so vigorously, and a deep relationship developed.

C.E.S. Wood, Nanny's future husband, as a
West Point cadet in 1874.
SOURCE: Private collection of John Gibbon Wood.

The young lovers became adept at devising ways to rendezvous away from their families. They discovered that they could meet with some privacy within the cemetery walls at St. Thomas' Church, directly across the Garrison Forest Road from Atamasco. Some of the graves have elevated stone slabs set on end pieces, like a table over the grave which is also covered with its own slab. In contrast to their somber surroundings, the young lovers would sit closely on the upper slabs of these grave markers, oblivious in the insouciance of youth to the evidence all around them that life is short.

She met Wood at the churchyard one evening, but the romantic mood was shattered when a male goat attacked her, and she had to escape by crawling under the huge stone slab of a memorial marker for her ancestor Samuel Howard Moale. For years afterward, both she and Wood laughed uncontrollably at the mention of this episode.

Nanny and Wood became more daring and risked scandal that summer. To obtain a greater measure of privacy, they began meeting regularly at 5:00 a.m. to ride horses, much to the clucking disapproval of her aunts, each of whom futilely tried to exercise authority over this motherless girl. On one occasion Wood wanted to take her to a camp meeting, a religious gathering, usually in a bucolic setting, where evangelistic preachers conducted revivals lasting for days at a time. Worshippers would camp out in wagons or large family tents, escaping the distractions of home and devoting themselves to the religious purpose of the camp meeting.

When Nanny and Wood arrived, a tremendous summer rainstorm drove them to seek shelter in a vacant tent, its owners being at the main site of the meeting. A deliciously naughty memory for Nanny all her life was that she and Wood had the tent all to themselves until midnight when the occupants returned.

Leaving the camp meeting, they journeyed home down the turnpike where they found the gatekeeper asleep and had to rouse him to let them pass. When they arrived at Aunt Augusta's they found the door locked. Not wishing to disturb the house with its many residents, they went to Wood's home at his insistence. There his sister Hannah welcomed the rain-soaked Nanny and led her to a dry, comfortable bed where she drifted off to sleep savoring the memory of another special evening with her beau.

The next morning she sent a servant bearing a note to Atamasco to tell the perturbed household of her whereabouts and to request a clean, dry dress. Upon her return to Aunt Augusta's home, Nanny received a scolding for having remained out all night unchaperoned with a young man, but, for her part, she always remembered how much she enjoyed being "talked about," as she termed it, by her aunts for her scandalous behavior.

Wood had the opportunity to show off his girlfriend to his fellow West Point cadets in March 1873 at U.S. Grant's second inauguration. Nanny's uncle, General Foster, was designated as commander and leader of the parade. In keeping with tradition, the U.S. Corps of Cadets from West Point would lead the parade, so almost the entire corps, about 400 at that time, came to Washington. Most of the cadets had family or friends in Washington, and they were allowed to stay with them. Those cadets without family in Washington stayed at the Ebbitt House, which was directly across the street from Dr. Lincoln's house at 1514 H Street NW.[3] The Ebbitt House, established in 1856 as a boarding house, became a favorite dining place for Presidents Grant, Andrew Johnson, Grover Cleveland, Warren Harding, and Theodore Roosevelt. Today, located two blocks from the White House, the Old Ebbitt Grill is a popular gathering place for Washington's political insiders.

The cadets were supposed to attend the inaugural ball, an excellent opportunity for the nation's political leadership to see the splendid future officers in their dress uniforms, and also an opportunity for the cadets to meet eligible young ladies of the Washington social scene. As usual, the independent-minded Nanny had her own ideas about how the inaugural evening should be spent.

She easily charmed General Foster into allowing a dozen or so cadets to come to her home for a small private party, and just as easily she arranged for a sufficient number of her girl friends to come and meet the handsome cadets. The young people danced, sang, and laughed the night away in a setting far more conducive to flirting and initiating friendships than the official inaugural ball. The girls stayed overnight at Nanny's house, and the cadets finally left in the early hours of the next morning.

The cadets had to march from their assembly point at the Ebbitt House to the train station for their return to West Point, and the formation occurred directly in front of Nanny's house. She and the other young women gathered at the front windows and on the porch to wave goodbye as the cadets marched away. One of her friends was Helen Coffin whose brother Billy (William Harrison Coffin, class of 1873) was a senior and the cadet in charge. Billy took advantage of his position as adjutant to break ranks and rush up onto the porch to kiss his sister goodbye, much to the merriment of the rest of the formation. Wood, a junior and therefore not a cadet officer, had to remain in the rank and file, but he did impulsively place his cap on the tip of his bayonet and twirl it in the air as a signal to Nanny to pick him out of the crowd. Had Cadet Coffin observed Wood's breach of military discipline, notwithstanding his own, Nanny's cadet would have been punished with walking extra tours of duty back at West Point.

Nanny is the center of attention on a visit to West Point in the summer of 1873. C.E.S. Wood stands behind her with his hand on his hip.
SOURCE: Private collection of John Gibbon Wood.

As her relationship with Wood grew more serious, Nanny arranged with her two general officer uncles, Foster and Gibbon, to take her frequently to West Point to see him. She could not have ventured to West Point on the train alone, nor would it have been acceptable for her to take a room by herself at the old West Point Hotel, no longer in existence, so her aunts and uncles chaperoned her.

Sometimes on special occasions at the academy the Gibbons and Fosters would go with Nanny together, but for some reason lost to time the two families were not getting along, so they stayed in separate hotels. The Gibbons usually stayed in nearby Highland Falls, while the Fosters favored the hotel at the "point" between the Plain and the Hudson River for which West Point is named.

Nanny preferred staying with her Uncle Foster and her chum Nannie Davis Foster because he allowed her to remain out late with Cadet Wood and did not object when he took her for a stroll on Flirtation Walk near the old West Point Hotel where cadets and their dates could enjoy their time together in privacy. One of Wood's functions in the corps was Master of the Revels; in that capacity he arranged all the parties and dances, called hops, and Nanny enjoyed being in the company of the cadet in charge. She also enjoyed visiting in the summer when the cadets were in camp on the Plain. Because classes were not in session, the atmosphere of the academy was more relaxed, at least for the upper class cadets, so Nanny could spend more time with her cadet.

Her visits to West Point were interrupted for a time in the Spring of 1873. Dr. Lincoln so opposed Nanny's deepening relationship with Wood that shortly after Wood came to Washington for the inauguration in March he ordered their correspondence to stop. He forbade her to write to him, and he would not allow letters from him to enter the home. Nanny obeyed her stepfather, and Wood devised a scheme of keeping a journal in the form of unsent letters, trusting that at some time he could deliver the journal to her so that she could see that he thought of her daily.[4] He occasionally called her

"Nannie," the diminutive form of her name. He also liked to address her as "ma Petite" and "Pet."

Wood's journal begins on 22 April 1873 with his adolescent suffering rendered in archaic diction, a knight writing to his lady fair: "I know not if you shall ever see this journal, dear, and do not think you will, but yet I am impelled to put down my thoughts. Ah, yes, and you shall read them tho' sometime, for until <u>you</u> make me I could not destroy them, and surely I know I shall see you ere long and then I shall show them to you."[5]

On 23 April he wrote,

> I heard from you today from Miss Whelan [a friend of Nanny in Washington who conveyed messages to him]. I heard that you were well (Thank God) and that you would write to me, my pretty one, if you dared. Ah, dear, you must dare to do anything you think is right. I hope it is not that you do not dare to write to me but that you are properly and lovingly respecting the wishes of your father.

He occasionally wallowed in self-pity: "I must bear all my young love's eager, craving hunger dumbly, and it has nothing but memory to feed upon. Oh, my dearest love, life is so short that at best we could live but a little while together then why should our destiny keep us apart another day? It is very hard."

His journal entry for 25 April is both poignant and maudlin:

> Saturday night. The dear, old, well-remembered night. Ah, how regularly I used to come to you week after week on this night. But they are all dead now. I can only think of you and that I do, not only on Saturday night but on every night. . . . Ah, how heartsick I was when I left you. . . . I have these precious pictures. You do not know how they comfort me in my loneliness, how they bring back so much to my mind of the days

when we were together. But, love, they make me very sad too. They show me the gentle, pure precious face I love so. Oh, so dearly, and then, too, they show me a very slight, delicate form. Oh, my darling, Oh my Nannie, I am haunted by my one terror, my one great, great fear. That you are not strong enough to live long in this world and soon will leave me—alone. Oh, God, how much alone. Oh Nannie, Nannie my wife, my only love. I cannot live without you. I may breathe and move but I cannot <u>live</u> with you gone from me forever.

In one entry he unwittingly offers a prophetic look at their future married life:

I used to think that I could have almost any woman I set to win because my conceit said, 'Look and look back and see you can,' and so I thought that I ought to wait and do something brilliant and dazzling and sell myself for a very high price. Ah, you will know when I changed and found you a treasure pure, heavenly, undefiled, and myself a weed, worthless, undeserving, and unworthy to even hold your hand in my keeping, still less your life. There will never be another change, dear. I am all yours forever.

In the 27 April entry he says, "Love, we will grow old together, we will cling to each other forevermore. Ah, I must have my Nannie, she is all mine, and if there be a merciful God he will bring her to me soon and make me happy."

In the next day's entry he feels the lover's gnawing fear of betrayal:

I cannot bear to think of <u>my</u> little girl giving her heart and love to someone else, and someone else being free to hold her in his arms while he whispered the love I had once told her and to kiss the lips I had once held as mine, mine alone.

On Sunday, 3 May, he walked alone on Flirtation Walk. He went to the bench where they had sat together:

> I thought of the times when we had sat there till the last minute that I had to spare was nearly gone and then I would take you back to the hotel and bid you goodbye, and go to my room feeling desolate even in that separation. Ah dear! When shall my home be your home and there be no shadow of parting.

During the summer of 1873, Wood and Nanny demonstrated increased maturity to Dr. Lincoln, and he lifted the ban on Wood and allowed him to visit her in Washington and at Atamasco, although he still did not think this future army officer was a suitable match for her. Despite the opposition of both sets of parents, the two young people had developed an understanding that they would eventually marry, but no formal engagement could occur until Wood gained some financial security, a condition exacerbated by the fact that he was expected to help pay for the education of his brothers and sister.

At just this time, a complication entered Nanny's comfortable world. A change was about to take place that would alter the course of her life.

Her Uncle Foster's new young wife, Nannie Davis Foster, had a good friend, Miss Jeanie Gould, from a distinguished family of lawyers and jurists in Troy, New York. Her father was Justice George Gould of the New York Supreme Court. Justice Gould's older brother William Tracy Gould was a justice of the Georgia Supreme Court. Jeanie's mother, Sarah McCoun Gould, was accustomed to wealth; her father was president of the New York State Agricultural Society and a successful importer and breeder of Durham cattle which he introduced in America from stock procured in England.⁶ When Jeanie's father died in 1868, Sarah Gould was determined that her sons and daughters would marry well, especially the unattractive but intelligent Jeanie.

A frequent visitor to Washington to see Nannie Foster, Jeanie made a point of currying Nanny Smith's friendship, for reasons that would become clear to her later.

When Jeanie invited Nanny to Troy to spend several weeks enjoying the glorious spring of 1874, the younger girl accepted, not out of any affection for Jeanie but simply because the visit would be a pleasant diversion en route to Wood's West Point graduation in June.

But, upon her arrival at the Gould home, Nanny became infatuated with Jeanie's handsome brother Tracy, then studying for the law, and spent most of her time there, as she worded it, "flirting desperately" with him. Distracted by Tracy Gould, she neglected to send love letters to Wood at West Point, and, worse yet, chose to stay in Troy with her new love interest rather than attend Wood's graduation, the crowning event of tremendous importance to any cadet who finishes at the academy. Wood was crushed that Nanny chose not to attend his graduation and to share his joy at this event marking the end of his life as a cadet and the beginning of his career as an army officer. Feeling jealous and betrayed, Wood resolved that he would not lose her to another suitor.

Wood made the short trip from Rosewood Glen in Green Spring Valley to meet her when she returned to Washington from Troy to try to renew her sense of commitment to their relationship. This trip would also, of necessity, be a farewell because he was under military orders to depart immediately for his first duty station, Fort Bidwell in far away northern California. Facing this long term and long distance separation, both young people wept at the prospect of ending their relationship. Still without a formal engagement but with a clear understanding that they would remain true to each other and eventually marry, they parted.

Clearly, Nanny was torn between Tracy Gould and Wood in the spring of 1874. When Wood obtained a recommitment from her, she wrote to Tracy to break off their budding relationship. Crushed by this rejection, Tracy wrote a long, sentimental poem—its diction and tone derivative of John Keats's "The Eve of St. Agnes" entitled *The Bride of the Broken Vow*. Published in Troy the same year he was spurned by Nanny, the poem is a highly romantic ballad about a young woman who becomes a nun when her betrothed, Lord Nevylle, rejects her after falling in love with the beautiful Edith whom he marries. The unnamed nun, who dutifully performs "the ritual of Romish pride," never forgets her first love. In prayer she confesses to Mary,

> My early love, but late forsworn,
> As Mother-Saint thou wilt not scorn;
> To thee alone can I confide
> The hopes that have forever died.

But Edith, sensing that Nevylle stills loves another, betrays him with an unnamed courtier who visits their manor. Her sin discovered, she flees from society to suffer the penance of guilt and shame. On her deathbed, Edith summons her former husband, unwittingly sending the nun—Nevylle's first love—as the messenger; he forgives Edith at the moment of her death. Then, years later, when Nevylle is dying, the nun delivers to him a box containing his love letters to her, reminding him that he betrayed her by marrying Edith. The overwrought poem concludes, "Oh! pow'r of woman, you conceal/The very woes you cannot heal."[7] There can be no doubt that Nanny was Tracy's "bride of the broken vow," and that he felt betrayed when Nanny resumed her relationship with Wood.

At first Nanny faithfully wrote letters to Wood after he became established in the West, but soon she began to be interested in other men again, and other social distractions occurred as well. She enjoyed being the head of her indulgent stepfather's house. Her devoted Cousin Nathan allowed her to do as she pleased, so Nanny's house became the meeting place for her and her girl friends to entertain themselves by making caramel and cake, sewing new party dresses, talking about potential husbands, and planning their imminent debutante balls.

When debutantes had their "coming out" in those days, they often had small parties at their homes in addition to a formal dress ball sponsored by the many exclusive private clubs. With this coming out, a young woman and her family publicly announced her eligibility to be courted by socially and financially suitable young men. Dr. Lincoln took no interest in such matters, so Nanny had to content herself with enjoying the cotillions, or Germans as they called them, at the homes of such friends as Hallie Patterson.

The Pattersons were one of Washington's most socially prominent families and held court at their mansion in Brentwood just north of Florida Avenue and 5th Street NE. Designed by Benjamin Henry Latrobe, the famous British-born Washington architect, Brentwood was named for Robert Brent, the first mayor of Washington, appointed by President Thomas Jefferson in 1802.[8] Hallie's father was Carlile Pollock Patterson, the son of Commodore Daniel Todd Patterson, a hero of the War of 1812 who won fame in the battle of Mobile Bay. Her mother, the beautiful Elizabeth ("Eliza") Patterson, was renowned in Washington for her Saturday afternoon receptions where other ladies would call, often bringing with them their bachelor sons to meet Hallie, Nanny, and their friends.

Through an intricate set of links, Nanny was related to her friend Hallie Patterson and to Emperor Napoleon I. Nanny's uncle, Wilson Cary Nicholas II, nephew of the governor of Virginia by the same name, married her Aunt Augusta Moale (Aunt Gussie who ruled Atamasco). Nicholas's cousin Mary married John Patterson, third son of William Patterson, a wealthy merchant of Baltimore of the same family as the distinguished Commodore Daniel Patterson.

John Patterson's sister Betsy married Jerome Bonaparte, younger brother to Napoleon, in Baltimore on Christmas Eve in 1803. Jerome was nineteen years old and Betsy eighteen and one of the wealthiest women in Maryland when they met and fell in love. The wedding of Betsy Patterson and Jerome Bonaparte caused a sensation in Baltimore and Washington social circles. In May 1804 the Bonapartes were guests of honor at a lavish dinner at the home of Alexander Hamilton in New York City two months before he was killed in a duel with Aaron Burr. Betsy Bonaparte's revealing dress scandalized the sixteen distinguished guests, prompting Margaret Bayard Smith to describe her as "an almost naked woman."[9]

Napoleon strongly opposed this marriage and ordered his brother to return to France without the young American beauty. Jerome and Betsy felt that she could charm Napoleon once they arrived in France, and, with Betsy pregnant, they sailed there in 1805. An emissary from Napoleon boarded their ship off the coast of Portugal and told them that she would not be allowed to proceed, so without ever touching French soil she was diverted to England to give birth to their child whom she named Jerome Bonaparte. Her husband continued to Paris where he capitulated to his older brother's wishes and agreed to an annulment in exchange for a kingship and a new wife through an arranged marriage. He became king of Westphalia and married Katherine Frederika, princess of Würtemberg.[10]

Betsy Patterson Bonaparte returned to Baltimore with her son and remained a local curiosity, albeit a wealthy one from an annual income provided by Napoleon. She frequently visited her cousin (and Nanny's uncle) Wilson C. Nicholas II at Atamasco[11] as well as the Patterson mansion Brentwood in Washington where her presence added allure to any event.

Hallie Patterson had at her disposal a much grander carriage than Nanny's phaeton; this enclosed spacious carriage had windows with green silk curtains. Hallie's elderly black driver, Neddy, endured taking the young women into the city to shop and to their friends' homes for visits. When he had to bring them home late at night from parties, he would scold them all the way, much to the mirth of the carefree debutantes who struggled to suppress their giggles.

In addition to her opportunities for flirting and enjoying her privileged youth, another major distraction caused Nanny's passion for Lt. Wood to cool. Jeanie Gould had cultivated Nanny's friendship with an ulterior motive: she had set her sights on the target of Dr. Nathan Smith Lincoln, Nanny's trusting and unsuspecting stepfather. The entry of Jeanie Gould into her secure, happy household would cause Nanny extreme distress.

Jeanie was plain and unattractive and too old to blend in comfortably with Nanny's friends. Still, she intended to win Dr. Lincoln and pursued him on a long visit to Nanny's home. Because she was not compatible with Nanny's set, she stayed in the home while Nanny continued her usual round of parties. Dr. Lincoln's life had settled into a quiet routine of reading from his extensive library in the evenings, and Jeanie joined him, at times reading silently and at other times engaging him in intelligent discussions about his work at the Providence Hospital and about literature, history, and current events.

Nanny's maid Clara drew her aside one night when she returned from yet another party and warned her, "Chile, you better stay home, 'cause while you is out to parties, Miss Jeanie she stay home and cook oysters for the Doctor." Nanny gave little thought to the possibility of a relationship between Dr. Lincoln and Jeanie. Born in 1828, Lincoln was almost twenty years older than Jeanie who was born in 1846. But Nanny ignored the example of her Uncle Foster's May-December marriage to Jeanie's friend, Nannie Davis.

Jeanie's mother took her on a tour of Europe, obligatory for wealthy young women in those days. After some weeks, Mrs. Gould telegraphed Dr. Lincoln saying that Jeanie was ill and they were cutting short their European tour and returning to New York City. She requested that Dr. Lincoln meet them there to attend to Jeanie's medical needs. The contents of this telegram were a complete fabrication and part of a grand plan to deceive Nanny.

Dr. Lincoln told Nanny that he really was not keen on going to New York City, but he would make the trip if she would accompany him. When the two of them arrived, Nanny's old flame Tracy Gould and his brother George met them at their hotel and took Nanny out to see the sights, elaborately entertaining her and making sure that she was in the best of spirits.

When the time came to meet the ship, Dr. Lincoln was nowhere to be found. Poor gentle Lincoln had sought refuge from the encounter that he knew was about to occur by going to the bookstalls to search for rare books. The Gould boys took Nanny to the docks and boarded the ship. Waiting at the top of the stairs, Mrs. Gould greeted her by demanding, "Where is the Doctor?" Shortly thereafter, Lincoln arrived and ascended to the deck where a perfectly healthy Jeanie Gould stood waiting. Nanny's mouth fell open in amazement as she watched Jeanie throw her arms around his neck and give him an enthusiastic kiss.

At last the truth was out and all revealed. While Jeanie was in Europe, Dr. Lincoln was supposed to have told Nanny of their intention to marry. Knowing that her world of carefree fun and gaiety would be forever altered, he could never find the courage to confront her. When the deceptive telegram summoned them to New York, he still could not reveal the plan. At the last possible time to warn her, just before meeting the women on the boat, he retreated to the bookstalls alone until he could delay the meeting no longer.

Later Nanny could laugh at the distress of her dear, sweet stepfather whose quiet, introspective, scholarly life ran smoothly in parallel to the giddiness of Nanny's adolescent pastimes, but at that moment this unpleasant episode caused her misery and anger.

She returned to the hotel with Tracy and George Gould in a state of shock, while her beloved stepfather went into the city with Jeanie and her mother. If Nanny had ever entertained thoughts of renewing a romance with Tracy, his subterfuge in the ensnaring of Dr. Lincoln quashed that possibility.

After a short time, the doctor returned to the hotel where, guiding her into one of the sitting rooms, he tenderly took her hand and told her that she was the dearest thing on earth to him. He promised her that this new situation would never alter his love for her. Amid her tears, Nanny could see the poor man's distress when he tried to convince her that he was doing this all for her sake because, in his words, she needed a mother. For all of her unhappiness, Nanny had to fight back the laughter when Dr. Lincoln offered this absurd justification for his actions.

The reasons Dr. Lincoln decided to marry Jeanie are subject to conjecture. Had Nanny's uninhibited behavior ironically brought about this event? Had her pursuit of parties, dancing, and laughter caused him to seek a helpmate in bringing Nanny's conduct into a more restrained, ladylike demeanor? Or did Dr. Lincoln realize that the captivating and delightful Nanny who chased away the gloom of his life as a widower would likely soon establish a serious relationship and depart his home for a life of her own, leaving him to a lonely existence? Or had the passive doctor simply surrendered to the formidable forces arrayed against him by the determined Gould women, mother and daughter?

No sooner had Nanny and Dr. Lincoln returned to their home in Washington than she discovered that the house was to be completely redecorated. Under instructions sent from New York by the imperious Mrs. Gould, carpenters, painters, plasterers, and wallpaper hangers descended upon the house—all at Dr. Lincoln's expense, of course.

Still more changes occurred. To her horror Nanny learned that she had to relinquish her large room to her stepparents for their wedding bower. Cinderella-like, she would be relegated to a small room on the third story where an indignant Nanny kept scornfully silent for the sake of Dr. Lincoln.

As the wedding arrangements proceeded, Jeanie asked Nanny to be a bridesmaid. While not wishing to give this tacit approval to the union by participating in the wedding, Nanny realized that for appearance's sake she would have to comply. Still, she retained enough independence—and immaturity—to walk down the aisle holding her head in a particularly impertinent way, wearing an unpleasant expression, to indicate that she was an unwilling player in the drama. To her vengeful satisfaction, word got back to her that guests in the church did indeed whisper that Jeanie was going to have a disagreeable and intractable stepdaughter.

The domestic situation deteriorated further still. Now married and somewhat older, Jeanie could not make friends with Nanny's crowd, and Dr. Lincoln's colleagues and their wives were too old for social interaction with her. Jeanie's younger sister Sarah came down from Troy, and the home was frequently filled with their friends from upstate New York, but they had little in common with the Washington girls.

Used to having her own way without restrictions, Nanny would walk out of the house, join her friend Hallie Patterson in the carriage, and ride away to their pursuit of pleasure, leaving the Troy visitors offended and insulted. The new Mrs. Lincoln felt particularly slighted because Nanny refused to use her influence with Hallie to obtain invitations to Mrs. Patterson's "at homes" at Brentwood mansion.

Because her situation at Dr. Lincoln's had become so insufferable, Nanny found reasons not to be in the house whenever possible. She made frequent trips to Baltimore where she could still find abundant love and warm receptions among the large Smith and Moale families.

Meanwhile, Wood had reported to his duty station at Fort Bidwell, California, and was missing Nanny. He wrote to her on 21 December 1875:

> My darling, darling, darling little girl how heartsick I am for you tonight. Oh, my sweetest one, I have thought of you so much today, thought of you lovingly and longingly till it seemed as if my heart would break. . . . Do you know ma Petite that I often picture to myself the first few hours after our marriage? How hard it will be to realize that we belong to each other and that this long, dreary waiting is actually passed. How we will talk it all over sweetheart, won't we? You

will rest your head on my breast and look up into my eyes and tell me of the hopes and fears that are past and tell me with your eyes of all the love and joy that is to be. . . . Oh, Nannie, I love you so, it can never fail.[12]

Wood's picturing the tiny Nanny with her head on his breast, in fact, became their intimate position after their marriage. Nanny's letters to Wood refer often to her sitting in his lap in a rocking chair. She was indeed a petite young woman. In his letter to Nanny of 22 December 1875, he says,

I am going to give you early warning. We will be married next May, my darling, so you must be all ready by the last of April. Now I mean what I say, and you must not let the time slip away so that when I come I will find you not ready and you will say you thought I was joking. . . . Oh, Nan, isn't it splendid to think this is positively the last Christmas we will ever spend apart? The very, very last."[13]

Unfortunately, Wood was not able to put aside enough money, and Dr. Lincoln still opposed the marriage. The marriage that they dreamed about for the Spring of 1876, two years after he left for duty in the West, was postponed indefinitely, and Nanny developed some serious new romantic interests. Their former relationship now fading, Nanny formed successive relationships with no less than four young men.

Nanny referred to these men as "lovers," and to their relationships as "love affairs," but those terms did not carry as much weight in the nineteenth century as they do at present. Indeed, the term "to make love to" someone meant at that time to express one's passion in a generally non-physical manner: writing love letters, sending romantic gifts, serenading the object of one's affection, or simply being in attendance. Nanny, for all her high spirits, still occupied a highly visible place in Washington society, and it is decidedly unlikely that she was ever promiscuous.

One of her suitors was the son of a wealthy banker in Washington. Another was a clerk in the State Department who relentlessly pursued her, frequenting her home so often that the usually unflappable Dr. Lincoln expressed his irritation.

A third relationship carried serious implications. A classmate of Lt. Wood, Wright Prescott Edgerton, was stationed at nearby Fort Monroe, Virginia. He had become acquainted with Nanny on her frequent visits to West Point when he and Wood were cadets together, and he could not resist pursuing her while his friend was in the West. Nanny's willingness to enter into a relationship with one of Wood's classmates represents a double betrayal; she should have known that the young men at West Point form bonds of loyalty. Her encouragement of Edgerton's attentions constituted an infidelity on her part and on Edgerton's as well.

On one occasion, Edgerton had to return to duty at the fort, and he came to Nanny's house to say goodbye. But she had contracted measles, and when Jeanie admitted him to Nanny's bedroom she covered her face with a shawl and refused to let him see her. Outside her window, Edgerton's fellow officers called up to her, "Throw down a measle! Throw down a measle!"

A fourth "lover" was a junior navy officer, the brother of one of her Washington girl friends. She admired him enormously but she thought he was too young and immature for marriage. Her decision to discontinue seeing him does show that she considered herself of marriageable age and that she was willing to wait for just the right person. Her instincts with regard to the navy officer must have been right; years later she learned that he had been married four times.

In 1878, Wood returned on a short leave from his duties in the West. He sent a message that he was coming to Washington to see her, but she tried to avoid him, going first to Green Spring Valley to visit the Moales, but he followed her there. Then she fled to the Smiths in Baltimore, and he pursued her there. She returned to Washington, but he shadowed her once again and finally confronted her.

He now considered himself a man of the world, a soldier who had seen combat, accomplished dangerous missions, and led troops in an austere and hostile place. Determined not to give up the fight, he pursued Nanny with all the competitive spirit he had acquired at West Point and in the army.

When he arrived for this long-sought audience, he angrily accused her of faithlessness and of not continuing their correspondence when he needed tender words of devotion while serving in the rugged and dangerous West. How dare she enjoy an active social life in his absence?

Softening, he declared his love once again and, implausibly, secured from her a renewal of their engagement before he returned to his western post. Her social calendar was full; she was a beautiful, lively addition to any festive occasion in Washington, commanding the attentions of a platoon of young officers or government officials. She could have chosen from any number of suitors, but she chose Charles Erskine Scott Wood. Given her efforts to avoid seeing him, why did Nanny finally accede to the persistence of this officer whom she had forgotten during his absence and whom she had avoided on his return?

While her family might have wished to see her happily married, Wood was not the one they would have selected for her. Dr. Lincoln specifically discouraged this relationship. In a rare moment of anger, he tried to dissuade Nanny from this commitment and asked her to release Wood from his proposal of marriage.

Lt. Wood was hardly unworthy. He deserved and had earned public approbation as a graduate of West Point and as an army officer who had served bravely in the West, but the Wood family could not match the Moales or the Smiths in social standing

To be sure, Lt. Wood's father occupied a socially acceptable position as a retired navy surgeon, now a country gentleman of some status in the Green Spring Valley society. Dr. Wood was one of the original members of the Garrison Forest Farmers Club in 1877, a group of leading citizens who promoted monthly lectures by "practical men on subjects of public interest."[14]

A major obstacle to their marriage was Wood's strong views on Roman Catholicism. In letters from the West, Wood told Nanny that she should leave the Catholic Church, and he voiced strong opposition to raising their children in that faith. He wrote to her on 27 December 1877, "The dogmas are to me such drivel, the talk of the priests out here so narrow, mean, and bigoted that I am almost becoming a bigot against the worm-eaten old institution."[15]

In a letter to Wood, Nanny reveals the emotional distress she suffered in the months before their marriage. She said,

> Remember, dear, how utterly alone I am in this world to help myself in the gravest and freightiest matters. Things have been different—all would be well if a mother filled my life, a father or sister. I am almost separated from my relations. Some of them love me, and I think care for my happiness, but the relatives with each other have not been intimate enough.

She emphasized to Wood her isolation: "I am left alone to help myself in all things." Then she addresses the matter of religion:

> I must tell you how perfectly I understand your feelings and your desires in regard to our religious beliefs. Ah, but what can I do, what can I say to you except that I cannot act hastily when thinking of my love for you. I know and feel I must be true to myself, but the struggle is so hard I have done nothing lately but think of this, and then the thought will come back to me—how would I act if my dear mother was here—that thought has kept me true and good so often I almost feel as if my mother was near me.

She confronts his monolithic attitude about her religion:

If you look upon the Catholic religion as such an awful despicable thing that you would rather kill your children than have them believe in it, then what must I be in your eyes? Remember, dear, you told me of your love before religion was spoken of between us. Did you consider such a loathing of me then. And yet you wished then that I belong and must belong to you. Catholic as I am, why did you love me and make me love you in return?

Almost in a presaging of their later relationship, she tells him, "You have outgrown me in all things. Perhaps I have not developed as you wished to have me. We do change each day dear, but how different when we are apart."[16]

Despite her family's opposition and discord over religion, Nanny had several reasons to marry the handsome young officer. The resistance of both families probably brought the two together in defiant independence, but, more than that, her marriage to Wood gave Nanny a chance for revenge against her stepfather for marrying Jeanie Gould, a wound that never quite healed. Her home life had become intolerable. Displaced as the mistress of Dr. Lincoln's house and resentful of her stepmother Jeanie Gould, Nanny wanted to leave this uncomfortable situation.

Her Green Spring Valley and Baltimore relatives had long since given up trying to tame the high-spirited girl, and they all had families of their own, so her presence in any of those homes for an extended time would have been a disruptive intrusion. Her aunts in Baltimore were becoming increasingly judgmental about her reputation as a social butterfly, and a marriage and departure for the West would allow Nanny to escape their constant criticism.

When Wood was still a cadet at West Point, he paled in comparison to the older men she had known in Washington and elsewhere, but now Wood presented himself as a mature, purposeful officer with a promising career. From time spent with her beloved uncles Foster and Gibbon, she was familiar with the peripatetic and sometimes adventurous life of an officer and his lady, and perhaps the prospect of escaping Washington and accompanying Wood to the exciting West enticed her as well.

Ignoring the difficulties of the past, the two handsome, intelligent, charming young people wed on 26 November 1878.

NOTES

1. *Atamasco* derives from the Virginia Algonquin Indian word *attamusco*, meaning lily. *Zephyranthes atamasco* grow in most areas of the southeastern United States.
2. Rev. Ethan Allen, *The Garrison Church* (New York: James Pott & Company, 1898), 189.
3. W. H. Boyd, *Boyd's Business Directory* (Washington: W. H. Boyd, 1879), 58.
4. Wood's journal of letters to Nanny is part of the Wood Papers at the Huntington Library. I gratefully acknowledge permission to publish excerpts from this journal.
5. C.E.S. Wood Papers, Huntington Library, WD Box 243 (6).
6. "George Gould." *The National Cyclopedia of American Biography* vol. 2 (New York: James T. White & Company, 1921), 355.
7. Tracy Gould, *The Bride of the Broken Vow: A Poem in Four Parts* (Troy, NY: William H. Young & Blake, 1874), 89.
8. Harold Donaldson Eberlein and Cortlandt Van Dyke Hubbard, *Historic Houses of Georgetown and Washington City* (Richmond, VA: The Dietz Press, 1958), 459.
9. Robert Hendrickson, *Hamilton:1789–1804* (New York: Mason/Charter, 1976), 625.
10. "Charles Joseph Bonaparte," *The National Cyclopedia of American Biography,* vol. 14 (New York: James T. White & Company, 1910), 22.
11. Robert Barnes, *The Green Spring Valley: Its History and Heritage,* vol. 2 (Baltimore: Maryland Historical Society, 1978), 218.
12. C.E.S. Wood Papers, Huntington Library, WD Box 243 (9).
13. C.E.S. Wood Papers, Huntington Library, WD Box 243 (10).
14. Dawn Thomas, *The Green Spring Valley: Its History and Heritage,* vol. 1 (Baltimore: Maryland Historical Society, 1978), 90.
15. C.E.S. Wood Papers, Huntington Library, WD Box 243 (13).
16. C.E.S. Wood Papers, Huntington Library, WD Box 260 (9).

CHAPTER FOUR

NEWLYWEDS

I
THE WEDDING

THE WEDDING OF NANNY MOALE SMITH and Charles Erskine Scott Wood took place at her Grandmother Julietta Smith's house at 89 Saratoga Street in Baltimore. Her grandfather, Dr. Nathan Ryno Smith (1797-1877), died just the year before. He was the son of the influential Dr. Nathan Smith who made tremendous contributions to the medical profession in New England. Nanny's imperious looking grandfather taught at the University of Maryland from 1827–67 and pioneered the procedure for thyroidectomy.[1] Her father, Berwick Bruce Smith, and stepfather, Nathan Smith Lincoln, studied with Nathan Ryno Smith at the University of Maryland medical school.

Given the bad feelings between Nanny and her stepmother Jeanie, Dr. Lincoln's home in Washington would have been an awkward venue for the wedding. Although she had spent much time at Atamasco, and although Wood's estate at Rosewood Glen was less than a mile away, the occupants of both houses had voiced opposition to the marriage, so neither of them would have been suitable. Nearby St. Thomas' Episcopal Church in the Green Spring Valley would not have served either because, unlike most of the Moales who were active in the congregation they helped establish, Nanny was Roman Catholic. Wood had a strong antipathy for Catholicism—and had expressed it in letters to Nanny imploring her to set aside her religion—so he refused to be married in a Catholic service.

A compromise of these conflicting interests occurred when Nanny agreed to a Protestant ceremony, performed by the Reverend Alfred Macgill Randolph of Emmanuel Protestant Episcopal Church of Baltimore, in the secular setting of her Grandmother Smith's home. Mrs. Smith was a member of Emmanuel Protestant Episcopal Church. In keeping with the social status of the Moales, the officiant was a distinguished clergyman. Five years after the wedding, the Reverend Randolph was elected Bishop of the Diocese of Southern Virginia. The Emmanuel Protestant Episcopal Church also produced a Bishop of Maryland, the Reverend Noble Cilley Powell. General George C. Marshall, of World War Two and the Marshall Plan fame, married Eleanor Tupper Brown at Emmanuel in 1930.[2] By coincidence, Nanny's oldest son Erskine became a friend of Marshall when the general commanded Vancouver Barracks, and later Erskine served as a trustee of the George C. Marshall Research Foundation in Lexington, Virginia.

About twenty of Nanny's school chums and friends from her social set came up from Washington. Wood's West Point classmate Wright Prescott Edgerton, who had energetically pursued Nanny while Wood served in the West, did not attend, but he sent her a beautiful and expensive lace fan as a token of his undying love. Her Uncle John Gibbon, home on leave from his assignment at Fort Snelling, Minnesota, attended, but his daughter Fanny Gibbon sulkily remained upstairs and refused to come down. In 1872 when they were both staying at Atamasco, Nanny and Fanny were rivals for Wood's affection. Nanny's horse and phaeton gave her the advantage over Fanny because she had the freedom to drive over to Rosewood Glen or to rendezvous with Wood in the cemetery at St. Thomas' Church as it pleased her. Fanny harbored bitter memories of her cousin's victory in winning Wood only to rebuff him during his cadet days and in the time he served in the West, so she refused to sanction their nuptials with her presence. Fanny was also devoutly Roman Catholic and did not want to attend a non-church wedding of her cousin.

Nanny wore a bridal gown designed by Charles Worth, one of the first male designers of women's clothes. He later was a force in the haute couture of Paris. Nanny's taffeta gown, slippers and gloves cost Dr. Lincoln $1000.[3] Years later, her family bequeathed this wedding gown to the Oregon Historical Society.

Following a ceremony at which relatives on both sides were uncomfortable, Nanny and Wood departed on the midnight train to Philadelphia for an odd honeymoon that presaged the unstable marriage that would ensue.

Having at last won the prize of one of Washington's most eligible young women, Wood seems almost immediately to have retreated into a daze of regret and confusion. Their honeymoon destination and purpose appear strange and implausible. Wood remembered from his youth that in a small town near Philadelphia there lived an old man who had made matches, and, incomprehensibly, he wished to go there to see if he were still alive. This bizarre circumstance hardly seems appropriate for the honeymoon of a handsome young army officer and his equally attractive and socially prominent bride. Rather than be forward looking and accept his responsibilities as a married man, Wood seems to have longed for a return to carefree memories of his youth.

What could Wood have been thinking as they made their way out of the city to the MacAfee House, not a plush hotel but simply a wayfarer's inn? Their marriage as yet unconsummated because of their night train journey, they arrived late on the afternoon of Thanksgiving Day. When they entered the front room of the house—lobby is too grand a term—many local elderly women ensconced there beside a stove scrutinized them. Still wearing her veil, Nanny lingered near the entry, not only because she was a properly shy and bashful bride, but also because she was taken aback by the modest lodgings where she would spend the next few days of her honeymoon. Wood strode to the desk and registered, writing "United States Army" after his signature. Not used to having such an attractive couple choose to spend their honeymoon at his modest establishment, the proprietor treated them as though they were visiting royalty.

The honeymoon became stranger yet. Wood further retreated into himself. Rather than take sleigh rides or carriage excursions or strolls through the Pennsylvania countryside, the newlyweds spent much time sequestered in their room, not in sportive pleasure, but with Wood neglecting his young wife, amusing himself with his lifelong interest in art by sketching as Nanny quietly sat nearby observing.

After a few days, they returned to Baltimore but did not stay with immediate family, further evidence that emotions still ran high against the marriage. Instead they stayed with her uncle Dr. Alan Penneman Smith and his wife Emily; he was a brother of Nanny's deceased natural father Dr. Berwick Bruce Smith. Alan Smith was a professor of surgery at the University of Maryland, a consulting physician at all the major hospitals in Baltimore, and one of the original trustees of the Johns Hopkins University.[4]

At the Smiths' they prepared for their journey across the country to Wood's duty assignment at the Vancouver Barracks in Washington Territory across the Columbia River from Portland, Oregon. Nanny's first extended trip away from familiar confines of Baltimore and Washington was to Troy, New York; but now she embarked on a trip that would end on the other side of the continent. This journey would test her mettle and begin the transformation from insouciant debutante into a capable, resilient woman.

By train they made their way to Chicago where they visited the wealthy merchant Charles H. Taylor and his wife. A year earlier Wood had accompanied Taylor on an expedition to Alaska Territory, then still largely unexplored, to assess investment opportunities in mining, timber, and fishing. When the United States acquired Alaska from Russia in 1867, the first military commander of the territory was General Jefferson C. Davis, who flirted with Nanny's mother in 1861 as a lieutenant when he was stationed with her Uncle John Gray Foster at Fort Moultrie and Fort Sumter.[5]

Wood and Taylor sailed to Alaska aboard the steamer *California* in April 1877, but Taylor returned home shortly after they arrived because their Indian guides refused to venture to the remote northern sectors on the dangerous open sea. The wild rivers were not navigable at that time of the year, and the expedition's necessary equipment and supplies made going overland out of the question. Wood decided to remain rather than return with Taylor, and he obtained permission for detached service, a three-year leave of absence from his regular army duties.

His commanding officer, General Oliver Otis Howard, a hero of the Civil War, had granted Wood his leave of absence, but now a rebellion by the Nez Perces caused Wood to truncate this detached service and return to his unit of assignment to assist Howard.

While he was in Alaska, Wood became interested in the indigenous culture. At one point, as a reward for applying simple home remedies and first aid to some members of an Indian tribe, he was rewarded with the gift of a niece of the chief. Wood's biographer says, "Out of chivalrous consideration for Nannie [sic], Wood said nothing more about their relationship, but there is little doubt that he and his Chilkaht companion were sexually intimate."[6] Wood knew full well that a public acknowledgment of this sexual relationship with an Indian woman would have obviated any possibility of marriage to Nanny; moreover, his army career would have been effectively ended.[7]

After a few comfortable days with Taylor in Chicago, the Woods set out for Fort Snelling, Minnesota, where her uncle, Brigadier General John Gibbon, who was in command there, had preceded them following their wedding in Baltimore. By now it was New Year's Day, 1879, and Nanny remembered years later how bitterly cold it was in that northern region where soldiers had to keep large fires going outside to enable them to perform their duties of maintaining equipment and horses. Following army custom, the officers had a New Year's Day reception, so the attractive niece of the post commander received ample attention from the young officers and the ladies as well.

Apart from a few long train rides and the numbing winter cold, Nanny's trip so far had been consistent with her comfortable Eastern life: a stay with the wealthy Taylors in the dynamic city of Chicago, and a visit with her officer husband to an army post commanded by her uncle. From Fort Snelling the couple began their cross-country trip in earnest by train.

II
THE TRIP WEST

Nanny was to see what life in the West was all about. Unlike her civilized and cultured home in the East, the interior of the country was still dangerous. Custer died at Little Bighorn less than three years before in 1876. Wood had been in combat with the Nez Perces as late as October 1877 when Chief Joseph surrendered. As an aide to General Howard, Wood had been at the center of the battle and at the actual surrender ceremony which he recorded and published.[8] Although armed conflict with Native Americans was effectively over, the deaths of 200 Native Americans at Wounded Knee would not occur for another thirteen years in 1890.

Nanny ventured into an American West that still was fraught with a variety of threats to health and safety—attacks from Indians, bandits, and wild animals; affronts from assorted desperadoes such as horse thieves and cattle rustlers; and threats from natural disasters such as prairie fires, searing desert heat, snowstorms, tornadoes.

Their itinerary would take them by train to San Francisco

NEWLYWEDS

Union Pacific train that took Nanny and her husband on their trip to Vancouver Barracks, Washington Territory, where they began their married life.
SOURCE: Union Pacific Railroad Historical Collection.

and from there by ship to the Vancouver Barracks. Travel by rail in the United States was rapidly improving when the Woods began their trip. The first transcontinental railroad was completed on 10 May 1869 linking two major lines, the Union Pacific and the Central Pacific.[9] The Northern Pacific ceremonially broke ground on 15 February 1870 near Duluth, Minnesota, with actual construction beginning in July of that year, so a section of this line was readily accessible from Fort Snelling. On 8 September 1883, the last spike was driven to make the Northern Pacific the first railroad by a single company to cross the continent.[10]

Nanny and Wood began their journey from Fort Snelling on the Northern Pacific line, went down through Iowa, and changed to the Union Pacific at Omaha, Nebraska. Then they went through Nebraska and Colorado to Ogden, Utah, the western terminus of the Union Pacific at that time.[11] From Ogden they continued through Utah and Nevada, passing through Winnemucca and Mills City and on to Reno before crossing the Sierras into California.

Nanny recalled that while on board a Union Pacific train—she thought that particular section of track was new because few towns had sprung up along this line—she had some adventures that caused her to wonder just exactly what her life in the West would be like.

At a particularly lonely spot their train stopped to take on wood and water and to allow the passengers to stretch their legs. Without her husband, Nanny walked down the track a little distance. From a nearby shack she heard someone incongruously playing beautiful music on a violin, not a fiddle sawing out a country ditty, but a genuine violin from which came classical music. As she approached the shack, the owner came out to greet her, happy to see someone new in this isolated place. Nanny complimented him on his playing and asked if he lived alone. He replied, "No, ma'am. I have a partner. We came out together to strike it rich. But three days ago he walked up the canyon by himself, and he hasn't come back. I'm afraid the coyotes have eaten him." Nanny shuddered and thought to herself, "My lord, if I've come to this kind of country, I want to go home."

In her second episode on this journey, Nanny's train collided with another. Fortunately, neither Nanny nor Wood was injured, but one of the passengers on her train had a leg cut off from the impact of the collision, and the authorities put the injured man in Nanny's Pullman berth to transport him to the closest settlement. Once again she witnessed the precarious way of life that was so unlike her safe world "back East."

From our vantage point today, we might think that simply riding on the train was the safest part of her honeymoon trip; however, train travel was, in fact, quite dangerous. As more tracks connected more towns in these early days of railroad travel, collisions occurred frequently. In the five years immediately preceding Nanny's trip in January 1879, from 1874–78, the *Railroad Gazette* reported 4,846 deadly railroad accidents; 1,698 of these occurred because of collisions.[12] Telegraph communications could be unreliable, and mechanical switching equipment could fail. In addition to the danger of collisions, trains could derail, catch fire, uncouple because of malfunctioning equipment, or suffer brake failure. Nanny deserves some admiration simply for embarking on this long and perilous train journey.

A third, even more dramatic event occurred on their cross-country trip. Isolated communities, little more than a few ranches located within a half-day's ride, could not afford a formal system of law enforcement. Most of the interior states were still officially territories with uniquely devised legal infrastructures. Unlike the popular image depicted in films, many towns did not have their own sheriff, and jails could be makeshift facilities. United States Marshals covered large judicial districts. Circuit judges, when available, traveled wide areas to dispersed pockets of population to hold court. Lacking a circuit judge, some communities elected a local citizen as justice of the peace, and, to a large degree, vigilantes dispensed swift justice without the benefit of any form of due process of law. The railroads also hired "agents," an armed constabulary, who could use force if necessary to protect their passengers and property and to maintain order on the lines.

About dark one evening, while making good time, the train began to slow and finally came to a standstill. The conductor came through Nanny and Wood's car telling the passengers to stay in their seats and remain silent. A few minutes later the conductor returned with several men, including one whose hands were bound. The conductor told the passengers that the local officials had just captured a murderer who had killed a railroad agent and his entire family on the prairie not far from there.

The men in charge led the prisoner through the car so that everyone could get a good look. As they passed, the leader announced that they were going to hang the prisoner and asked everyone to remain quiet and witness the event. When she realized the enormity of what was about to take place, Nanny began shaking. Wood, who had seen far worse than this fighting Plains Indians, remained calm.

The party exited the train and assembled just outside Nanny's window. She heard the leader ask, "Have you anything to say for yourself?" And then they hanged the murderer from a telegraph pole a few feet away from Nanny. She tried not to look, but, like the other passengers, was compelled to witness the fellow's last moments. She thought, "Oh, I wish I were back in Baltimore. Why did I ever come to this wild country?"[13]

This prisoner was John Vassar, a young man from Dakota who was arrested just a few days before. As one Union Pacific Railroad official said, he had "committed enough crimes to hang him a dozen times." A newspaper account said, "The Union Pacific is making an organized and successful effort to break up the gangs of robbers who have been committing depredations in the country along the line."[14]

Frontier justice, as it was called, was the norm, not the exception, in the time that Nanny and Wood crossed the country. Groups with names such as the Regulators, the Moderators, the Committee for Safety, and the Vigilance Committee could, and did, hang, maim, brand, or whip their victims.[15] Their actions engendered a macabre sense of humor; victims would be invited to a "necktie party," "a hemp stretching," or a "tree decorating." Perhaps this dark humor indicates the intolerance of the vigilance committees to those lawless men who chose to take self-serving advantage of others in a place where people depended upon mutual trust and decent behavior for survival.

Some of the executions, such as the one Nanny witnessed, were carried out with at least a measure of decency. In Idaho a vigilance committee condemned to death two highwaymen. One asked for time to pray and became silent, but the other swore furiously and cried out, "Hang me first, and let him pray!"[16]

Although Nanny's eyewitness experience with lynching was disturbing to her personally and a shock to her refined eastern sensibilities, such activities frequently occurred. In South Dakota in October 1878, just three months before Nanny passed through that region, two separate lynching events occurred: one near Fort Pierre when two bandits from a larger gang were captured and hanged; and another near Rapid City when a horse thief and highwayman named "Lame Johnny" stretched a rope while being taken to jail.[17]

These dramatic incidents—the man apparently "eaten by coyotes," the train wreck and dismemberment of a passenger's leg, the lynching of a murderer—might have caused a less plucky young woman to turn back. Nanny could have said, "This is a mistake. I'm not meant to be in this place. Take me home where I belong." But she did not. These events were beginning to shape her character; the Washington debutante was being left farther behind with each mile as the train carried her deeper into this new phase of her life.

III
THE WEST COAST

When Nanny and Wood crossed the border from Nevada to California, passed through Placer County on the western slope of the Sierras, and entered Sacramento, she must have felt that they were at last returning to civilization. From there they could take any number of trains of the Central Pacific through Vacaville, Vallejo, Oakland, and, finally, by ferry, San Francisco.

Exhausted from the cross-country trip, they were also hungry and broke. When they left Baltimore, they carried with them a basket of treats prepared by the famous Maryland Club, the most prestigious social club, founded in 1858. The first president of the Maryland Club was Jerome Napoleon Bonaparte, son of Nanny's cousin Betsy Patterson Bonaparte. One historian said that for Baltimoreans "the presidency of the Maryland Club is just about the highest social honor."[18] That food got them as far as Fort Snelling where, once again, they started their long trip with a large hamper of edibles prepared by the ladies of the post. But by the time they reached Sacramento, the food was depleted, and for the last two days of their journey they subsisted on anchovy paste that they brought all the way from Baltimore.

A small menu of food was available in dining cars on most of the larger railroad lines by this time, but passengers usually purchased food that was fresh, hot, and ready at the stations along the way. They could also buy baskets of food for about $1 to take with them for long stretches of unpopulated road.[19] Unfortunately, the Woods could not purchase meals because they had no money.

Although Nanny had enjoyed a life of luxury among her distinguished relatives, she had not inherited any money from the Moales nor the Smiths. Nathan Smith Lincoln and his wife Jeanie Gould Lincoln felt no obligation to support Nanny who had married Wood over their objections. In short, she was penniless, dependent upon her husband's meager army wages.

Charles Erskine Scott Wood always lived beyond his means, a habit he inherited from his father. Nanny's husband insisted on the best, especially with regard to his tailored suits, silk ties, and custom-made stickpins; his home furnishings—silks, damasks, statuary, paintings, wallpaper, crystal, fine wine, custom leather bound books—all had to be the best. For much of their married life they teetered on the edge of bankruptcy because of the disparity between his lavish tastes and small income.

When they arrived in Sacramento, Wood spent the fifty cents he had been hoarding to send a telegram to friends in San Francisco saying that they would be arriving soon. When they finally did reach San Francisco, he had not a penny in his possession. Nanny, who had been accustomed to enjoying life without regard to cost, now found herself transforming into the marriage partner who had to learn how to live practically and frugally.

Before they departed Baltimore, Wood had drawn his month's pay in advance. Officers could go to the nearest military installation, present their pay book, and draw cash from the Quartermaster. The Quartermaster would keep detailed records of his disbursements and send copies to

Washington for reconciliation with individual officers' pay records. Officers could draw several months in advance, but eventually the pay records might reveal profligate living, gambling debts, an inclination to alcohol, or other indications that an officer was living beyond his means. Antiquated as that system sounds today, it actually was quite feasible given the small size of the standing army, and no other system could have worked as well given the state of communications at that time.

Although the MacAfee House near Philadelphia where they spent their first married days had been modest, Wood had, nevertheless, exhausted his entire month's advance pay on the train trip. Perhaps Wood felt that the honeymoon really could begin now that the arduous trip was behind them and Nanny had proven that she could be brave and spunky. The ordeal of the cross-country trip elicited from Nanny a resolution and determination that had never been required of her in her pampered eastern life. Nanny might have felt in her element back East, but now Wood felt that he could show her his world of soldiering and the energetic West Coast societies of San Francisco and Portland.

They went at first to the home of Dr. and Mrs. Alfred A. Woodhull, an army surgeon, who insisted that they stay with them. They had expected to remain in San Francisco for just a few days, but General Howard sent a telegram saying the Columbia River was blocked with ice and the boats could not get to Vancouver Barracks. He advised that they stay in San Francisco until the river thawed. This unexpected vacation gave Nanny a chance to see the city and to visit with prominent members of society. In a letter to her grandmother Smith, she said, "Mrs. Louis McLane and daughters came out to see me, also the Bowies, and others I had a letter of introduction to. A Mrs. Griffith and daughters which Mrs. Patterson sent me. I find they and the McLanes are decidedly the ultra nice people of the city." She also takes some pride in the fact that "we haven't quarreled yet and are still very happy—and good to each other."[20]

After a few days with the Woodhulls, the Woods relocated. Rather than seek out a modest hostelry in San Francisco, Wood checked them into one of the "most ornate and splendid hostelries in the world."[21] True to form, he took Nanny to the Palace Hotel, William Ralston's grand enterprise modeled on Europe's finest hotels. With its four hydraulic elevators that whisked guests to their floors, the Palace's luxury and elegance were unmatched in San Francisco when it opened on 2 October 1875, just three years prior to the Woods' marriage. Because of financing problems with the Bank of California, William Ralston never got to see his dream realized; he drowned himself in San Francisco Bay two months before the hotel opened.[22]

They checked into a suite consisting of two rooms furnished with French chandeliers, English marble fireplace surrounds, a Persian bedspread, and Turkish carpets.[23] They stayed only a few nights in the Palace. Apparently Wood had been saving this surprise as a reward to his bride for her bravery in surviving the trip. Leaving Nanny to enjoy the opulence of the Palace, Wood went to the Quartermaster Office in San Francisco to draw against his next month's pay.

After this brief stay at the Palace, Nanny and Wood relocated to the mansion of her cousin, Louis McLane (1819–1905). As we have come to expect of her relatives, this branch of Nanny's family was extraordinary in many fields, in this case politics and finance. Louis McLane married Nanny's great-aunt, Sophie Hoffman of Baltimore in 1849. Sophie was the daughter of Ellen Moale (Nanny's grandfather's sister) and Samuel Hoffman.

This branch of the family had its roots in Delaware where Louis McLane, Sr. (1784–1857) was first a Representative to the United States Congress, then a Senator. Louis McLane, Sr., helped defend Baltimore when he commanded a company against the British in 1812. Then the family became associated with Baltimore and Maryland politics. Later, President Andrew Jackson appointed him minister to the Court of St. James's in London, the most desirable ambassadorship. He became Secretary of the Treasury, and, finally, Secretary of State.

Leaving public service he became president of the Baltimore and Ohio railroad company and established the family in Baltimore. He was also the president of the Morris Canal and Banking Company.

Nanny's cousin Louis McLane, Jr., followed his father's footsteps in becoming associated with banking interests. After a career in the United States Navy where he served with Colonel John C. Fremont in the California Battalion during the Mexican War, he resigned his commission in January 1850. He entered the steamboat business where he continued to amass his fortune. In June 1866 he became the president of the famous Wells Fargo Bank. In 1875, he became the president of the Nevada Bank of San Francisco, the position he held when Nanny and Wood arrived in San Francisco.[24] A history of San Francisco calls Louis McLane one of the "people that made San Francisco's world go round" and "one of the blue-blooded elite of the fashionable South Park and Rincon Hill society crowds."[25]

Just as she had enjoyed the lavish hospitality of the Taylors in Chicago, she was happy to arrive at the home of people who could accommodate her with servants, luxurious rooms, and elegant meals. She must have felt that she had made the right decision to persevere on the overland journey, and her first impressions of her new life on the West Coast were pleasant indeed.

The next few days in San Francisco would extend her education in being an officer's lady beyond what she had observed from her aunts who married generals. Officers and their ladies who were stationed at interior posts such as Fort Custer, Montana; Fort Halleck, Nevada; Fort Bridger, Wyoming; and Fort Apache, Arizona, had a much harder time of it than Nanny and Wood at Vancouver Barracks, Washington Territory. Still, the social niceties, even in those remote areas, survived despite the isolation, deprivations, and genuine danger. The possession of a few pieces of valuable furniture, a silver tea service, a china set, reminded these ladies that they represented civility in this wild region.[26] Ladies at these interior posts would hold teas, holiday receptions, poetry readings, chorales, musicales, and similar events to introduce a bit of culture.

At San Francisco, the main army post was The Presidio, a former Spanish garrison guarding the Bay. General Irvin McDowell, the commander of the entire Military Division of the Pacific from 1876–82, invited Wood and Nanny to a dinner party, along with General and Mrs. Oliver Otis Howard, Wood's commanding officer of the Department of the Columbia, who at last had been able to navigate the frozen Columbia River at Vancouver Barracks. Nanny did not understand that McDowell's command was huge; she thought he simply commanded The Presidio. Years later, from 1901–04, Nanny's dear Uncle Ned Moale would command the Presidio as his last assignment before retiring from a career that began at Fort Moultrie and Fort Sumter.

General McDowell was a West Point classmate of General Pierre Gustave T. Beauregard who commanded the attack on Fort Sumter in 1861. The members of their class still on active duty split when the Civil War occurred. Of the forty-four members who graduated with them, nine became generals in the United States Army, and seven became generals in the Confederate States Army.[27] Charles Erskine Scott Wood was drawn to General McDowell through their similar interests. Educated in France before graduating from West Point in 1838, McDowell had a reputation in the army as an intellectual. He enjoyed music, painting, architecture, and landscape gardening, all of which appealed to Wood.[28]

General and Mrs. McDowell were known for entertaining lavishly because of McDowell's personal fortune.[29] The officers, most of whom were generals and colonels, wore their dress uniforms bedecked with campaign ribbons, and the ladies wore their finest gowns. Fortunately, Nanny had shipped some boxes containing a few nice dresses that arrived with them on the train.

Wearing the best dress in her wardrobe, Nanny arrived at the dinner party with her handsome new husband and made a late entrance because their hack driver got lost, despite the explicit instructions provided by Louis McLane; Nanny thought their driver must certainly have been drunk. Because she was related to the McLanes, well-known in San Francisco society, and because she was a Washington belle just arrived from the East, Nanny received the attention of the older women who normally would have expected her to defer to them, owing to their husbands' higher rank. Nanny remembered, "I was made something of."

    Nanny's hostess, Mrs. McDowell, paid great attention to the newcomer to army life, insisting that they must be related because she was a Poultney. Samuel Thomas Poultney (1797–1864), born into a family with roots in Pennsylvania and Maryland, married Ellin Moale Curzon (1799–1880) on 20 September 1828. Ellin Moale Curzon was the daughter of Richard Curzon Jr. and Elizabeth Moale, sister of Nanny's great-grandfather Samuel Moale. Indeed, the Poultneys could claim high social standing in those days and for years later. In the first two decades of the twentieth-century, one of Baltimore society's best known figures was Ellin North Moale's great-grandson, Walter de Curzon Poultney. A history of Baltimore calls him "a bachelor of ancient and honorable lineage. . . . He was known to the town as Sir Walter. No social occasion was complete without his presence."[30] Not known is whether Nanny discovered that Mrs. McDowell was the former Helen Burden of Troy, New York, where she certainly must have known Jeanie Gould whose marriage to her stepfather had brought much misery into Nanny's life.

    Elizabeth ("Lizzie") Howard, whose husband far outranked Lieutenant Wood, became miffed that Nanny received so much attention from Mrs. McDowell. The normal pecking order would not put the wife of a lieutenant in this favored position. Mrs. Howard became even more distressed when the other ladies made plans to call upon Nanny at Louis McLane's sumptuous home at a time when Mrs. Howard had to sail with her husband for Vancouver Barracks. Doubtless the officers' ladies saw Nanny as a means to rise in social prominence in San Francisco by meeting the McLanes.

The women did call on Nanny over the next several days, and protocol demanded that she return their calls. She did so and found amusing the fact that she had to travel by rowboat to The Presidio, but this method was quicker and easier than travel by carriage. These visits became part of her education. When in private with each lady, she heard the latest gossip about the other wives, and learned that many of them were not on speaking terms with each other. Military housing, while occasionally quite fine (such as that appropriated by her Uncle John Foster during the New Bern campaign in the Civil War), could also be incommodious at other posts. At The Presidio the officers' apartments shared stairwells, and Nanny learned that the wives quarreled because they could not agree on whose turn it was to clean this common space.

Shortly before the Woods left San Francisco, Nanny had a thorough medical examination by Dr. Woodhull who pronounced Nanny pregnant after scarcely a month of married life.

Later in January 1879, when the ice cleared from the Columbia River, they sailed aboard the *George W. Elder* steamship for Portland where they checked into the Esmond Hotel on the waterfront. General Howard, who had preceded them from San Francisco, met them at their hotel to escort them across the river to the Vancouver Barracks. Accompanying Howard was James T. Gray, captain of the steamer *Lurline*, who presented a gift of a silver service to the newlyweds. Shortly thereafter Captain Gray married Grace Ellen Howard, the general's daughter. For their wedding gift, Nanny and Wood presented them with a large watercolor painting by Wood of an island in the Columbia River.

Lt. Wood had served with General Howard his entire brief military career, and Howard had entertained hopes that Wood might marry his eldest child, Grace, whom Wood had gallantly "beaued" around before his marriage to Nanny. Because the house that was being constructed for the Woods was not completed, General and Mrs. Howard invited them to lodge with them, and Nanny dreaded it.

Howard had ordered this house built in August 1878 and the Howard family occupied it in the second week of January 1879, so the house was brand new when the Woods arrived that same month. Costing $10,000, the house contained work rooms and servant quarters at the rear. In October 1879, former general and president Ulysses S. Grant and his wife stayed at the house on their round-the-world tour, and a year later President Rutherford B. Hayes stayed there two nights. Grant, as president, had personally appointed Wood to West Point in 1870. As a key member of Howard's staff, Wood—and Nanny—were included in the festivities surrounding visits such as these.

General Howard was known in army circles as the "Christian General." Highly religious, he not only recited long prayers but also led the singing of hymns at breakfast, dinner, and supper. Nanny recalled that every time she thought about Mrs. Howard she pictured her in a brown alpaca dress with a high neck and stiff linen collar, her hair drawn tightly back into a bun. The fun-loving Nanny chafed under all the religious rituals, not to mention the loss of privacy that newlyweds might wish to enjoy.

When an officer and his lady arrived at a post, army etiquette required that his commanding officer allow the other officers to meet them by hosting a reception. Mrs. Howard proposed such a reception. The other wives knew Lt. Wood, but they were eager to meet his bride. Nanny was in a familiar element with receptions or social events of any kind.

Mrs. Howard had developed a method of conducting these affairs. She sent an enlisted soldier around to the officers' quarters with a sheet of paper, and the ladies would write down their names if they planned to attend—a typically military efficient way of issuing an invitation and receiving an instant R.S.V.P.

The day of the reception was dismally rainy, so the ladies arrived wearing long raincoats to protect their dresses. One lady wore a handsome sealskin coat; this unique and attractive garment efficiently shed the rainwater and gave panache to its wearer. Scoring a social coup with her unique attire, Alice Sawtelle captured Nanny's fancy right away, and they became friends. She was the wife of Major Charles Greene Sawtelle, West Point class of 1854, a classmate of General Howard. Sawtelle held the regular army rank of major when Nanny met him, although he had held brevet brigadier general rank during the Civil War. He retired in 1897 as a regular brigadier general and chief of the Quartermaster Corps.[31]

Their class included George Washington Custis Lee, son of Robert E. Lee, and James Ewell Brown Stuart, the great cavalry leader of the Confederacy. Lee finished first in the class of forty-five graduates; Howard was fourth; J.E.B. Stuart was thirteenth; and Sawtelle was far back at thirty-seventh.[32] Nanny Wood and the Sawtelles had similar backgrounds. Major Sawtelle's father had served two terms in the United States Congress as had several of Nanny's relatives, and Alice Chester Monroe Sawtelle was the daughter of the president of the New York Produce Exchange and was used to the finer things in life.[33] They recognized in each other the social graces that came with their upbringing, and although Alice was older than Nanny, she had just the sort of outgoing personality that would mirror Nanny's own and counterbalance Mrs. Howard's stuffy Victorian morality. Knowing that Alice Sawtelle would be a friend and neighbor made Nanny comfortable in this new place.

The Vancouver Barracks, situated on the Columbia River with a view of beautiful snow-clad peaks, was not the grandest of posts, nor was it a post of particular hardship compared with those of the interior. Large, heavy Victorian furniture popular at that time could not practicably be shipped from the East, so the army wives had to make do with locally handmade items. Instead of freestanding breakfronts, built-in sideboards and cupboards had to suffice. Army-issue tables, not known for elegance of style but for their ability to be dismantled and roughly transported, were painted and covered with cloths to conceal their crude construction. Rugs were impossible to obtain, so animal skins from Alaska covered the floors. Colorful Native American baskets woven from cedar root, beargrass, cherry bark, raffia, and strips of seal skin served as interior decorations. Women accomplished both a social and a domestic purpose when they gathered to make lace for inexpensive but attractive window treatments.[34] Quilting parties provided an opportunity for conversation and produced a utilitarian item of bed clothing to ward off the severe winter cold.

Domestic help was readily available, and officers' wives could pick from many nationalities of workers. Chinese laborers were in plentiful supply as cooks, gardeners, and housekeepers. Native American women cooks, Irish nannies, and even Russian women housekeepers from Alaska were hired for small salaries.[35]

Another source of cheap labor for the officers' wives were young enlisted men, called "strikers," who, in many cases, almost became members of the family. For $5 to $10 a month, the strikers performed repairs around the house and maintained their officers' tack and equipment.[36] In return the young soldiers could receive an occasional home-cooked meal and enjoy the warmth and cheer of a home with children.

Accessible to sea shipping, Portland regularly received delicacies from California—oranges, melons, mushrooms, and pineapples. A variety of fish and wild game of all sorts was plentiful: ducks, geese, deer, rabbits, and squirrels. A creative army wife could enjoy a measure of comfort using some imaginative culinary and decorating skills.

Nanny and Wood remained with General and Mrs. Howard for about two months until their house was habitable. The Woods' next door neighbor was a bachelor, Captain Thomas William Symons, a classmate of Wood, who was the first honor graduate of the class of 1874. She had met Symons during their cadet days at West Point, and she also knew him later when he was stationed in Washington, DC. Symons was enthralled with Nanny and considered it an honor to render her any service, large or small. He began to eat breakfast with them every Sunday, even when Wood was away for several days on a mission. Nanny's Chinese cook, Dock, did not approve of Symons' eating Sunday breakfast there without Wood present and banged pots and pans while muttering his disquiet in Chinese.

Shortly after Nanny and Wood moved into their own house, an important court-martial brought many young officers to Vancouver Barracks from outlying posts. They would serve as prosecuting and defense counsels and as members of the jury. Nanny came up with the idea of entertaining these young officers at a dinner party, and she determined that she would show them how it was done back in Baltimore and Washington society.

She and Dock—who had become quite a good cook under her guidance—planned the menu with enthusiasm, and Wood and some of his friends went out into the nearby forests to acquire the ingredients for a "game dinner" in imitation of the pheasant and terrapin delicacies served back home in Maryland. Nanny's menu consisted of little native oysters on the half shell; trout à la Meuniére, with Saratoga chips, roast grouse with bread crumb sauce and guava jelly, terrapin prepared Maryland Club style, with thin tea biscuits, roast saddle of venison with sweet potatoes, port wine sauce with melted currant jelly, and lettuce salad. She complemented the food with Rhine wine, Madeira, and Champagne.[37] This meal was the talk of the post for weeks afterwards, and Nanny was recognized thereafter as one of the officers' ladies who had style.

Younger than the other officers' wives, Nanny did not have many intimate friends, but she and Wood did enjoy the company of Captain Joseph Alton Sladen and his wife Martha Frances Sladen and became close friends with them. Wood and Captain Sladen had come to depend upon each other as they often rode together on missions into the interior, monitoring the peace and checking on the Indian reservations in their sector. At this time the Sladens had a five year old son, Fred W. Sladen who later had a distinguished career in the army as a major general. He returned to serve at Vancouver Barracks, 1904–05, and later became Superintendent at West Point, 1922–26.[38]

Pregnant with their first child, Nanny had to accept the separations that occurred when Wood left for patrol missions. She wrote an endearing letter to Wood in May 1879:

> Dearest heart,
> How often I have come to you through these poor letters for comfort and consolation. Nights when I felt just how terribly long the distance is between us. And I thought the day till we wedded would never come! I am almost that unhappy tonight my darling. I want you so. The nights are so long. Will you never, never come, sweetheart. I am so tired tonight and would give all that I possess, but you my precious one, if I could be sitting with you in the big rocking chair before the fire, my head resting on your dear breast. Oh, what happy moments those are—and what shall I do to realize your pleasure when you come back home![39]

A month later, when she has just learned that Wood's unit is homeward bound, she wrote of her excitement at seeing him again:

> Oh, Sweetheart, can't you hear me call for you and say how impatient I am? It seems now that I just couldn't wait for your return now that your face is turned homewards. I want to fly to you and meet you half way. It would lessen the distance between us a little. . . . I want to fall in love with you all over again, my dear precious husband, who is all, all my own. What a blissful thought. . . . Oh, my darling, I wish I was a thousand times better, worthier, prettier for your dear sake—I pray God to spare my life that I can devote all of it to you, dear heart. . . . You are the dearest, most devoted lover and husband in the world. I am so glad when you tell me you miss me. . . . Our love is indeed a sweet, sweet blessing. . . . My arms are waiting to welcome you home.[40]

Nanny delivered her first child, Erskine, on 1 September 1879, scarcely ten months after her wedding. Nanny was able to obtain the services of a "fat old English woman" as a nurse and helper. As is customary in army communities, other women rejoiced in the birth of Nanny's son and also offered help.

Two days after Erksine's birth, Nanny once again came to understand the character of the rowdy Pacific Northwest when Wood was called upon to lead a group of soldiers from the 21st Infantry Regiment to raid a scow anchored in the Columbia River between Portland and Vancouver Barracks. Aboard the scow were a large supply of whiskey and prostitutes. Wood's military unit teamed up with civil authorities from Portland and swooped in aboard the steamer *Vancouver* to overwhelm the floating brothel. The customers on the scow resisted, and, after a reinforcement unit arrived, the soldiers and police took more than thirty-five prisoners to the guardhouse at the barracks for the night. The next morning when the authorities sorted out the customers, twenty-five soldiers and a dozen citizens of Portland were handed over to the military or civil courts for punishment.[41]

Thus began Nanny's assimilation into the life of an army wife. She was welcomed as one who could brighten the social scene with her charm, good looks, and sense of humor. She and her husband made a handsome pair who would be welcome guests at any table. Her savoir faire at social gatherings and her taste in clothing made her one whom the other wives would want to befriend.

Nanny's marriage brought about an unexpected maturity, a departure from her largely self-centered world. In the nineteenth century, marriage meant that two people became one, and that one was the husband.[42] Her situation, as with most women of that day, required that she follow her husband wherever his orders took him. The other officers' wives helped acquaint her with the role of a dutiful military spouse. Having her first child so soon after her marriage also forced her to assume complex responsibilities that would have been foreign to her one year earlier. In short, Nanny was no longer the spoiled adolescent.

As part of General Oliver Otis Howard's team, the Woods, Sawtelles, and Sladens would go with him to their next duty assignment, the United States Military Academy at West Point.

NOTES

[1] Oliver S. Hayward and Constance E. Putnam, *Improve, Perfect, and Perpetuate: Dr. Nathan Smith and Early American Medical Education* (Hanover, NH: University Press of New England, 1998), 256.
[2] Thomas L. Culbertson, Letter to author, 19 April 2001. Dr. Culbertson is the rector of Emmanuel Episcopal Church.
[3] Suzanne Richards, "Historic Wedding Gown on Display," Portland *Journal* 12 March 1971, sec. 2, p. 1. Nanny's taffeta gown was faced in book muslin. It had a tucked front, draped sides and tulle at the neckline and sleeves. A shell motif of taffeta appeared on the train of the dress. She wore simple white slippers and had white mitts. The dress was donated to the Oregon Historical Society where it remains today.
[4] "Alan Penneman Smith," *The National Cyclopedia of American Biography* (New York: James T. White Company, 1893), 154.
[5] Robert M. Utley, *Frontier Regulars: The United States Army and the Indian, 1866-1891* (New York: Macmillan Publishing Company, Inc., 1973), 187.
[6] Robert Hamburger, *Two Rooms: The Life of Charles Erskine Scott Wood* (Lincoln: University of Nebraska Press, 1998), 39.
[7] For an account of the consequences of an Eastern young white man's marrying an Indian woman, see James Willard Schultz's *My Life as an Indian: The Story of a Red Woman and a White Man in the Lodges of the Blackfeet* (New York: Doubleday, Page & Company, 1907). Schultz says, "My people would never forgive me for making an alliance with [an Indian woman]. They were of old, proud Puritan Stock, and I could imagine them holding up their hands in horror at the mere hint of such a thing" (99). When, in 1870 in Montana, Schultz took an Indian

woman as wife without the benefit of religious sanction, he severed all ties with his family back in New England.

8 Charles Erskine Scott Wood, "The Surrender of Chief Joseph." *Harper's Weekly* 17 November, 1877: 906.

9 John S. Bowman, ed., *The World Almanac of the American West* (New York: Pharos Books, 1986), 218.

10 Edward W. Nolan, *Northern Pacific Views: The Railroad Photography of F. Jay Haynes, 1876–1905* (Helena, MT: Montana Historical Society Press, 1983), 63.

11 Don D. Snoddy, Letter to author, 3 January 2001. Dr. Snoddy is the historian for the Union Pacific Railroad.

12 Charles Francis Adams, Jr. *Notes on Railroad Accidents* (New York: G.P. Putnam's Sons: 1879), 265–266.

13 Dr. Norton H. Moses of Montana State University–Billings, who wrote the authoritative book on lynching [*Lynching and Vigilantism in the United States: An Annotated Bibliography* (Westport, CT: Greenwood Press, 1997)] reveals that 326 vigilante movements in America killed at least 729 people. But the exact number cannot be determined because annual national statistics were not collected before 1882, three years after Nanny's journey and the lynching she witnessed.

14 "A Ruffian's Career Checked," *New York Times* 14 January 1879: 1.

15 Matt Dodge, "The Vigilantes: Nebraska's Public Defenders." *Real West* 27 (October 1984): 15.

16 John W. Clampitt, "The Vigilantes of California, Idaho, and Montana." *Harper's New Monthly Magazine* 83 (August 1891): 148.

17 Wayne Gard, *Frontier Justice* (Norman: University of Oklahoma Press, 1949), 191.

18 Francis F. Beirne, *The Amiable Baltimoreans* (New York: E. P. Dutton and Company, 1951), 30. The first president of the Maryland Club was Jerome Napoleon Bonaparte, nephew of the emperor and Nanny's relative.

19 Don D. Snoddy, Letter to author, 9 January 2001. Union Pacific historian Snoddy estimates that Nanny and Wood's trip from Fort Snelling to San Francisco took about six days.

20 C.E.S. Wood Papers, The Huntington Library, WD Box 261 (15).

21 Barnaby Conrad, *San Francisco* (New York: Bramhall House, 1959), 24.

22 Charles Caldwell Dobie. *San Francisco: A Pageant* (New York: Appleton-Century Company, 1939), 150.

23 Gordon Thomas and Max Morgan Witts. *The San Francisco*

NEWLYWEDS 83

Earthquake (New York: Stein and Day, 1971), 20. When the Palace Hotel was built, San Franciscans said that if the Palace ever burns down, the city itself would also be gutted. Thirty-one years later, in the aftermath of the earthquake of 1906, flames engulfed the original Palace.

[24] "Louis McLane." Biography File. Sacramento: California State Library, 1952.

[25] Robert O'Brien, *This Is San Francisco* (New York: McGraw-Hill, 1948), 48.

[26] Michele J. Nacy, *Members of the Regiment: Army Officers' Wives on the Western Frontier, 1865-1890* (Westport, CT: Greenwood Press, 2000), 21.

[27] Paul W. Child Jr., ed., *Register of Graduates* (West Point, NY: United States Military Academy, 1990), 263.

[28] Dan L. Thrapp, *Encyclopedia of Frontier Biography*, vol. 2 (Spokane, WA: The Arthur H. Clark Co., 1990), 901.

[29] Robert M. Utley, *Frontier Regulars: The United States Army and the Indian, 1866-1891* (New York: MacMillan Publishing Co., Inc., 1973), 35.

[30] Francis F. Beirne, *The Amiable Baltimoreans* (New York: E. P. Dutton and Company, Inc., 1951), 296.

[31] "Sawtelle." *New York Times* 5 January 1913: 17.

[32] Paul W. Child Jr., ed., *Register of Graduates* (West Point, NY: United States Military Academy, 1990), 278.

[33] "Charles Greene Sawtelle." *The National Cyclopedia of American Biography* vol. 28 (New York: James T. White & Company, 1940), 360.

[34] Mary Rose, "150 Years at Vancouver Barracks: Life of an Army Wife." *The [Vancouver] Columbian* 28 March 1999: D7. Rose's article mentions that Nanny, "the Washington, D.C., belle" arrived with her husband at the Vancouver Barracks in January 1879 and enlivened the winter months there.

[35] The Russian women became available as servants to American officers when Alaska, which had a large Russian population, was incorporated into the Department of the Columbia in 1867.

[36] Michele J. Nacy, *Members of the Regiment: Army Officers' Wives on the Western Frontier, 1865-1890* (Westport, CT: Greenwood Press, 2000), 58.

[37] Erskine Wood, *Life of Charles Erskine Scott Wood* (Vancouver, WA: Rose Wind Press, 1991), 28-29.

[38] "Fred Winchester Sladen." *The National Cyclopedia of American Biography*, vol. 34 (New York: James T. White & Company, 1948), 255.

[39] C.E.S. Wood Papers, Huntington Library, WD Box 260 (18).
[40] C.E.S. Wood Papers, Huntington Library, WD Box 260 (9).
[41] I am grateful to Mary Kline Rose who supplied a typescript of a news item appearing in the *Vancouver Independent*, 3 September 1879, for the account of the floating brothel.
[42] Jane H. Pease and William H. Pease, *Ladies, Women, and Wenches* (Chapel Hill: The University of North Carolina Press, 1990), 2.

CHAPTER FIVE

WEST POINT

WHEN THE WOODS RELOCATED in 1880 from Vancouver Barracks to the United States Military Academy at West Point, New York, they returned to one of the scenes of their courtship in the early 1870s. Both had fond memories of that time, but their return also awakened in Wood memories of his chafing under the restrictions and discipline of cadet life. While he was a cadet he informed his father that he wanted to resign from the academy and undertake a career in writing, but Dr. Wood furiously forbade his son from pursuing this impulsive idea.

Although he had successfully performed the duties of an army officer, Wood never really assimilated his free spirit with the demands of rules and regulations that governed the daily life of a career officer. Soldiering in the West was a young man's adventure, and, from all accounts, Wood faithfully contributed his intelligence and energy to his various missions, but his heart was never in it.

He participated dutifully in the battles with the Nez Perce and sensed that he was witnessing a moment in American history with the surrender of Chief Joseph, but he was dismayed by the treatment of the Indians by agencies of the federal government.

His dissatisfaction with military life would become increasingly evident during their time at West Point. As part of General Howard's personal staff, he enjoyed privileges that come with being part of the commander's inner circle. His duties, first as aide, then as post adjutant, were not physically onerous compared to his duty in the West. Ever urbane and gregarious, Wood was at his best when distinguished visitors came to the military academy. In those quasi-social situations, his wit, erudition, and striking good looks made him a valuable protocol officer and commander's representative.

As was the case when they moved to the Vancouver Barracks, the Woods' assigned house at West Point was not ready, being occupied by a departing officer and his wife who had not yet vacated the quarters, so Nanny stayed for a few weeks with her Grandmother Smith in Baltimore. Now that she was a mother, she enjoyed better relations with her Baltimore family than she did at the time of her marriage. Little Erskine charmed all the Smith and Moale women.

The Woods occupied a small house near the old hospital and the cadet mess hall in the center of the post, known then as South Gate.[1] Erskine enjoyed watching the cadets march past on their way to meals in the mess hall. He soon became the darling of the post. Once he played in the middle of the street with a huge drum that the drum major had given him. He was so absorbed in his playing that the cadets had to break ranks and march around him.

West Point occupies one of the most beautiful spots in America where the Hudson Highlands rise sharply out of the Hudson River, an American fjord. Although only fifty miles from New York City, West Point, even today, is isolated and creates its own social structure. In Nanny's day, a trip to New York City had to be carefully coordinated with riverboat or train schedules. Both means of transportation were available but not always reliable. A day-trip to the city might result in an unplanned overnight stay if mechanical problems arose with either conveyance. A coach or buggy ride was not feasible for a day-trip because of the rugged terrain of the Highlands.

In addition to its isolation, West Point was a small army post in those days. The Corps of Cadets totaled only about four hundred (in contrast with four thousand today), and the staff and faculty was comprised of less than fifty officers. Officers and their ladies had to develop their own amusements: holiday parties, receptions for newly assigned officers, promotion celebrations, and the like. Officers wives organized book clubs, poetry readings, arts and crafts activities, and musicales. Cadet dances, or "hops," highlighted special occasions, and the staff and faculty and their ladies enjoyed these events as well.

Young married officers, such as the Woods, occupied a special place in the unique social order of West Point. Cadets could develop with impunity platonic crushes on the beautiful wives of junior officers. Bachelors could visit in the homes of their married brother officers and provide dotingly witty attention, all within the bounds of propriety, on the young wives. The teenaged daughters of senior officers and the wives of younger officers had standing invitations to join the cadets in the afternoon for dancing lessons. The army felt that "officers and gentlemen" needed to know how to dance in order to acquit themselves properly in social situations. If an insufficient number of wives and daughters showed up at dancing classes, the cadets danced with each other.

Although she had not suffered many deprivations at Vancouver Barracks, Nanny felt at home on the east coast, just a day's journey from Baltimore by ship or train, and she continued to enjoy her role as an officer's wife. She delighted in looking across the Hudson River from her home on the bluffs high above. Large, steam-powered ocean-going boats could travel the deep river from New York harbor as far up as Albany. The "point" of West Point obtrudes into the Hudson which otherwise runs almost due north and south, so the large ships would have to slow to make the turn. At night the ships would be ablaze with light, and Nanny thought they looked like floating palaces.

One boat in particular became important to her, the night boat that took passengers and cargo from New York City to Albany. The *Mary Powell* had made this night run for over twenty-five years, and successive generations of West Point officers and their ladies had come to know the captain and crew. With her characteristic charm, Nanny was able to enlist the services of the captain and the ship's caterer to obtain delicacies from the fresh food markets in New York City. When the ship stopped at West Point's South Dock going south, she would give the caterer her shopping list and money; then, on the northbound return to Albany, she would receive her order. Although Wood's army pay was still meager, Nanny prided herself on her gift for setting an attractive table and entertaining guests. Her experience growing up in Baltimore and Washington taught her how to provide good food and drink, pleasant conversation, and comfort for her guests.

One particularly distinguished visitor—Mark Twain—sorely tested both her skills as a hostess and her patience. Wood met Mark Twain when the writer came to West Point on 28 February 1881 for a cadet celebration known as One Hundredth Night, so named because one hundred days remained until graduation. Over the years this celebration had become elaborately entertaining with skits lampooning the staff and faculty, songs, and, in the case of Mark Twain, the telling of stories and jokes. Cadet Andrew Hammond, class of 1881, was a parishioner in the Hartford, Connecticut, church of the Reverend Joseph Twichell, Mark Twain's good friend and spiritual advisor. With Twichell's assistance, Hammond persuaded the famous writer to come to West Point and entertain the cadets, staff, and faculty. As adjutant and protocol officer, Wood met Mark Twain and arranged the details of his visit.

Mark Twain so much enjoyed his time at the One Hundredth Night festivities with the class of 1881, that he readily returned with Twichell in June for their graduation, this time staying with Nanny, Wood, and his unmarried sister Hannah Wood who was visiting from the Green Spring Valley to help care for young Erskine while Nanny was approaching the birth of her second child.

For the June 1881 visit, Mark Twain and Twichell traveled

in distinguished company on a train from his home in Hartford. Secretary of War Robert Lincoln (son of Abraham Lincoln), General W. T. Sherman (an old friend of Wood's father Dr. William Maxwell Wood), General and Mrs. Nelson A. Miles (Miles did not like Lt. Wood), General Stewart Van Vliet, General J. Tidball, General Horace Porter, and three Connecticut politicians, Governor Hobart B. Bigelow, and two ex-governors Marshall Jewell and Richard D. Hubbard. Former Confederate generals "Fighting Joe" Wheeler and Milo T. Polk also were among the notables. The most distinguished military and political visitors stayed at the West Point Hotel or with General Howard, and other officers accommodated the others as they were able.

Lt. Wood, whom Mark Twain liked right away and teasingly addressed as "Colonel," was delighted to have a famous writer stay in his home. Nanny and Hannah were less pleased. Hannah occupied the only decent guest bedroom in the Woods' modest house, so the family had to improvise and hastily decorate the attic room where Mark Twain and Twichell would have to share a bed. With the same ingenuity she used to decorate their Vancouver Barracks quarters, Nanny went to the post sutler and bought some cretonne, colorful cotton or linen used for slipcovers or draperies, and arranged this material over simple packing crates to conceal their lack of proper furniture. In the village of Highland Falls outside the main gate, Wood bought some paint, but the only colors available were white, aquamarine blue, and scarlet. Calling upon his skill as an artist and his knowledge of literature, Wood painted the ceiling white and blue to resemble the sky; he decorated the borders of the ceiling with quotations from Shakespeare, Chaucer, and other notable English authors. Using an ornate "fractur" script, he embellished characters to simulate an antique English Gothic style.

The boat with the distinguished visitors was late and arrived at dinnertime. Mark Twain knew that Wood was married, but pretended not to know. As he entered the house and saw Nanny, he exclaimed, "Oh, are you a married man?" Nanny was unfamiliar with Mark Twain's brand of humor, having read none of his work, and was initially offended. When he saw that the table had been prepared and ready for dining, Mark Twain insisted upon shaving before he would eat, perhaps to further amuse Wood and irritate Nanny.

Everyone was invited to attend the graduation hop, the June Ball, but Nanny, only weeks away from giving birth, could not attend, so Wood, Mark Twain, and Twichell went and stayed out late. Mark Twain enjoyed the company of young people, and the sight of the handsome cadets and their special partners for the evening was a delight for him.

Only a few short years before Nanny had been one of those vivacious dance partners when Wood was a cadet. Now a mother expecting her second child, Nanny felt forlorn and unattractive as she remained at home with her spinster sister-in-law Hannah.

The next morning, Mark Twain continued to be a nuisance. Already annoyed by his apparent lack of gracious behavior, Nanny and Hannah remained at their breakfast table and refused to send the only maid to the attic room with breakfast for her two guests when they did not come down. To keep the peace, Wood sent his enlisted orderly with a tray of food, but shortly thereafter Twichell came down alone and politely inquired whether it might be possible for him to have some breakfast. Surprised, Nanny asked, "Didn't you have some breakfast in your room?" He replied, "Mark got absorbed in reading the literary excerpts on the wall and ate both breakfasts."

Later, Mark Twain also descended and joined Twichell at the breakfast table for coffee. Hannah Wood brought little Erskine into the room and asked, "Don't you adore babies, Mr. Clemens?" Mark Twain replied, "No, I hate them." The shocked Miss Wood and Nanny both stood astonished and offended. Then the humorist launched into an impromptu rendition of a comic sketch about babies, giving the ladies a free performance.[2] But they did not understand his humor and found Mark Twain impossibly offensive. He and Twichell remained for another night, and Nanny arranged a stag dinner—men only—for her two houseguests, her husband, and some of his officer friends. Nanny had become an accomplished cook, and she prepared some of her favorite dishes for Mark Twain to be presented by her servants after she and Hannah departed to visit friends. She began with soufflé de fromages, cherries on stem in cognac, and Nymph Aurora. The main courses were Sorbonne chicken custard with cream sauce; roasted lamb with mint jelly; and artichokes stuffed with chestnuts. These were followed by Salade La Haute with green mayonnaise; La Belle Creole dessert; flower ices, French pasties, and curaçao.[3]

Nanny thought the decorations in the attic room looked cheap and grotesque, but Mark Twain was captivated by Wood's clever extractions from literary masterpieces, and his discovery that Wood was a serious student of literature led to a historic collaboration of one of Mark Twain's most infamous writings. He and Wood began a friendship and a correspondence that would span many years. On 3 February 1882, Wood wrote the following:

> My dear Mr. Clemens,
> I take my pen in hand to let you know that one of my unreconstructed friends in Norfolk sent me a boxful of diamondback terrapins, the creeping things, & I suppose I must eat them. So Mr. Blackburn of Kentucky—a reconstructed southerner who says he's not afraid of them, is coming up from Washington on or before the 21st of this month. On the night of the 21st we are to have some cadet foolishness as last year when you were here, after which there will be a ball. I know you dote on balls and on the 22d an Officers Hop. Mrs. Wood has gone to Baltimore to stay till April and I want you and Mr. Twichell and Mr. Blackburn and Mr. [Alexander W.] Drake, Art Supt of the "Century" [Magazine] and Mr. Jones, a young artist lately from Russian & Parisian wilds to occupy my

sanity, destroy the terrapins, play whist and use up that Scotch Whiskey you left here.
  Please communicate with Twichell and let me know. The invitation stands until supper is announced. Feb. 21 11 P.M.
  With best regards
    I am Yours Sincerely,
      C.E.S. Wood

  P.S. I have moved into a larger house. You need not this time be "Enskied and sainted" but you'll have to take a room in common with Twichell.[4]

This letter reveals Wood's eagerness not only to see the famous writer again, but also to enjoy himself fully while Nanny was visiting family in Baltimore for two months. Mark Twain was unable to come to Wood's stag party because serious illness struck both the Clemens and Twichell households.

In a letter dated 11 February 1882, Wood expressed his disappointment that Mark Twain and Twichell would not be able to return for the proposed stag party. He said, "I myself had anticipated some medieval rambles with you; for until Prince & Pauper I had no idea you were a student of dead days."[5] Wood's remarks sparked an idea with Mark Twain; he had been trying to arrange for a printing of his bawdy Elizabethan tale *1601*. He replied to Wood on 21 February 1882:

> My dear Wood,
>   Twichell's Tribe and mine are still in the doctor's hands. The circumstances remain in both cases about as they were before. Do not let the charming Kentucky school girl [Terese Blackburn, daughter of Wood's Kentucky friend] get away from there: put her under martial restraint until we come,[6] for Joe and I are certainly coming, just as soon as things will permit.
>   We bear your proffered hospitality in mind, and

propose to take advantage of it as early as we can. Speaking of dead days: Have you seen my 1601?[7] Did not Gen. Sherman or Gen. Van Vliet have it when I was at West Point? It's [sic] circulation is quietly enlarging: A copy of it has just gone to Japan. I shall get into trouble with it yet before I die. With warmest regards to yourself and Mrs. Wood.
    Yours faithfully,
    S. L. Clemens

P.S. Excuse haste and a bad pen.[8]

Mark Twain wrote *1601* in 1876 and sent copies to close personal friends. The scatological humor of Queen Elizabeth I, Sir Walter Raleigh, Shakespeare, Ben Jonson, and other Elizabethans discussing the breaking of wind and the emitting of noxious fumes at a small gathering shocks some readers. Told from the point of view of the queen's cupbearer, *1601* is salty language indeed. Having distributed all his copies, Mark Twain made a quiet visit to West Point some time between the end of February and early April 1882 to inquire about Wood's using the West Point printing press to produce about fifty copies of *1601*.

On 3 April 1882, Mark Twain sent the original of the manuscript, pointing out in this letter that it contained many errors of spelling and giving Wood complete autonomy to "make any and all corrections that suggest themselves to you."[9] Wood entered into the spirit of the project. He and the print shop foreman, Sergeant Tucker, soaked handmade linen paper in a weak coffee solution, then placed the pages in a warm room to mildew. He also altered some type to give it an antique appearance and corrected a few spelling errors. Then he and Tucker ran off sixty copies, fifty of which went to Mark Twain; Wood kept ten copies which he distributed to friends.[10]

The story of Wood's developing relationship with Mark Twain indicates the growing estrangement between Nanny and Wood. Wood enjoyed associating with the rich and famous, but Nanny was becoming maternal; Wood wanted to fulfill his dream of becoming a writer, perhaps a successful writer of caustic wit and political commentary such as Mark Twain, but Nanny was not clever in literary matters; Wood wanted to be like Mark Twain, a man of the world, but Nanny was becoming content to manage a household.

Having babies and being a good mother allowed Nanny to become closer to her own family and especially to Wood's family. She had viewed her sister-in-law Hannah Wood as cold and imperious, but Hannah's visit to West Point brought the two into a close friendship. After Nan Wood (future Representative to the United States Congress) was born, Wood's mother and his younger sister Roberta ("Berta") came for a visit. Berta was a pretty girl, and the word soon spread through the cadet corps about her presence, and the Wood household was filled with cadets vying for her attention. Remembering her own experience of coming to West Point to see her beau, Nanny happily played hostess to these youthful gatherings.

The Woods remained at West Point for two years. During that time Wood obtained from General Howard permission to take courses at Columbia University in New York City. Taking courses in law and political science, Wood earned the Bachelor of Philosophy (Ph.B.) degree, and had plans to continue until he earned his doctorate in a related field, perhaps with an eye toward becoming a professor at a university or a writer of political commentary.

But General Howard received orders in 1882 to relocate to Omaha, Nebraska, to assume command once again of an army department in the West. As part of Howard's staff, Wood—and Nanny—would be expected to accompany him. Wood did go to Omaha, but Nanny returned to Baltimore to stay with relatives who were delighted to see her and to have the opportunity to spoil her two small children, Erskine and Nan.

She still loved her stepfather Dr. Nathan Smith Lincoln and had softened her view of Jeanie Gould Lincoln who had become a mother also, but Nanny was never close to Dr. and Mrs. Lincoln again. Neither of them was her biological parent, and she harbored lingering resentment over Jeanie's intrusion. Moreover, Dr. and Mrs. Lincoln now had two children of their own to occupy their time and concerns.

Both of Dr. Lincoln's children obtained stature as writers. Attaining prominence in journalism, G(eorge) Gould Lincoln (1880–1974) became known as the dean of Washington political writers. During his sixty-year career he covered every presidency from Theodore Roosevelt's to Gerald Ford's. He graduated from Yale in 1902 and worked at the *Washington Times*, the *Washington Post*, and the *Washington Evening Star*. He accurately predicted in print the outcome of every presidential election he covered. In 1970, President Richard Nixon awarded him the Medal of Freedom.[11] He resigned from *The Star* as an active reporter at age 84, but he continued to write a weekly column for that paper until shortly before his illness and death at age 94.[12]

Natalie Sumner Lincoln (1881–1935) was a writer of detective fiction and editor of the magazine of the Daughters of the American Revolution for twenty years. Natalie Lincoln was the society editor of the *Washington Herald* newspaper from 1912 to 1914, when she began writing novels. She wrote twenty-two mystery and detective tales, all but one having a Washington setting. She also contributed mystery stories in *Smith's Magazine, McCall's, All Story,* and *Detective Story*.[13]

An interesting episode in Natalie Lincoln's life occurred when she made one of the great finds in American stamp collecting. In April 1930, while sifting through some family papers she found a stamp on one of Dr. Lincoln's letters that was postmarked in Baltimore, May 1847, two months before the federal government began to issue stamps. Affixed to the envelope was one of the rare "provisional issues by postmasters." The letter and stamp had lain neglected in a wicker basket in her workshop for at least nine years. Only about half a dozen other "postmaster" stamps are known to exist. Within two weeks of her discovery, in the Great

Depression, she sold the stamp to the Nassau Stamp Company for $10,000.[14]

Natalie was following her mother's lead as a novelist. Jeanie Gould Lincoln (1846–1921) published several novels, among them *A Chaplet of Leaves* (1869); *Marjorie's Quest* (1872); *Her Washington Season* (1884); *A Genuine Girl* (1896); *The Luck of Rathcoole* (1911); and *A Javelin of Fate* (1906). *A Javelin of Fate* is set in Baltimore during the Civil War and reflects the rebel sympathies that divided Nanny's family.[15]

This was a time of change for Nanny and Wood. The Lincolns were involved with their own two children, and Nanny became less dependent on her Washington and Baltimore relatives. Wood realized that he had lost his enthusiasm for soldiering and that he had become intrigued with the idea of becoming a lawyer. He obtained Howard's permission to continue his studies at Columbia University on detached service (and half pay).

He returned to Columbia to pursue his legal studies, and at first stayed with old friends of his family, the Peter Brysons (Wood's brother Peter Bryson Wood was named for this family, and Wood and Nanny named their daughter Lisa Bryson after Mrs. Bryson). Then he took a small apartment of his own and lived what Nanny called "a bachelor's life." During this time he became friends with several artists and writers who formed part of New York's bohemian scene, and the contrast between their independent, free-wheeling lives and the necessarily regulated, rank-bound strictures of life as an army officer caused Wood to question the path his future should take. Artists Albert Pinkham Ryder, J. Alden Weir, and Childe Hassam became his dinner companions. Over wine, their conversations about art, travel, and literature awakened new interests in Wood.

After he took his law degree, Wood returned to the West, this time to remote Boise Barracks, Idaho, and a few weeks later Nanny, pregnant again, made another wintry cross-continent journey in December 1883 with her two small children, taking with her an elderly woman as nurse and companion. Her family in Baltimore engaged the services of this woman, refusing to allow Nanny to undertake the arduous journey alone. Nanny could have remained in comfort through the winter with her large family in Baltimore, but she had learned that she could deal with adversity. She knew what childbearing entailed and felt confident that she would again have a fat, healthy baby. She also wanted Wood present at the birth of their third child.

Suitable army quarters were not available, so General Howard's wife had arranged for Nanny to take room and board with the wife of an ex-steamboat captain in familiar surroundings at Vancouver Barracks. Because she could not join Wood at Boise Barracks, having two small children and being pregnant with a third, Nanny was lonely and depressed at Christmas 1883. One of the officers went into the nearby woods and cut down a Christmas tree for her and the children, and she decorated it as best she could with a few trinkets and homemade items.

Showing remarkable intrepidity and devotion to Nanny, Wood came down the partly frozen Columbia River as far as he could by ship, then completed the journey by jumping from ice cake to ice cake to join Nanny and the children. Thus Wood was with her when she gave birth to their third child, William Maxwell Wood, on 23 January 1884.

Wood's military career had become tenuous. General Nelson A. Miles, now one of the most powerful generals in the army and overriding General Howard's protective mentorship, harbored a grudge against Wood because he felt that his published accounts had diminished Miles's role in the capture of Chief Joseph, shining a more flattering spotlight on General Howard. When Wood asked for a re-assignment from the remote interior post at Boise, Idaho, to familiar Vancouver Barracks, an irritated Miles let it be known that Wood's career as an army officer was perilously close to being terminated because of his pertinacity in placing his personal comfort above the needs of the service.[16]

Resigning a commission in the post-Civil War era usually

resulted from one of two situations. Either the officer had significant business prospects in the civilian world or his career had become besmirched in some way. Wood had not tarnished his personal name through ignominious acts, but he had run afoul of the protocol system traditionally entrenched in the military. Officers of Wood's era remained in the army at the rate of 81 percent. From 1874, when Wood graduated from West Point, until 1897, the army consisted of approximately 2,100 officers. For seventeen of these twenty-four years, less than one percent resigned.[17] With the threat of a court-martial for insubordination looming, Wood wisely resigned from the service. That he chose to resign is yet another indication of his unwillingness to accommodate himself to an institutional structure. It also indicates his confidence in himself to make his way in the world with his growing family.

Armed with his recently acquired law degree, his confidence, easy charm, and good looks, Wood took Nanny and their children to Portland and began a new phase of their lives, a period that would provide Nanny with much joy as a mother and much emotional pain as a wife.

NOTES

[1] The old hospital currently houses the Admissions Office, and the old cadet mess hall, now called Grant Hall, is a reception room and cadet lounge in the central post area.

[2] See Dixon Wecter, *Mark Twain in Three Moods* (San Marino, CA: Friends of the Huntington Library, 1948), 27–32. Wecter relates C.E.S. Wood's version of Mark Twain's story. No other record of this story exists; it is not the famous "To the Babies" toast Mark Twain delivered at the reunion of Civil War veterans of the Army of the Tennessee in Chicago, 13 November 1879. Wood's version contains several errors: the date of this visit was June 1881, not July 1882; nor had Nan been born yet.

[3] I am grateful to Nanny's granddaughter Nancy Wood Robinson von Gimbut who possesses Nanny's handwritten recipes and menus for providing copies of them. Some of these were written on West Point stationery, thus indicating that these were her favorite dishes for entertaining at that time.

[4] Philip W. Leon, *Mark Twain and West Point* (Toronto: ECW Press, 1996), 225–26.

[5] Leon, 227.

[6] Wood tried to entice Mark Twain to come for a visit by invoking the name of young Terese Blackburn. Late in life, Mark Twain had an inordinate affection for young girls, calling them his "Angel-Fish" and organizing an "Aquarium." See John R. Cooley, "Mark Twain's Aquarium." *Mark Twain Journal* 27 (1989), 18–24; John R. Cooley, *Mark Twain's Aquarium: The Samuel Clemens Angel-Fish Correspondence, 1905-1910* (Athens: University of Georgia Press, 1991); also Doris Lanier, "Mark Twain's Georgia Angel-Fish." *Mark Twain Journal* 24 (1986), 4–16.

[7] The complete title of Mark Twain's bawdy story is *[Date, 1601.] Conversation, as it was by the Social Fireside, in the Time of the Tudors*. Students of Mark Twain refer to this work by the abbreviated title *1601*.

[8] Leon, 227–28.

[9] Leon, 228.

[10] Mark Twain, *1601*. Franklin J. Meine, ed. (Mattituck, NY: Amereon House, 1938), 17.

[11] "G(eorge) Gould Lincoln," *Contemporary Authors* vol. 113 (Detroit: Gale Research Company, 1985), 290.

[12] "G. Gould Lincoln, 94, Political Reporter," *New York Times* 2 December 1974: 36.

[13] "Natalie Sumner Lincoln," *Who Was Who in America* vol. 1 (Chicago: The A.N. Marquis Company, 1942), 730.
[14] "Natalie S. Lincoln, Author, Is Dead," *New York Times* 1 September 1935: 18. Her novels include *The Trevor Case* (1912); *The Man Inside* (1914); *The Official Chaperone* (1915); *I Spy* (1916); *The Moving Finger* (1918); *The Three Strings* (1919); *The Red Seal* (1920); *The Unseen Ear* (1921); *The Cat's Paw* (1922); *The Meredith Mystery* (1923); *The Thirteenth Letter* (1924); *The Missing Initial* (1925); *The Blue Car Mystery* (1926); *Dead Man's Bluff* (1928); *The Fifth Latch-Key* (1929); *Marked "Cancelled"* (1930); *No. 13 Thirteenth Street* (1932).
[15] "Mrs. Jeanie Gould Lincoln," *Book Review Digest* vol. 2 (Minneapolis: The H.W. Wilson Company, 1906), 207.
[16] Robert Hamburger, *Two Rooms: The Life of Charles Erskine Scott Wood* (Lincoln: University of Nebraska Press, 1998), 74.
[17] Edward M. Coffman, *The Old Army: A Portrait of the American Army in Peacetime, 1784-1898* (New York: Oxford University Press, 1986) 283.

CHAPTER SIX

PORTLAND

I
STARTING OUT

WHEN THE WOODS ARRIVED in Portland in 1884, they already had three children: Erskine (born at Vancouver Barracks, Washington Territory, 1 September 1879, named after Wood); Nan (born at West Point, 15 July 1881, named after Nanny); and Max (after Wood's father William Maxwell Wood and elder brother Max, in Vancouver, 23 January 1884).[1]

Nanny took to the role of mother naturally and with surprising patience. Because Nanny was so young when her mother died she remembered little about her. The various Moale and Smith aunts who tried to influence the exuberantly adolescent Nanny were a temporary succession of mother figures. Certainly her stepmother Jeanie Lincoln provided no direction or example in the short time Nanny lived with her and Dr. Lincoln. So Nanny, having no long-term maternal role models, followed her instincts and became a devoted mother who would provide a home abounding with grace and love.

With his customary bravado and confidence, Charles Erskine Scott Wood embarked upon his career as a lawyer in Portland in March 1884, an exciting time in the city's history. New municipal improvements—water and sewage systems, public transportation, gas and electric utility systems—were making the quality of life in Portland as convenient and comfortable as any large city in the country. He already knew many of the leading citizens from his time in the army as a key aide to General Howard at Portland and nearby Vancouver Barracks, and he was quick to capitalize on these friendships. Wood acquired a reputation as a young man of many talents who had an ability to get things done. Soon he joined other forward-looking, civic-minded leaders of the community who promoted the arts through the founding of libraries, museums, art galleries, and performance halls. He found himself appointed to various governing boards, advisory committees, and task forces.

Wood was one of those that Rudyard Kipling described in *From Sea to Sea* when he visited Portland in 1889, five years after Nanny and Wood settled there: "You could find men who had thrown in their lives with the city, who were bound up in it, and worked their life out for what they conceived to be its material prosperity."[2] Portland's energy, its railroads, docks, and wharves, made a great impression on Kipling.

Nanny and Wood were to live in Portland longer than any other place, but what should have been a time when their marriage quietly matured into a blend of professional career, family concerns, and community interests became instead a period of marital discord.

Wood, it seems, discovered that women found him irresistible. As he became established in the professional and social spheres of Portland, he realized that the civilian world allowed relatively more freedom than had his army life with its strict rank protocols and codes of conduct. Always uncommonly handsome, his face now radiated maturity and warmth; women thought his alluring eyes projected a soulful sensuality. His reputation as a West Pointer and as an Indian fighter elevated his status among the leading men of the city. Moreover, as a prolific publisher of magazine articles and poetry, he acquired an intellectual aura. His lavish entertaining, his cultured mannerisms, his dandyish dress—silk shirts, rings, stickpins—all made him a bon vivant for whom the doors of Portland, including bedroom doors, were opened.

In contrast to her youthful flirting and vivacious personality, Nanny evolved into a modest, cultured nineteenth-century woman—wife, mother, and promoter of civic pride through gardening. Much of the credit for Portland's sobriquet as the "Rose City" goes to Nanny for her sponsorship of horticultural events.

Cicero H. Lewis, one of the leading men of Portland who had amassed great wealth in the mercantile trade, insisted that Wood, Nanny, and their three children join him, his wife, and their ten children in his mansion at no expense. The Woods enjoyed Lewis's generosity for two months while they searched for a house to rent.

Their first house was located at 433 Tenth Street.[3] Shortly after they established themselves at this address, they received an invitation to a fancy-dress ball from the Henry Failings, one of Portland's most prominent families. Mr. Failing, whose father had twice been mayor of Portland, was the president of the First National Bank from 1869 until 1898, and he served three terms as mayor.[4] Being invited to a grand social occasion at the Failings' home was an important entrée to Portland society.

Nanny did not own a suitable dress to wear to the Failings' party, so she crafted one out of muslin curtains. Having no proper carriage in which to transport Nanny through the snow, Wood placed a large wooden box atop Erskine's sled, lined it with Alaskan furs, and pulled Nanny to the Failings' mansion at the corner of King and Main Streets. Despite her lack of material wealth, Nanny was comfortable and undaunted at the opulence of the Failing mansion and in the homes of other established families of Portland. All those evenings with the Pattersons at Brentwood back in Washington and the formal military balls at West Point had prepared her well to present herself as a cultured, attractive young wife of a promising lawyer.

She moved easily and graciously in Portland society with

young friends as well as the more established families. One of the younger set was Stewart B. Linthicum (1850–1949), an attorney who joined Wood's law firm. From a distinguished old Maryland family, Linthicum followed the pattern of many wealthy young men from the East who ventured west to seek independence. His cousin Congressman J. Charles Linthicum introduced the bill that became law making "Star Spangled Banner" the National Anthem. Stewart and Charles Linthicum were descendants of Abner Linthicum Jr., a captain in the War of 1812. The town of Linthicum, Maryland, founded by his family, is located near the Baltimore-Washington International Airport.

Young Linthicum missed Baltimore and practically lived at the Woods' house, where he doted on the still attractive Nanny, frequently escorting her to parties when Wood was unable to go. Linthicum was devoted to Nanny in the same manner that Captain Thomas Symons was at Vancouver Barracks. Nanny was accustomed to having unmarried young men as admirers, but no hint of scandal ever attached to her. Eventually Linthicum married the Woods' friend Marie Louise Wilson and was always a favorite male friend of Nanny. When Nanny's son Erskine graduated from Harvard and could not decide on a career, Linthicum, who by 1910 had become a partner in Williams, Wood & Linthicum,[5] counseled him to pursue the law and join his father's firm. Erskine studied law with Linthicum and at Oregon State University, passed the bar examination, and was admitted to practice in 1912.[6]

Having so recently left the army, Nanny and Wood still had many young friends stationed nearby. One of them, Captain Elijah Merrill, West Point class of 1878, commanded the artillery unit at Fort Stevens which, along with Fort Canby, guarded the entrance to the Columbia River that runs sixty miles inland to Portland. In the summer of 1885 he offered his house to Nanny and the children for the entire summer. Nanny's friend Emma Lewis, daughter of Cicero H. Lewis, stayed with her the whole time, and the two young women enjoyed each other's company and planning the social season to come in Portland.

The next summer Nanny's uncle, General John Gibbon, who was at that time commanding the Department of the Columbia, gave her the use of a beach house at Fort Canby. Instead of having one constant houseguest, this summer she had many visitors from Portland who came and stayed for varying lengths of time. Stewart Linthicum was a frequent guest, and she also played hostess to some of the finest families, including the Failings and Kathryn (Kitty) Seaman Beck. Kitty Beck would become one of Wood's first mistresses.

In those early years the Woods' best friends in Portland were Captain and Mrs. Charles Ridgly Barnett, West Point class of 1868. The Barnetts had three children the same age as Erskine, Nan, and Max, so they became steadfast playmates. These were happy times for the growing, gregarious family, and Nanny was comfortable in the roles allowed women in that time and place.

II
MOVING UP

Wood enjoyed entertaining beyond their means, and the couple acquired a reputation for serving the best food and finest wines in their group of young friends. Years later Nanny recalled, "We were noted for our nice supper parties." They were able to afford a Chinese servant, Guy, who cooked, babysat, and did house and yard work. Guy stayed with the Woods for fifteen years.

From their cottage in South Portland, now S.W. 12th Street, the Woods moved, after two years, to a larger rented house atop a hill at the corner of King Street and Salmon Street.[7] At this location their close friends were another substantial Portland family, the Winslow B. Ayers; Daisy Ayer became Nanny's closest friend. Winslow Ayer (1860–1935) arrived in Portland one year before the Woods settled there. He made a fortune in the lumber business and, like his friend Wood, contributed to the cultural life of his adopted city. In the Central

Library of the Multnomah County Library, a plaque honoring his efforts to establish the library reads, "To his creative imagination and constant labor the public library system of Multnomah County is a monument." The Ayer and Wood families shared Thanksgiving dinner for many years. In 1914, when he was away from Portland and could not be present for the traditional meal, Wood sent a light-hearted twenty-four line poem entitled "Thanksgiving at the House of Ayer." The last two lines read, "Here's to the stars above us! Here's to all who really love us:/ Here's to all at Daisy's table my love and my goodnight."[8]

Lisa and Berwick were born in this house on King Street. Nanny's three older children had been born while Wood was an army officer and were delivered without expense by an army surgeon. Now, however, they had to seek the services of Dr. Holt Wilson, father of Marie Louise Wilson whom Stewart Linthicum married. On 15 December 1885, Dr. Wilson delivered Eliza "Lisa" Bryson. On 28 May 1887 Berwick Bruce, named after Nanny's father Dr. Berwick Bruce Smith, was born. By 1891 the Woods had moved from the King Street home to a larger house at 761 Flanders.[9] Their friends in the old neighborhood were unhappy that this move took them so far away, but the new house signaled their upward mobility as Wood took on more important and lucrative legal work.

The Wood boys had the run of the new neighborhood. Wood had bought them a pony, and they all had bicycles, so they could roam at will with their playmates. Their father encouraged them to be fearless and independent. On one occasion the boys rode their pony down the hill to the streetcar tracks where they halted the pony as a car was approaching. The conductor just kept going until a horrified passenger called out, "Slow down! You're going to kill those children!" The conductor calmly replied, "You can't kill them. Them's Woods."[10]

The Woods' next door neighbors were Captain and Mrs. William Logan Geary. He had been a classmate of Wood at West Point, so they had all known each other for years. Nanny remembered Geary from her visits to Wood when he was a cadet. The Gearys had five sons who became the constant companions of Nanny's boys. Guy, the Chinese servant, complained loudly about having so many rowdy boys in the house.

While they were still at the Flanders Street home, Nanny received some unusual visitors. In 1889, Chief Joseph (1840–1904) of the Nez Perce tribe came to Portland where Wood had arranged for his friend the sculptor Olin Warner (1844–96) to execute the Skidmore fountain, a public monument named for a Portland businessman. Warner arrived in Portland in 1888 to oversee the erection of the fountain. Warner is famous for many sculptures, including the bronze entry doors to the Library of Congress.[11] Wood asked Warner to create a bronze medallion of the chief.

Accompanying Joseph were seven other chiefs. Normally these Indians would have been confined to a reservation, so their presence in Portland was noteworthy. Wood had known some of them from his days as an Indian fighter in the army years earlier as an officer on the staff of General Howard when they captured the Nez Perces at the battle of Bear Paw Mountains in Montana in 1877.

Warner made three bronze medallions of Chief Joseph. One is in the Oregon Historical Society, one is at the entrance to the Chief Joseph Dam on the Columbia River, and one went to Erskine Wood, Nanny's oldest son.[12] His medallion includes his Nez Perce name, Hin-Mah-Too-Yah-Lat-Kekht, and the date 1891. Nanny's grandson, John Gibbon Wood of San Mateo, California, owns medallions of two other chiefs who visited Nanny. Among them are a bas-relief, eleven inches in diameter, of "Poor Crane," whose Indian name was Ya-Tin-Ee-Ah-Witz. Inscribed beneath his image are the words "A mighty warrior—friend to the whites—thrice wounded for them—he slew Ehegant hostile chief—1878—Yakima War 1855—Piute 1867—Bannock & Piute 1878—Snake 1879." John Wood also owns a medallion, eight inches in diameter, of "Lot," Chief of the Spokanes. Warner completed the medallions of Poor Crane and Lot in 1891. Other subjects include Moses, Encheaskwe, and Seltice.

On this first visit by Warner, C.E.S. Wood commissioned no less than eight cast bronze busts of himself, five of which were later distributed to his children. One of them is on exhibit at the Portland Art Museum, a gift of Helen Ladd Corbett, one of Wood's mistresses.

As word spread through the neighborhood that a procession of Indians was coming up the hill, children lined the streets and adults hung out of their windows to see the show. Nanny, ever the gracious hostess, stood at the front door to greet them and was annoyed when they wordlessly filed past her. The visitors trouped into the parlor and lounged about on Nanny's divan. Then, when the luncheon was ready, they marched single file into the dining room where one of them accidentally knocked over a stack of cups and saucers on the sideboard causing great confusion and embarrassment all around.

Nanny, who took pride in her lavish dinner parties, did not know what to serve them, but she and her household staff were able to put together a simple meal of sandwiches with coffee. She was astonished to see her guests stir their coffee with their fingers. She served watermelon for dessert and was speechless when she saw them spit out the seeds on the floor. Although the Indians knew English, they chose to talk to each other in their own language. Nanny asked an interpreter what they were saying, and he said that her children reminded them of their boyhood days and the fun they had on hunting trips.

Then Nanny received a shock. Chief Joseph asked that Erskine come visit him the following Spring and accompany him on a hunt. Wood and Erskine thought this was a capital idea, but Nanny wanted nothing to do with this scheme and told them so. Nanny's objections notwithstanding, in July 1892, twelve-year-old Erskine traveled to Chief Joseph's camp at the Nespelem Agency in northeast Washington. Following their defeat by General Howard, the Nez Perces were relocated to the far northern region of Washington State near the Canada border, so Erskine's journey was not easy.

Chief Joseph. Nanny's oldest son Erskine stayed with Chief Joseph for part of two years. Her husband, C.E.S. Wood participated in the battles that led to Joseph's surrender in 1877.
SOURCE: Library of Congress.

First he traveled to Fort Spokane where Wood had arranged for him to stay for two days with the commanding officer of the post. From there he was escorted to Joseph's camp, a step back in time, for little had changed since the days when the Indian land was taken by the whites. Erskine lived in a teepee with Chief Joseph and his two current wives (his first wife had died) and another family for six months and loved every minute. These two wives were the widows of Nez Perce warriors who had fallen in battle.[13]

He hunted deer, fished, learned about the outdoors, and cared for Chief Joseph's herd of about fifty ponies. Wearing buckskin and moccasins, often sleeping under the stars on extended hunting trips, Erskine learned how easy his life had been in Portland and how difficult life could be for some segments of American society. He turned thirteen on 1 September 1892, the classic age for a boy's recognition of his new status as a man. Wood was delighted that his eldest son could experience this archetypal rite of passage, but Nanny wanted Erskine to return to Portland, and he did so shortly before Christmas 1892.

The next year he returned to Chief Joseph's camp and stayed from September until nearly Christmas 1893. These months spent with Chief Joseph remained one of Erskine's fondest memories. When he was ninety-eight years old, Erskine recalled, "Although I was only a boy, I knew that with Joseph I was living with a great man. He was a father to me, guiding me, providing for me, occasionally, when needed, rebuking me, and guiding me in the Indian way of life."[14]

On one occasion Erskine was eating too greedily from the meager pot of stew that all the occupants of Chief Joseph's teepee shared. Quietly, Joseph told Erskine that the food was for everyone, not him alone. Another time, on a deer hunting trip, Erskine ineptly allowed a buck to escape when the family needed venison. Chief Joseph did not utter a word, but by a knowing look and a sad shaking of his head let Erskine know that he expected better results from his hunters.[15]

When the time came for Erskine to say farewell to Chief Joseph and the Colville Indian Reservation, Erskine asked him if his father could do anything for him. He expected Chief Joseph to request permission to return to his native land in northeastern Oregon. Instead, the old chief asked for a good stallion to improve his herd of horses. Erskine thought that this was a trivial request and never told his father about it. Years later, his granddaughter Mary C. Wood said, "That was his major regret in his life." In 1997, led by Mary C. Wood and Nanny's grand-daughter Katherine S. Livingston, the direct descendants of Erskine and the extended Wood family, fifty-five in all, raised the money to buy a magnificent black and white Appaloosa stallion and delivered it to Chief Joseph's great-great-grandson, Keith Soy Redthunder. Participating in the presentation ceremony was N. Scott Momaday, the Kiowa novelist who won the Pulitzer Prize in 1969 for *House Made of Dawn*.[16]

The most sumptuous of Nanny's homes was the final one on the corner of Ford and Main;[17] Ford street was renamed Vista Avenue. At this house Nanny began to plant the flowers, trees, and shrubs for which she became known in Portland society. See Appendix 2 for an inventory of these plants. Although the house no longer exists, still standing is a holly hedge that surrounded the land. This property was later donated to the Portland Garden Club which acknowledged Nanny's contribution to the beautification of the city with a plaque, still affixed to a brick wall in the garden: "In memory of Mrs. C.E.S. Wood, whose home once occupied these grounds, now given to the club by her heirs."[18]

Nanny and Wood shared a large bedroom looking east to majestic Mt. Hood; Lisa and Nan shared another large room looking east. Erskine had his own small room at the top of the stairs on the second floor, and the other boys shared a large room down the hall. In the summertime the boys would use a "sleeping porch." The cook and the maid had quarters on the third floor, and Guy's quarters were in the basement.[19]

Guy loved all the children and told them bedside stories, escorted them to circuses, watched over their play, and helped them make kites and Chinese lanterns. The family was devastated when Guy ran away with Nanny's Swedish second maid. Although Nanny genuinely cared for Guy, she feared for the safety of her maid in China and attempted to find out where they went, but she never heard from them after they eloped.

Nanny's sons continued to be popular and had many chums come to their house to play football in their spacious yard. Her daughters Nan and Lisa were becoming proper society girls and had many friends coming in and out of the house, reminding Nanny of her schoolgirl days in Washington with Hallie Patterson.

Nan and Lisa attended St. Helen's Hall, an Episcopal school for girls located just across the street from the Wood home. The first Episcopal schools in Oregon date to 1852. Two years later the Episcopal Missionary Diocese for the states of Oregon and Washington encouraged more schools, and soon Bishop Scott Academy, St. Helen's Hall, and others were established in Portland.[20] St. Helen's Hall opened in September 1869 and moved to the Vista Avenue location in 1890. The catalogue of St. Helen's Hall for 1900 shows that the curriculum was expressly designed to parallel the entrance requirements for Vassar, Smith, Wellesley, and Bryn Mawr colleges for women.

Just as Nanny's sons drew a crowd to their home, Nan and Lisa's friends also felt welcome. Every day at noon the girls would come from St. Helen's Hall with their lunches to sit beneath the trees and fill the garden with laughter and gossip.

When Miss Mary Rodney, the headmistress of St. Helen's, died, school officials telephoned Nanny and requested that Erskine go over and toll the bell, a task he decidedly did not want to perform. But Nanny insisted that it would be a worthy deed and instructed him to ring the bell of the carillon somberly and with dignity suitable to the occasion. At 2:00 p.m. the next day, as the funeral procession was to begin, Nanny heard the bell ringing violently, followed by Erskine's lively playing of a circus tune on the carillon. The mischievous Erskine Wood, oldest of the children, was one of the most popular boys in Portland and destined for a lifetime of achievement.

Years later, about four o'clock one morning in 1914, Nanny heard screams coming from across the street. Fire engines rushed up the hill, and Nanny looked out to see St. Helen's Hall ablaze. One boarding student, a lay teacher, several sisters of the Order of St. John the Baptist who were also teachers, and the maids were living in the building, but they escaped without injury.[21] Nanny remembered that she threw on a golf cape, rushed across the street, and found a teacher who had sprained her ankle huddled on the stairs outside the dormitory. Nanny had neglected to pin up her hair which, after the fashion of the day, reached almost to the ground. To see a woman with her hair down was a sensual privilege only husbands could enjoy. After Nanny draped her cape around the teacher and comforted her, she realized what a sight she must have presented to the firefighters and other men as she stood there clad only in her nightgown with her hair flowing down. The fire destroyed all except the south wing of the building, but soon the school was rebuilt and continued to educate the young women of Portland society. In 1964 the school moved to its present suburban location in Raleigh Hills.

Beginning in 1889 Nanny's health began to fail. She became ill with typhoid fever, a common infection obtained from contaminated food or water. This debilitating disease, afflicting Nanny with intestinal hemorraging and high fever, marked the first time that she was seriously ill. Part of Nanny's charm and vivacious personality derived from her energetic good health.

Soon afterwards, another event occurred that would cause her health to deteriorate further. When her sixth and last child was born 3 May 1891, Nanny named her Katherine Gordon Wood after a favorite neighbor. Nanny, thirty-six years old when Katherine was born, had a difficult labor. Unlike her other children, this child was never robust and died four months later. Nanny, of course, was devastated emotionally and physically. Although she would live forty years more, she was never strong again.

Nanny's health would take her away from C.E.S. Wood for months at a time when she would go Colorado Springs to a spa, the standard regimen in those days. She would take the five children with her, hardly a respite from maternal responsibilities, leaving Wood alone in Portland, a situation that prompted his infidelities.

In the winter of 1892 Max Wood, Nanny's third child, came down with scarlet fever, another common nineteenth-century disease, occurring predominantly in children. Nanny was afraid that her other children would succumb to this highly contagious disease, but they were spared. Max was sick for an extended period, and when he finally recovered, Nanny was exhausted. Wood took the train down to Colorado Springs from Portland and arranged for a woman to stay with the children while he and Nanny made a convalescent vacation trip to Mexico.

Indeed, this trip seems to have been a tonic for Nanny's health and for their marriage. In Mexico City they stayed at a hotel that had once been a convent, and from the balcony of their room they could enjoy pleasant sensual indulgences. They could see the beautiful flowers in the garden below, breathing in their aroma like an elixir. They could hear the street vendors crying their wares, including fresh strawberries for their breakfast.

Shortly after their arrival in Mexico City, Mrs. Holt Wilson, wife of the doctor who had delivered three of Nanny's children, came there from Galveston, Texas, with three old family friends, so the Woods now had a group with whom to walk about during the day. They went shopping in the markets, took carriage drives to see the old city, bought fresh flowers, and occasionally bought pulque, a milky, fermented drink made from the tropical, fleshy agave plant. Sometimes they would forego a carriage and stroll contentedly along the city streets where pretty senoritas under the watchful eyes of their duennas sat on the balconies of fine homes waiting for their lovers to come and flirt.

An interesting interlude occurred when Mrs. Wilson had an attack of gastritis one night. When she traveled Dr. Wilson would give her a list of names of physicians in the places she would visit. The hotel sent a servant to summon a doctor who turned out to be Austrian and who claimed to have been the physician to Emperor Maximilian (1832–67), the Austrian archduke who was appointed Emperor of Mexico (1864–67) by the French. He was executed by Mexican republicans.

The doctor's English was poor, so he wrote out a prescription in Spanish, and Wood got directions from the hotel staff to an apothecary shop. Wood should have insisted on having a servant accompany him, but, with characteristic confidence, he set out in the middle of the night to have the prescription filled. He wandered through narrow, dark streets, unable to ask directions or to explain his destination. To reveal his disorientation in halting Spanish might have been dangerous.

Finally, he found the place and tapped on the wall. A narrow window opened, revealing only darkness and silence. He proffered the prescription and some pesos, a hand took them, and the window closed. Wood waited on the street until, finally, the window opened and the unseen druggist placed the medicine on the ledge. They had exchanged not a word of conversation.

Wood hurried through the streets back to the hotel, and when he arrived they found that the medicine was nothing but a flax-seed poultice to be applied to the stomach and licorice powders for drinking mixed with water. But, the two substances proved efficacious, and the next morning Mrs. Wilson was much improved.

This little story became a favorite family tale for several reasons. Nanny found the cultural differences amusing with the unexpected presence of the odd Austrian doctor in Mexico City, and she liked the mysteriously silent transaction with the unseen chemist. Wood enjoyed his role as the gallant knight who ventured into the dark labyrinths of the city on behalf of a woman in distress.

Nanny and Wood traveled by train to Guadalajara, to the north and west of Mexico City, to see the bullfights. Wood was eager, Nanny reluctant. She deplored violence. The stadium was full of aficionados, and many soldiers sat among the crowd on the stone seats. Nanny wanted to be as far away as possible from the bullfight, so she sat on the top row of seats, but Wood went alone to the front row where he could observe the centuries-old ritual.

Nanny was determined not to look and sat with her eyes closed, but a roar from the crowd during the placing of the banderillas, staves that are thrust into the bull's shoulders, made her look momentarily. She was appalled at the horror of the scene and angry that Wood seemed to be enjoying himself, watching as the matador prepared to kill the bull.

Standing alone, his muleta or short cape over his left hand, the matador thrust his sword at an angle into the bull's shoulder, severing the aorta. During this final phase of the bullfight, called the Hour of Truth, the crowd reached a frenzied state, and Wood enthusiastically joined in the cheering. At this moment of jostling exuberance, someone in the crowd picked Wood's pocket. Under normal circumstances, Nanny would have been distressed at this thievery in a foreign land, but she told Wood it served him right for taking her to this dreadful event and abandoning her to be closer to the action.

The vacation ended when Wood was called back to Portland on business, and Nanny accompanied Mrs. Wilson back to Galveston where they stayed for about ten days. Then Mrs. Wilson returned to Portland and Nanny to Colorado Springs and the children.

Her actions during these years at the turn of the century reveal that Nanny was turning increasingly to her children as her primary concern. Her husband was busy with his law practice and his involvement with artistic and social causes. Her houses ran smoothly with staffs of maids, cooks, and yardmen. By tacit agreement, Nanny and Wood were going their separate ways.

III
GROWING UP

For Nanny to immerse herself in motherhood might seem to some as mere reconcilement to her role as a second-class person in those years. But, in many ways, Nanny's care of her children as they approached adulthood shows strength and resolve that had never been required of her before that time. Erskine's extended illness illustrates how she could rally her energy and intelligence and become decisive and resourceful without being guided in every action by her husband.

During Erskine's senior year at Harvard in 1900 he entered a period of his life beset with illness. He appeared so run down and weak while spending his Christmas break with Helen Ladd Corbett in New York City that he left college to spend the winter in the mountains of North Carolina near the famous Biltmore estate. The crisp, clean air of the mountains helped but did not completely restore Erskine to good health.

He then went with the Corbett boys to Eastern Oregon, hoping to enjoy a salubrious climate, but nothing seemed to help. Nanny relocated to LaGrange, Oregon, to look after Erskine. She stayed in a small cabin, and Erskine lived in a tent so that he could breathe the high altitude air. Dr. Bryson Wood, C.E.S. Wood's brother who had studied medicine in Baltimore with Nanny's uncle Alan Penneman Smith, came to offer medical assistance, but his efforts produced no improvement in Erskine's condition.

In 1902 Erskine was diagnosed with the family disease tuberculosis, and Nanny accompanied Erskine to Arizona. They stayed there for the remainder of the winter. In Phoenix, Nanny was reunited with her dear cousin Annie Foster Seton who had been with her at Fort Sumter just prior to the start of the Civil War. Annie's son William Henry Seton was also ill, and he died soon after Nanny's visit, further deepening Nanny's concern for Erskine. Annie's other son, John Foster Seton, died in 1897.

Nanny developed a new sense of initiative and independence because of Erskine's prolonged illness. In Arizona she assumed the responsibility for finding lodging for herself and Erskine, but this proved difficult because landlords did not want anyone with a disease renting from them. Erskine, as had become his custom, lived in a tent, both to be able to breathe the fresh air and also to reduce exposing anyone else to the tuberculosis bacilli.

The summer months in Phoenix were not pleasant. Erskine's lack of progress toward good health depressed him and discouraged Nanny. Arizona was often recommended as a place for tubercular patients to convalesce because of the hot, dry climate, but the heat caused both Erskine and Nanny misery.

Fortunately Nanny was able to hire a small staff to assist her. She brought a maid with her from Portland to Arizona, but this servant soon returned home. Then she hired a Negro woman as cook and a young girl from the nearby Indian School to do the housework. She also rented furniture for the small house. Forced by the circumstances of Erskine's illness, Nanny made decisions on her own and in doing so discovered a capability she did not know she had.

When the weather turned cool, Erskine had not shown any improvement, so they decided to seek help elsewhere. In 1903, they went to Chicago where Wood met them to decide what to do next. In Chicago there resided a German physician whose brother Wood had known in eastern Oregon. This doctor told them that Erskine should go to a sanitarium in the Black Forest region of Germany, but this seemed too ambitious and Germany seemed so far away.

In the Adirondack Mountains of New York state, Dr. Edward Livingston Trudeau (1848–1915) operated a camp similar to the famous Western Health Reform Institute directed by Dr. John Harvey Kellogg (1852–1943) in Battle Creek, Michigan. Camps such as these became enormously popular in North America and Europe, treating patients for a variety of ailments with proper diet, herbal concoctions, and much pampering by a professional staff.[22]

Dr. Trudeau, born in New York City in 1848, came from a long line of French medical doctors. In 1873, when he was twenty-six years old, he fell victim to tuberculosis and, ironically, went to Aiken, South Carolina, as Nanny's mother had done a few years earlier, but his condition worsened there.[23] He then went to the Adirondack Mountains where he spent a winter in the bracing cold air. In 1876, the year Kellogg became the director of his camp at Battle Creek, Dr. Albert Loomis of New York City published a paper in the *Medical Record* extolling the value of the Adirondacks region. In 1884, Trudeau opened his camp at Saranac Lake. Well-respected among his peers, Trudeau was president of the National Association for the Study and Prevention of Tuberculosis and president of the Association of American Physicians in 1904–05.[24]

Trudeau believed that a cure for pulmonary disorders could be effected if patients would spend as much time as possible in the outdoors, eat plenty of good food, and practice rest and discipline. This natural approach appealed to Wood who had frequently taken his children, the girls also, on camping trips. Wood happily accompanied Nanny and Erskine to Trudeau's camp seeking a cure, but they were dismayed to discover that at that time he took charity patients only.

In earlier years Robert Louis Stevenson took the cure under Trudeau's direction in 1886, and, in later years, legendary New York Giants baseball pitcher Christy Matthewson was there in the 1930s. Famous people visiting friends who were taking the cure included scientist Albert Einstein, New York City mayor Fiorello LaGuardia, writer Ernest Hemingway, and bootlegger Legs Diamond.[25]

Because the family had made the difficult journey expressly to see him, Trudeau did examine Erskine, and he agreed with the Chicago physician that the sanitarium in Nordrach, Germany, would be ideal for treatment of tuberculosis. Before the family left Trudeau's camp, Nanny prevailed upon him to give them prescriptions (including one for her for the treatment of itching of the vagina). Nanny took this prescription with her to Germany and had it filled by Dr. Gleiss of Hamburg. She also refilled a prescription for a skin rash written for her by Dr. Stone of Phoenix, Arizona, at the pharmacy of Frank E. Kendall of Saranac Lake. When she became settled in Germany, Nanny found the Englishe Apotheke, an international pharmacy in Munich where she had several prescriptions filled that she had wisely obtained from her brother-in-law Dr. Peter Bryson Wood and her uncle Dr. Samuel Theobald, both of Baltimore.[26]

Once again we see Nanny rising to the occasion and assuming new responsibilities. Wood could not leave his law practice, so Nanny arranged to accompany Erskine to Germany. She sent for Lisa to join them in New York City and booked passage for the voyage to Europe. Wood returned to Portland and Nanny stayed on Governors Island, the former army base guarding the entrance to New York harbor, for about a week with her old friends, Brigadier General and Mrs. Thomas J. Barry, with whom they had many connections. Barry was on the staff of Eastern Division Headquarters.[27]

The headquarters for several important commands were located at Governors Island—Eastern Division, Division of the Atlantic, Department of the East—and assignments to this post were desirable. Some of the important army generals who served there as commanders were Oliver O. Howard, Nelson A. Miles, Wesley Merritt, Arthur MacArthur, Tasker Bliss, and Leonard Wood.[28]

Mrs. Barry was the former Ellen Bestor, a native of Washington, DC, where Nanny grew up. General Barry and Wood were at West Point together, Barry graduating in 1877. They had known each other during the Indian wars, and he had been an adjutant general at Vancouver Barracks.[29]

Nanny did not know Lisa's travel plans from Portland, so she sent telegrams trying to find her, all to no avail. Finally, on the very day their ship was to sail, Lisa arrived at Governors Island. Barry had his private launch take Nanny, Erskine, and Lisa to the ship, causing quite a stir among the others passengers who wondered who these important people were who deserved such personal treatment.

The passage was pleasant, although Nanny kept to herself. Erskine and Lisa, both attractive and intelligent young people, made friends easily and enjoyed their time aboard ship. The ship docked at Hamburg, and the family proceeded to a hotel to rest and get their bearings in this new place. Nanny had hoped that Lisa, who knew a little German, could translate for them, but when she was confronted with conversational German, Lisa could not understand anything. They had difficulty asking directions to Nordrach, and when they finally could frame the question, no one knew where it was.

Nanny had not corresponded with anyone at the clinic in the Black Forest, and the Wood family was not expected. From Hamburg Nanny sent a telegram to Dr. Otto Walther, but he never replied. After several days there, they departed by train for Frankfort, heading for the Black Forest region. While Erskine rested in his room, Nanny and Lisa strolled about the city and felt homesick and lonely. They spent one night in their two luxurious hotel rooms, then departed for Nordrach. On this portion of the journey, they traveled by "a funny little country train," as she described it. Once again, they had difficulty expressing themselves, and no one spoke English. They just kept repeating the name "Nordrach," and the trainmen told them when to get off, not at Nordrach but at Gengenbach, the closest train station to their destination. Nanny could see that the train station sign read Gengenbach, and she became agitated and confused.

As they stood on the platform, they had no idea what to do or where to go. At just that moment a carriage arrived bearing an elderly English couple who had taken their grandson and granddaughter to the clinic for treatment. The English couple told them to take their carriage, which was returning to the clinic anyway, so Nanny finally had some good luck after a difficult trip by ship, train, and now carriage.

Nanny was not traveling as a tourist, and she was oblivious to the beauty of the Black Forest. She thought the fir trees looked like the ones back in Oregon, and she thought the little thatched-roof cottages they passed looked humble and rustic, not charming and quaint. But when they approached the valley in which the sanitarium lay hidden, she was struck by the beauty of the setting and her spirits lifted at the sight of this place where she hoped her son would be healed.

Below the former imperial town Zell-on-Harmersbach two mountain streams flow together: the swift Nordrach and the placid Harmersbach form the Kinzig River. Following the river's course, a road winds through many curves to the valley floor where the Nordrach-Kolonie sanitarium was established. Today, the site houses the Rehabilitationsklinik Klausenbach.[30]

This modern facility receives patients from the state insurance agency of Baden for treatment of lung disease.

In the 1880s Dr. Otto Walther, whose wife suffered from pulmonary disease, searched the Black Forest for a suitable location on which to build a sanitarium for lung patients. When he came to the lower Nordrach valley, he found an existing cluster of buildings, a former monastic glass and paint factory. The great forest region belonged to the Gengenbach Benedictine monastery. The monks established dairies in the high pastures as a colony to the Gengenbach monastery.

Abbot Augustinus Müller established a glass factory in 1700 high up in the forest region; in 1750 Abbot Benedikt Rischler added a paint factory. The two enterprises provided income for the monastery, not only through sales of their products but also through investments of capital by the mayors of nearby imperial towns. When the church sold its interest in the glass and paint factory, the shareholders moved the business to its present location in the valley floor. After secularization, the factories were unable to make a profit, and the German workers resettled, at government expense, to America.

All the elements Dr. Walther was seeking were here: water from the river was plentiful; the altitude was favorable, not too high in the mountains, but not so low that fog would present a problem; the valley received plenty of sunlight for much of the day; and the valley was protected from cold northern winds.

On 30 August 1889, Dr. Walther purchased the buildings and began to expand the campus and build his clientele. Most of his patients were English, like the couple who conveniently gave their carriage to Nanny and her children at the train station. Word of Dr. Walther's clinic was just beginning to spread to America, and Erskine was one of the first non-English patients. Fortunately, the language problem disappeared when Nanny reached the clinic because the hospital staff spoke excellent English.

Dr. Walther was ahead of his time in realizing that some degree of isolation was necessary to prevent the spread of the bacilli that are pathogenic for tuberculosis. Erskine was not confined to a large hospital ward but to an individual cottage. Common buildings included an observation tower that allowed some patients to monitor their progress by their ability to climb the stairs to enjoy the panoramic view of the valley; a large gazebo on the lawn provided a place for patients to socialize in pleasant weather; a solarium enabled patients to sit in the warm sun and bake the congestion in their lungs; and a Speisesaal (dining room) where patients could converse during meals.

Nanny could not stay in Erskine's cottage, so she lived in Karlsruhe, a two hour journey from the Nordrach sanitarium. When she visited, she would join Erskine and the other patients in the dining room where Dr. Walther had individual meals prepared to exacting requirements. He regarded food as having the same importance as any prescriptive medication, and he insisted that the patients eat the heaping mounds. Nanny's refined sensibilities were shocked when she watched Dr. Walther hover over the patients and not allow them to leave the table until they had eaten everything.

For two years Erskine lived at the Nordrach clinic. Lisa stayed for much of that time, and Erskine's brother Max came over as well. Nanny remained there the entire two years. Nanny, Erskine, Lisa, and Max became devoted friends with Dr. Walther and his family, son Heinz, who became a surgeon, and daughters Mara and Gerda. Lisa found a good friend in Mara who later moved with her husband to Montevideo, Uruguay, before the beginning of World War Two. Six-year-old Gerda worshipped Erskine and Max and remained close to the Wood family all her life. Gerda took a Ph.D. in philosophy from the University of Munich in 1921 where her dissertation was "On the Ontology of Social Intercourse."[31]

C.E.S. Wood struck up a correspondence with the socialist-leaning Gerda, whom he never met. She spoke and wrote excellent English and was conversant in French, Italian, and Spanish.[32] In 1920, shortly after Wood left Nanny, he wrote a long letter to Gerda explaining how his marriage inhibited his creativity. She answered him with sympathy, but then gave him a cautionary lecture:

> Will you please greet Mrs. Wood very much when you see her, and tell her I am so very sorry for her, and feel all I can with her, too? And please remember me to Miss Field, too, though I don't know her. Maybe she is all you see in her. My father, too, loved a young girl very much in the last years of his life. She <u>was</u> and <u>is</u> very nice, but I don't know if she really was all he thought. At least I'm glad he thought so and I'm glad he had that sunbeam before parting, having at last found out—after a marriage of nearly 14 years, that what his children and friends had known from the very beginning—his wife absolutely <u>wasn't</u> what he thought, not the least bit of a loving, deep woman, but only a very selfish and cold being in the end, though she certainly <u>can</u> be very amiable if she pleases to.[33]

Dr. Walther died 6 April 1919, so his marital experience was still very much in Gerda's thoughts when she wrote to Wood in 1920.

Gerda became a university lecturer in philosophy, and she developed an interest in psychic powers, writing English translations of horoscopes and writing a psychic-religious novel. In 1941 she was arrested by the Gestapo, as were many other known psychics, to reveal what they foresaw as the future of the Third Reich. Because of her superior linguistic skills, she was forced to work as a military translator in the department that censored the foreign mail coming into Germany. She tried to pass as much anti-Nazi information as possible. In 1944 she converted to Catholicism as a spiritual stronghold against Nazism.[34]

After the war, the Woods sent her packages of food, magazines, paper, ink, and other scarce items. She maintained a correspondence with various members of the Wood family until 1954 when she lived in Munich[35] where she died 6 January

1977. Her biographer, Andreas Resch described her as "one of the most significant personalities in the area of mysticism and parapsychology in the [twentieth] century. In addition to an analysis of the external forces of phenomenology. . . she has written an examination of the effects of personal experience in the breadth of the human spirit. She formulated a model for understanding this mystical union."[36]

When Nanny and Erskine returned to Portland from Germany in 1904, Wood met them at the train station with a carriage and two horses. Family lore holds that Wood became engrossed in talking with Nanny and Erskine and gave the horses their heads to proceed through the streets of Portland. An awkward moment ensued when the horses stopped and the occupants of the carriage looked out to find that they were not at their home but in front of Helen Ladd Corbett's house.

Erskine resumed an active professional life, became a lawyer in his father's firm, and fathered four children. Despite his health problems as a young man, he died at 104 years of age. Erskine said of his stay at Nordrach, "During all this time, my mother gave up her home and her life with my father in order to be with me. It saddens me to think that she made this great sacrifice, for as I now look back on it I think it was inevitable that my father, during these absent years, drifted more away from her toward other women."[37]

NOTES

[1] I am grateful to Patty Johns of Bainbridge Island, Washington, for information obtained from her copy of a handwritten journal in which both Nanny and Wood recorded births, marriages, and deaths.
[2] Rudyard Kipling, *From to Sea to Sea: Letters of Travel* vol. 2 (New York: Doubleday & McClure Company, 1899), 26.
[3] *Portland City Directory* (Portland: R. L. Polk & Company, 1885): 417.
[4] "Henry Failing." *The National Cyclopedia of American Biography*, vol. 34 (New York: James T. White & Company, 1949: 171.
[5] *History of the Bench and Bar of Oregon* (Portland: Historical Publishing Company, 1910), 172.
[6] Erskine Wood, *Life of Charles Erskine Scott Wood* (Vancouver, WA: Rose Wind Press, 1991), 92.
[7] *Portland City Directory* (Portland: R. L. Polk & Company, 1886): 467.
[8] Edwin Bingham and Tim Barnes, *Wood Works: The Life and Writings of Charles Erskine Scott Wood* (Corvallis: Oregon State University Press, 1997), 212.
[9] *Portland City Directory* (Portland: R. L. Polk & Company, 1891), 996.
[10] Katherine Smith Livingston, Letter to author, 23 March 2002. Ms. Livingston is Nanny Wood's granddaughter.
[11] Carl Abbott, "Portland: Civic Culture and Civic Opportunity," *Oregon Historical Quarterly* 102 (2001): 21.
[12] Mary Rose, "Foreword," *Days with Chief Joseph* (Vancouver, WA: Rose Wind Press, 1991), vi.
[13] Merrill D. Beal. *"I Will Fight No More Forever": Chief Joseph and the Nez Perce War* (Seattle: University of Washington Press, 1963), 298.
[14] Erskine Wood, *Life of Charles Erskine Scott Wood* (Vancouver, WA: Rose Wind Press, 1991), 111-12.
[15] Erskine Wood, *Days with Chief Joseph* (Vancouver, WA: Rose Wind Press, 1991), 35.
[16] Courtenay Thompson, "After 104 Years, Family's Gift Fulfills Chief Joseph's Request," Portland *Oregonian* 27 July 1997: C1, C5.
[17] *Portland City Directory* (Portland: R. L. Polk & Company, 1896), 666.
[18] Patty Johns located the memorial plaque at the Vista Avenue location.
[19] Marian Wood Kolisch, Letter to Author, 16 March 2002.

[20] Oscar Osburn Winther, *The Great Northwest: A History* (New York: Alfred A. Knopf, 1948), 213.
[21] Sally Reed Stout, *St. Helen's Hall: The First Century, 1869–1969* (Portland, OR: St. Helen's Hall, 1969), 26.
[22] For a hilarious spoof of nineteenth-century health camp fanaticism, see T. Coraghessan Boyle's novel *The Road to Wellville* (1993).
[23] Edward Livingston Trudeau, *An Autobiography* (Garden City, NY: Doubleday Page & Company, 1916), 73.
[24] "Edward Livingston Trudeau," *The National Cyclopedia of American Biography*, vol. 13 (New York: James T. White & Company, 1906), 564–5.
[25] Mark Caldwell, *Saranac Lake: Pioneer Health Resort* (Saranac Lake, NY: Historic Saranac Lake, 1993), 29.
[26] I am indebted to Nancy Wood Robinson von Gimbut who has her great-grandmother Nanny's collection of prescriptions from the early 1900s.
[27] Edmund Banks Smith, *Governors Island: Its Military History Under Three Flags, 1637–1922* (New York: Valentine's Manual Inc., 1923), 218.
[28] R. Ernest Dupuy, ed. *Governors Island: Its History and Development, 1637–1937* (New York: The Governors Island Club, 1937), 40.
[29] "Thomas Henry Barry," *The National Cyclopedia of American Biography*, vol. 21 (New York: James T. White & Company, 1931), 116–117.
[30] I am grateful to Hr. Ehret, chief of administration for the Rehabilitationsklinik Klausenbach, for sending several pamphlets and brochures regarding the history of Dr. Walther's sanitarium and its present use.
[31] Gerda Walther's other publications include *The Phenomenology of Mysticism* (1923) and *On Other Shores* (1960).
[32] Wood Papers, Huntington Library. WD Box 213 (33).
[33] Wood Papers, Huntington Library, WD Box 213 (35).
[34] Wood Papers, Huntington Library, WD Box 213 (42).
[35] Wood Papers, Huntington Library, WD Box 213 (54).
[36] See Andreas Resch, *Gerda Walther* (Innsbruck, Austria: Resch Verlag, 1983).
[37] Erskine Wood, *Life of Charles Erskine Scott Wood* (Vancouver, WA: Rose Wind Press, 1991), 126-27.

CHAPTER SEVEN

INFIDELITY

I
DRIFTING AWAY

NANNY DID NOT RECORD HER THOUGHTS about Wood's straying from his marriage vows. She seems to have erected a protective barrier separating the sorrow and the joy caused by her marriage to Wood. When he finally summoned his courage to leave her, she pretended that he was away on an extended business trip from which he would soon return.

Because this is Nanny's story, Wood's escapades with other women will receive only brief mention here; details of Wood's affairs may be found in Robert Hamburger's excellent biography *Two Rooms*. But an account of Nanny's life, bound so inextricably with Wood's, must include some attention to his dalliances.

Kathryn Seaman Beck, or Kitty, was one of Wood's first mistresses. The Becks, mentioned as favorite summer houseguests, were one of Portland's most distinguished pioneer families, going back to the earliest days of the city. When the vivacious Kitty divorced her wealthy husband, a bold and scandalous move in those days, Wood hired her as his personal secretary, and soon she became his lover. Their affair continued intermittently for several years.

Another mistress was Helen Ladd Corbett. The Ladd,

Failing, and Corbett families figure prominently in Portland's cultural and civic history. When William S. Ladd arrived in Portland in 1851, he and his friend Charles E. Tilton formed a partnership and established Ladd & Tilton, the first bank north of San Francisco. In 1925 Ladd & Tilton became the United States National Bank of Portland.[1] Acquiring fabulous wealth, Ladd became one of Portland's greatest benefactors. His younger daughter married Frederick B. Pratt, son of one of the principals of the Standard Oil Company.[2]

Helen Ladd married Henry J. Corbett, son of Henry W. Corbett. In 1851 Henry W. Corbett took a shipload of goods from New York City around the Horn to Portland to sell to the gold miners. He made a profit of $20,000 and soon thereafter made Portland his home. With his brother-in-law Henry Failing he founded the firm of Corbett, Failing & Company, the largest hardware dealer in the city. He acquired prime real estate and properties in the heart of Portland, and in 1867 he was elected to one term in the United States Senate. When he died in 1903, the elder Corbett had constructed more buildings in Portland than anyone in the town's history.[3] His son, Helen Ladd's husband, had been groomed to succeed his father in running the family's huge financial investments, but he died suddenly in 1895 at the age of thirty-eight.[4]

When Wood made Helen Ladd Corbett his conquest, all of Portland society knew of this liaison, but Nanny seems not to have noticed or, more likely, not to have acknowledged it publicly. Instead, she simply distanced herself emotionally from Wood and lavished her attention on her children.

Wood's sexual escapades, already the topic of whispered gossip among the women and backslapping humor among the men, increasingly became too much for Portland society to bear. A recent history of Portland says Wood's actions "antagonized the city's prim social circles. Wood was, quite simply, like no other lawyer Portland had known."[5]

Had Wood's private behavior been more orthodox, he could be remembered as one of Portland's leading citizens

Nanny about 1905, Portland's grande dame.
SOURCE: Private collection of Marian Wood Kolisch.

because his civic life was exemplary. For instance, he enjoyed public acclaim in 1895 when his old friend Mark Twain visited Portland, hosting a lavish supper for him at the Arlington Club in the company of two dozen of the leading men of the city.[6]

At the same time that his extramarital escapades were becoming the subject of gossip, Wood increasingly annoyed and angered disparate groups of citizens. In July 1907 he delivered a graduation address to the University of Washington at Seattle, and his remarks received wide coverage in the Portland newspapers. To a mixed class of men and women, Wood expressed his ideas on freedom of thought, speech, and action. The ministers of the First Presbyterian Church and the First Baptist Church charged Wood afterwards with "infidelity, atheism, and socialistic anarchy." Wood countered by saying in an interview in the *Oregonian,* "These gentlemen seem to me today really possessed of the same spirit of intolerance, the same worship for what they honestly believe to be the only truth and the same determination not to have that truth attacked, which led to the crucifixion of the Christ they profess to follow."⁷

In late December 1907 he angered the members of the Oregon Chapter of the United Daughters of the Confederacy when he referred to the South as "an area of barren and unproductive land where the most degraded order of slavery known to history was maintained." The sub-headlines name him and indicate the extent of the resentment he caused: "Colonel C.E.S. Wood Charged With Insulting Daughters of Confederacy/ Speech in Bad Taste/ Lawyer, Essayist and Poet Delivers Address at Meeting of Local Chapter and Stirs Up a Hornet's Nest." He declared that slavery in the South "represented only the desire of the people to live off the labor of others." The audience, all of whom were women, were furious. One woman said, "He would not have dared to deliver the same address before an audience of men from the Southern states without running the risk of being called to account before he had made a good start."⁸

Then, in 1908, he offended the directors of the Portland Y.M.C.A., when they refused to allow the radical Emma Goldman to speak in their auditorium. A newspaper article called her the "high priestess of anarchy" and quoted Wood as saying Portland's attitude toward her was a factor of "illiberal and bigoted ignorance."⁹ Goldman lectured around the country on birth control, woman's suffrage, and other causes considered immoral at that time.

In November 1909, speaking to five hundred members of the International Workers of the World, Wood publicly declared himself an anarchist in support of Spokane Socialists imprisoned on charges of inciting a riot. An article in the *Oregonian* identified Wood as a "member of the Portland law firm of Williams, Wood and Linthicum." Wood said, "I am an anarchist. That's my ideal. I believe in the anarchistic theory."¹⁰

In 1916, when birth control advocate Margaret Sanger arrived in Portland as part of a national speaking tour, she was promptly arrested and jailed because her sixteen-page booklet *Family Limitations* was considered obscene. Wood defended her before a city judge who fined her $10.[11] While technically Sanger lost the case, the small fine was a victory for planned parenthood and further established Wood's reputation for championing liberal causes as well as a reputation for being an astute lawyer. Wood and Sanger shared views on sexual liberation. When Sanger separated from her husband in 1914 she began affairs with several well-known figures, including psychologist Havelock Ellis and writer H.G. Wells.

Wood also was deeply involved in defending Dr. Marie D. Equi, a Portland physician, against charges of sedition and espionage. The Espionage Law was enacted during World War One to quell pro-German activities by American citizens and also to counter the rising interest in communism. The Russian revolution of 1917 caused many Americans to become curious about socialism and communism. Uttering unpatriotic sentiments could result in charges of espionage. A longtime radical and advocate of women's rights, Dr. Equi spoke out against the war, calling it "The Big Barbecue." When authorities thought her remarks lent aid and comfort to the enemy they charged her with eight counts of violating the Espionage Law. She was found guilty and sentenced to three years in prison. Wood took up her defense.

On 6 June 1919 in San Francisco, Wood argued before three judges of the circuit court of appeals that the sedition laws of the United States were unconstitutional. Equi, lost the appeal, and she served over two years in prison.[12] Some in Portland considered Wood's remarks about "free speech or bombs" threatening and further evidence that he was unfit for polite society.

Wood had already angered many people in Portland in 1917 when he defended Floyd Ramp, a Socialist farmer from Eugene, Oregon, against charges of violating the Espionage Act. Wood lost this case also, and Ramp served eight months in a federal prison.[13]

Nanny's son Erskine recalled that one of the few times Wood became angry with him occurred when Erskine suggested that his championing radical causes had hurt their law practice by driving away some important clients.[14]

Nanny remained silent on Wood's political activities and continued to associate with her friends at the Town Club. She and the children, all adults now, were increasingly uncomfortable with Wood's unseemly sexual conduct that ran counter to her upbringing and the way she was attempting to guide their children. Wood soon abandoned all pretense of covering up his affairs and lost his restraint against speaking out for social causes he deemed important. The relationship between Nanny and Wood was about to alter irrevocably with the arrival in Portland of the woman who would become the great love of Wood's life.

Nanny seems to have been oblivious to Wood's willingness to stray from their marriage. In July 1910 she went on an excursion to Alaska with their two daughters Nan and Lisa. On 28 July she wrote to Wood, "How glad my heart would be, dear heart, if you, too, were enjoying this beautiful trip and delightful rest. Then, indeed, I could be content.... As it is now I miss you all the time, wish for you, and think you ought to be with me. As I have told you often before that pleasure taken without you is only half pleasure."[15]

In October 1910, the famous labor lawyer and supporter of anarchistic causes Clarence Darrow introduced Wood to Sara Field Ehrgott, the wife of Albert Ehrgott, the minister of Portland's East Side Baptist Church who had recently arrived with Sara from Cleveland. Sara's sister Mary Field was one of Darrow's lovers. On at least one occasion Darrow, who was married, also attempted a physical familiarity with Sara. Thirty years younger than Wood, both beautiful and intellectual, Sara seemed to be everything he desired in a woman. She did not have the social standing or wealth of a Kitty Beck or a Helen Ladd Corbett, but she equaled them in physical attractiveness and surpassed them in her ability to articulate social and political concepts that were important to Wood.

Wood offered to use his contacts to help Sara publish some of her writings, and she became his assistant, proofreading and editing his work. Within a few months they declared their love for each other and began a relationship that would last until death. When Kitty Beck learned of Wood's affair with Sara, she married an alcoholic, Dr. Lloyd Irvine, a mad, impulsive act of retaliation that provoked possessive jealousy in Wood. Grudgingly though, he admired Kitty's willingness to risk all and be decisive. Wood struggled to find the courage to leave Nanny.

Wood wanted to be with Sara Field Ehrgott whom he regarded as the perfect complement to his social anarchism, his intellect, his love of writing. Nanny was none of these. Her role had evolved into that of mother, grandmother, and promoter of civic pride. Wood and Sara each felt trapped in their marriages. In 1910, in an impromptu ceremony beneath an oak tree, Wood and Sara pledged their love to each other and considered themselves married after that, but they lived apart, unable to break the tie with their spouses.

For all his devotion to Sara, Wood still had other love interests. Wood began an affair with Frances Burke, a pianist. To Sara's jealous inquiries, Wood insisted that they were not sexual partners, but Sara did not believe him.[16] Then Helen Ladd Corbett complicated his situation further by seeking to renew their intermittent affair just at the time Wood wanted to break from Portland altogether.[17]

In 1912 Sara told Wood that she was pregnant with his child, and they agreed that she should have an abortion as soon as possible, but a miscarriage terminated the pregnancy. Sara was suffering from tuberculosis, spending most of her time in Los Angeles. Wood also experienced a brief illness when he contracted an infection of the inner ear, and he remained at home with Nanny for several weeks.

Shortly after these two distressing incidents, Wood felt the need to get away from Portland for a rest, so he went to see his friend Bill Hanley on his ranch at Burns in eastern Oregon. Ever faithful and loving, Nanny sent him a touching letter on 30 August 1912 with the tone of a mother caring for a sick child:

> My dear Scotty,
>   I was relieved to receive your telegram announcing your safe arrival at Burns, for I feel none too easy about automobiles and bad roads these days. Do try and rest all you can and get some enjoyment out of the time. That means you are not to talk all the time with Mr. Hanley or anyone else, especially late at night, but go off by yourself. If you can't sleep long, then go out before others in the fresh air, paint the morning skies or the shadow of the hills and get your sleep by being early to bed.[18]

Letters to Wood from this period are usually signed "your affectionate wife," as though to remind him of the primacy of her claim to him, or she would sign them "your loving Sippy," using their private term of endearment, a nickname derived from the way she pronounced her maiden name, Smith, when she was a little girl.

In May 1913, Wood received the first of two $100,000 payments for his commission on the Willamette Valley & Cascade Mountain Wagon Road Land Grant. On condition of building a wagon road, the original grantees received the rights to the land from the United States in the early 1900s. But soon Lazard Freres, the international banking firm that had subsequently obtained the grant, was beset by lawsuits. Wood represented Lazard Freres, symbol of old-fashioned capitalism, at the same time he was championing anarchistic causes on behalf of the labor movement. The case dragged through the courts, and Wood finally argued the case successfully before the United States Supreme Court.

The same month that Wood received his large commission from Lazard Freres, Sara journeyed to Goldfield, Nevada, for the purpose of obtaining a divorce from Ehrgott. In this act, as in so many others, she and Wood were breaking new ground. Nevada had only recently become known as a place where one could obtain a "migratory divorce," that is, a divorce granted by a state other than one's legal residence. She lived in Goldfield with her sister Mary and her four-year-old daughter Kay for six months until the divorce was granted. [19] Sara moved to San Francisco, expecting Wood to divorce Nanny and follow her, but Wood remained indecisive. He could not bring himself to confront Nanny.

Sara demanded that Wood effect a complete break with both Frances and Nanny. Wood was able to summon the courage to dissolve the relationship with Frances, telling her that he loved only Sara, but he was non-committal with Nanny, telling her that Sara was his soul-mate and that their relationship was not sexual. Whether Nanny was convinced or not is unknown, but she refused to grant him a divorce, then or ever, and things stood as they were. Nanny continued to be an active member of the Town Club and to be listed, along with her daughter-in-law Rebecca (Mrs. Erskine) Wood and sister-in-law (Mrs. James McIntosh Wood), in *The Portland Society Annual, 1914–1915*. Despite her husband's increasingly unacceptable behavior, the Woods were included in "the 400 families . . . from Portland's most exclusive circle."[20]

In 1915 Wood began an affair with Dr. Janina Klecan, an immunologist who had been treating him for rheumatism. Sara immediately sensed the sexual attraction between them, but, true to form, Wood denied that sex was a component of their friendship. Amazingly, his ex-lover Kitty Beck advised Wood to break off the relationship with Janina and return to Sara.[21]

Wood dropped hints to Nanny that his friendship with Klecan was growing. In February 1916, Nanny went to New York City with her friend Daisy Ayer, staying at the Hotel Gotham. In a letter to Nanny, Wood urged her to go see J. Alden Weir to have him sketch her portrait. He adds, "Dear strange shy Dr. Klecan brings me (and Max) Bulgarian milk every day."[22]

Sara, meanwhile, was finding her own public voice and a cause; she had become increasingly involved in the women's suffrage movement, going all over the nation to speak at rallies. She was an electrifying speaker, eloquent, passionate, and physically attractive. George West, a young reporter who heard her speak, fell in love with her and proposed marriage. In February 1916, Sara told Wood that she was growing tired of his procrastination and that she was thinking about marrying West to achieve stability and companionship in her life.

Wood swore to Sara that he would end his affair with Janina Klecan, and left Portland to spend a month with Sara in San Francisco. After returning to Portland, Wood received a letter from Sara telling him that she was again pregnant as a result of their month together. The sixty-four year old Wood arranged for Sara to return to Portland where Janina performed an abortion on her. Whether Janina intended it or not, the operation was not skillful, and Sara suffered with an inflammation of the uterus for several weeks afterwards.

Nanny and C.E.S. Wood in 1917
with some of their grandchildren.
SOURCE: Private collection of Marian Wood Kolisch.

Wood was in San Francisco with Sara when he sent Nanny a Valentine gift. Still struggling to keep her marriage intact, she sent him a note on 17 February 1918, saying, "I received the sweet violets and lovely tulips on St. Valentine's Day. I send you my love for your thought of me. It was dear of you. Lovingly, your Sippy."[23]

Dispirited and physically spent, Sara felt that Wood lacked the courage to make his break with Nanny whose letters still expressed her love for him. Then, in August 1918, Wood won for Lazard Freres the right to sell the grant they held, over 860,000 acres, and they did so for $6,000,000. Wood's commission on this sale was reportedly $1,000,000, paid over several years.[24] This commission ensured financial security for Wood, Nanny, and their children, but it also gave him the freedom to leave Nanny and go to California with Sara.

In October 1918, using a political campaign in California as an excuse to be away from Portland, Wood received a letter from Nanny that uses rare testy language: "My dear Scotty... Why did you go to any political campaign... to speak for a woman candidate whom you acknowledge has not the ghost of a show. Still my words have no weight with you."[25]

Late in 1918 he cleared out his law office and left Portland for San Francisco. In July 1919 when he was sixty-seven and Nanny was sixty-four, he returned to beg her for a divorce, but she adamantly refused, not so much out of loyalty to her Roman Catholic faith, but because she was a Moale, a Smith, a Lincoln, and a Wood. Her upbringing in Baltimore and Washington would not allow her to disgrace herself through divorce. She knew her past and her present place in Portland society, and she would not be humiliated, no matter what. She would be the only Mrs. C.E.S. Wood as long as she lived.

Facing facts, Wood left Nanny for good and lived with Sara without the benefit of a divorce from Nanny. Having made his decision after so many years, Wood ceased to have affairs and settled into the intellectual, bohemian life he had imagined and yearned for. He had plenty of money to support himself and Sara, and he made legal arrangements for the comfort and security of Nanny and their grown children. Freed from his former life in Portland, he could indulge himself in his lifelong desire to be a writer, either of poetry or social diatribes, as the occasion suited him.

On 12 October 1918, Wood and Sara went on a picnic outing accompanied by Sara's two children Kay and Albert.

Sara was driving her new car that Wood had insisted that she buy. When she lost control on a steep embankment, the car went over the edge and crashed. Sara was seriously injured, and Wood and Kay slightly injured. Young Albert was killed.

This was a bad time for both Nanny and Wood. The United States had entered World War One, and their son Erskine was ordered to report for artillery training in Kentucky, and their son Berwick reported to a camp in Eugene, Oregon, where influenza raged. On 17 October 1918, while Sara lay near death in the hospital in her grief over Albert's death, Nanny wrote to Wood that Berwick had come down with the influenza and that his temperature was 103 degrees. Of the fifty thousand men in the camp, fifteen thousand were seriously ill. Wood had not given Nanny Sara's address, so she had to write to him at the Anglo London and Paris National Bank.

Nanny went to Eugene and took rooms at the Osburn Hotel. She went to the camp and removed Berwick to the hotel where she could care for him. On 20 October 1918, still unable to communicate directly with Wood, she sent a message to the Western Union Telegraph Office at San Rafael, California, to be forwarded to E. L. Smith at San Anselmo. Beset with his own problems, Wood neglected his wife and son during this terrible time.[26]

Erskine was rejected for military service when he arrived at Louisville because of the condition of his lungs, ravaged years earlier by tuberculosis. He was greatly disappointed because he wanted to serve in the artillery. Nanny had urged him to apply to the Judge Advocate General Corps as a lawyer, but Erskine wanted to see combat as his father had before him.

While Nanny dealt with illness and the stress of military service at home, Sara's former husband, the Rev. Albert Ehrgott publicly accused Wood of causing his son's death through his scandalous seduction of Sara that resulted in her deserting and divorcing him. Had Wood not interfered, he alleged, his son would be alive and his marriage intact. In a lengthy article in the Portland *Oregonian*, Ehrgott declared the "self-confessed anarchist and practicer of free love, C.E.S. Wood,"[27] unworthy of associating with decent men and women.

With Wood's departure now an accomplished fact, and faced with the certainty that he would not be returning home, Nanny was forced to deal with issues as they arose, and she seems to have found a new, independent voice. When Wood came into some money from an insurance settlement, he asked her about the distribution of it. She replied on 22 October 1920,

> In one of your late letters you said the insurance money should be divided among the children. . . . I do not want any of that money—not for a minute. I did not mention your suggestion to Nanny [Honeyman], nor did I to Becky [Erskine's wife] or to Berwick.

She brings up a subject that must have been painful for her:

> I forgot to speak of Mrs. Corbett and her inordinate curiosity and meddlesome tactics. I am wondering how it is that she and I can speak. . . . I heard of her inquiries of the furniture in your library. I thought we were done with Mrs. Corbett's gifts and belongings, that her pillows, rugs, and desk were sent out of this house. Please tell me truly if there is anything else here she is liable to consider her property, for it has always been embarrassing and most distasteful for me. What she wants to know now about our affairs I cannot tell.

Further, Nanny acquaints Wood with the public humiliation she suffers in Portland, telling him someone asked her when he was coming home and why he stayed so long in San Francisco:

> My dear Scotty, please talk and write a bit more plainly. In your letter you write, 'This is not any criticism of you.' No, I know that. . . . Please explain just to satisfy

> my stupidity. I never speak to Mrs. Corbett. You know what a gossip she is. Then she questions and draws people out, especially some of Nanny's set. She makes intimates and pets of [them] just as you allowed Nanny to be whilst I was in Germany. I have heard some of these girls tell how curious she is with her questions and drawing out.

Then Nanny concludes this letter by softening her tone: "In many of my conversations, especially when talking of old days or past doings of our life I frequently quote you or bring your name in most naturally and affectionately, as if nothing had happened to change our lives. . . . And that's all, my dear. Again, your Sippy."[28]

Just before Christmas in 1920, Erskine's wife Becky wrote to Wood, saying that the family does not understand why he cannot come home for Christmas. She tells Wood that

> It is just because [Nanny] has never spoken the least disapproval or has ever said a word against Mrs. Field, that I admire her so. I think if she were like other women, and had attempted to prejudice me against you or Mrs. Field, or your present life, I would not admire her in the same way, and I certainly would not consider her feelings. But when I think of her, it is almost with a feeling of awe at her saint-like nature.[29]

That same Christmas, Nanny was making a waistcoat for Wood, but ran out of the silk material she had ordered especially from London. She promised to finish the waistcoat when the extra bolt of silk arrived: "Anyhow, accept it please as a handmade gift for Christmas, such as it is, and I am wishing it was a thousand times better thing for you, dear one. Yours as ever, Sippy."[30]

A week later she writes to Wood to thank him for a roll of black velvet material he had sent her: "I am delighted at such a gift, but wishing you could see for yourself and that I could speak with my lips than on dry paper. It is a generous, beautiful Christmas gift, and I hope to show [you] myself arrayed in my suit [that she would make using this fabric]." Then Nanny allows herself a melancholy moment:

> When alone in my room I so wish that we could see back when and how we first took comfort in each other's hearts. If that could be possible, I don't know. Feelings are mingled with heartache and memories of vanished days of happiness, and the day will come when the eyes of one will be closed, the lips silent and only memories left. Let us live, if we can, with our grandchildren. They at least are not sad. Good night, dear heart. Your Sippy.[31]

While Nanny seems to have come to a reconciliation of sorts with her own situation, all was not well, neither in Portland nor in San Francisco. Six months later, in June 1921, depressed by the death of Albert and Wood's inability to obtain a divorce from Nanny, Sara attempted suicide.

Some months after his departure from Nanny and Portland, Wood received word that Janina Klecan had committed suicide. Although his leaving was not the primary cause of her emotional distress, Klecan's affair with him had complicated her life and created a fair measure of despair that indirectly led to her suicide. Her death, of course, focused public attention once again on Nanny as a long-suffering, proper matron while Wood was a sexual libertine who devoured women.

After Sara recovered from her attempted suicide, they moved to the little town of Los Gatos where they built a retreat from the world in the Santa Clara Valley near San Jose and named it "The Cats." Still flanking the entrance to the driveway today are two nine-foot tall sitting cats, a male and a female. Leo has his eyes open, while Leona has her eyes closed.

Nanny's son Max died in 1921 of blood poisoning from kidney failure. His siblings felt the absence of their father during

Nanny's time of grieving, and a schism occurred. Nan and her husband Dave Honeyman remained loyal to Nanny, as did Berwick and his wife Alice, and Erskine and his wife Becky. Erskine recalled pleading with his father to return: "'Why cannot you take Mrs. Field as your mistress, but still make this your home and not leave my mother?' He replied, 'No it is better to cut the cord completely.' But he was in anguish."[32] Lisa and Kirk Smith, who lived in San Rafael, California, regularly visited Wood and Sara at The Cats and accepted her with love. The Smiths also became friends with Sara's daughter Kay and her husband Jim Caldwell, a Chaucer scholar at the University of California, Berkeley. Wood and Sara, Lisa and Kirk, and Kay and Jim often spent days together enjoying each other's company.

Although grown and married, Nanny's children were hurt by Wood's departure. Erskine hated choosing between his parents, but he sided with Nanny: "I have said that I am very sorry [for shunning Wood]. I am. But this does not mean that I regret my conduct as it bore upon my mother. She needed me, and I gave [her my loyalty]. I only mean that, in giving it, I had to hurt my father, and for that I am sorry."[33]

In addition to Erskine's pleas with Wood to remain with Nanny, Berwick Bruce Wood (1887–1970) wrote to his father 21 June 1921 imploring him to return. Wood's response shows insight into his relationship with his wife.[34] He tells Berwick that he has for Nanny a "love with all affection for her true, fine nature, and I do not believe she thinks she is either wrong or selfish. I think according to her bringing up and her lights she thinks she is doing exactly right, and that to have been quiet and made no trouble is all that should be asked of her. She has been most patient, most dignified and above praise in the way she has acted." He explains that he has no power to resist being with Sara because she brings out his creativity in a way that Nanny never could.

The letter reveals that Nanny had not taken the event of Wood's desertion as an opportunity to seek public sympathy for herself and condemnation for Wood. Even within the family, as Wood acknowledges, Nanny's reaction to his departure derived from "her bringing up." He also mentions that Nanny "has been most patient, most dignified and above praise in the way she has acted." Without explicitly revealing her feelings to her children, as Becky Wood's letter records, Nanny had nevertheless communicated to them her sense of hurt and disappointment.

Nanny and Wood had grown apart. He had always been drawn to women for their beauty—even Nanny when she was young—and when Sara, thirty years younger than he, beautiful, highly creative, intellectual, alive with dedication to social causes, entered his life, he found the person who could match his interests as well as gratify his sexual needs. In March 1942, nine years after Nanny's death, Becky Wood wrote to Wood and Sara, thanking them for their hospitality during a recent visit to Los Gatos: "Well, they were three heavenly days with you two darlings. I don't believe there is a more peaceful, hospitable place in the world, filled with love and friendliness—to say nothing of intellectuality and art!"[35]

That Nanny did not sue for divorce in light of Wood's extramarital affairs could be a testimony to her dignity, as many in her family prefer to see it, or it could be a statement about the options available to women in the first two decades of the twentieth century. Although Nanny had grounds for divorce and could have been provided for financially, in those days a divorced woman, not the man, bore the brunt of public opprobrium. If the marriage failed, it must be her fault. What did she do wrong? Why could she not keep him?

Although Nanny clearly did maintain her poise and equanimity, transforming in her final years into acceptance and stoicism and earning the continued respect of her friends, Wood's life was stained with further ignominy.

In September 1922 Wood and Sara visited Kitty Beck and her third husband, another alcoholic, George Vanderveer in Seattle. Their visit renewed Kitty's disappointment at losing Wood and her dissatisfaction with her current husband. On 31 October 1922 Kathryn Seaman Beck Irvine Vandemeer committed suicide by inhaling chloroform. She was the second of Wood's mistresses to commit suicide. Kitty, just as Janina Klecan before her, and as Sara had attempted to do, sought to disentangle herself from Wood through self-destruction.

II
FINAL DAYS

At the beginning of 1930, Nanny's health, which had been poor for several years, declined. In a shaky handwriting, Nanny sent a letter in February to Wood:

> My dear Scotty, I feel that I should always begin any note or letter by explaining that the reason for my writing such a scratchy lot of letters is because my hands tremble all the time. I can do no better than to hold a pen. I always want to thank you for your kind and generous thought of me with your present. Did you receive the photograph I sent you in [the] mail? . . . I feel particularly blue this afternoon, having just heard of the death of our kind old friend Mr. Koehler. He died this afternoon of bronchial pneumonia.[36]

At this point the letter degenerates into undecipherable scrawl.

Nanny ceased to write letters and sent telegrams. For example, on 9 February 1932, she telegraphed him, "I wish you a happy birthday with our children."[37] Nanny never failed to send Wood a Christmas and birthday telegram during the thirteen years of their separation.

As her strength diminished, Nanny sensed her own mortality. In one of her final walks around her property she made an inventory of the dozens of trees and flowers that made her garden a showplace and an inspiration to others in Portland. Her nurse and amanuensis Dean Fischer recorded the name and location of each plant : "in the grove"; "under the south bank by the steps"; "in the northeast bed at the north of the lawn." In some cases, she left instructions for caring for the plants after her death: "It needs a soil of rich top dressing"; "needs plenty of sun"; "protect in winter." Like her attractive and talented children, this lavish garden was her legacy. Appendix 2 contains the record of the contents of her beautiful plantings.

In July 1933 Nanny fell and broke her thighbone, and Wood wrote to her on 16 July[38] using her pet name from childhood:

> My dearest Sippy, Kirk [Smith, Nanny's son-in-law, married to Lisa] told me on Thursday of your most unfortunate accident the news of which gave me a great shock and you know you have my deepest sympathy. . . . I understand your fracture is about as fortunate a kind as you could have and will not have to be put into a plaster cast. I understand it is not the neck of the femur but a simple fracture of the thighbone below the femur.

Wood might have sensed that the delicate Nanny could not survive this injury, and he wrote in detail about his pride in their children. He said their daughter Lisa "brings love and cheer and joy with her wherever she goes." He described Nan Wood Honeyman as "a lovely girl, sweet, demure, not brilliant perhaps but almost better, arriving at her goal by hard, hard work." He expressed his love for Lisa and Kirk's children, their granddaughter Katherine Smith, "our dear honest old Tashie, so full of commonsense, is a delight. . . a decided leader everywhere." Tashie's brother Alan is "the quiet young giant. . . a hardworker [who] gets there in both studies and athletics." He voiced his concern of their son Berwick: "I do hope he will be careful of diet and drinking. These ulcers may lead on into cancer." He praised their daughter Nan's children, "the quiet little Judy and fine manly David." Perhaps Wood felt compelled to describe their children and grandchildren to Nanny, who would have known all this anyway because most of the family was there with her in Portland while Wood had removed himself to Los Gatos, as a way of paying tribute to her, a recognition of her contributions in the form of their progeny.

In September she declined into semi-consciousness.[39] Wood was full of guilt and regret when Erskine telephoned to tell him that Nanny was near death, but he declined to come see her in her final days. He did write to Erskine that his "greatest regret is that I could not bring to your mother a realizing sense that I had not ceased to love her."[40]

That final December her spacious bedroom was decorated with Christmas items—toy elves and Santas, poinsettias, a silver tree laden with tinsel. Her four-poster bed was festooned with evergreen garlands and bright glass Christmas balls. Clusters of roses crowded personal memorabilia—photographs, paintings, and bronze reliefs of her children. Many of her surviving children and grandchildren were with her when she died 18 December 1933.

Nanny is buried in River View Cemetery overlooking the Willamette River. Her friends Henry W. Corbett, William S. Ladd, and Henry Failing purchased 350 acres of land for $79,000 in 1879 to found this cemetery. Nanny's grave marker resides between two sequoias and is oriented toward Mount Hood and Mount St. Helens. She is flanked by her sons William Maxwell Wood, who died in 1921, and Berwick Bruce Wood, who died in 1970. Her daughter Lisa, who died in 1958, lies nearby as does C.E.S. Wood's brother, James McIntosh Wood, who died in May 1944. Nan Wood Honeyman's grave is in her husband's family plot nearby. Erskine is buried near Vancouver, Washington, where he spent most of his life.

C.E.S. Wood suffered a heart attack on 16 September 1937. After two weeks near death, he recovered and came to the realization that he and Sara, despite their adherence to unconventional behavior, must marry in order to protect any money or property that he would leave her upon his death. On 20 January 1938, they married in a ceremony performed by Rabbi Jacob Weinstein, Wood's former paperboy in

Portland. Even Erskine, who had so opposed his father's affair with Sara, relented and acknowledged that "my father and Sara spent the last twenty years of his life [at The Cats]. In her he found perfect companionship."[41] In an interview in 1985, Kay Ehrgott Caldwell agreed with her step-brother: "If you ever saw a model of a deep and rich companionship, there it was between Colonel Wood and Mother."

At their Los Gatos retreat they could receive famous visitors such as Lincoln Steffens, Robinson Jeffers, John Steinbeck, and others. Wood became a dedicated vintner and enologist, producing his own variety of red wine. He who despised the Roman Catholic Church and tried unsuccessfully to get Nanny to forsake her religion became good friends with the monks and priests in a monastery about a half mile away from his vineyard and delighted in spending hours with them talking not only about wine but on many subjects.

Wood lived eleven years after Nanny's death. When he died 22 January 1944 he was ninety-two years old and the last surviving member of his West Point class of 1874. Certainly he left his mark on Portland, particularly the Portland Art Museum, but he had disgraced himself to the extent that not even a street is named for him.[42] Sara Bard Field (born in 1882) died 15 June 1974. She is remembered as one of the brightest stars in the constellation of women who were the leaders of the national suffrage movement.

Although both Wood and Sara outlived her, Nanny was a survivor. She had survived the dangers of the Civil War, the loss of both parents when she was young, the peripatetic life as an army wife, and the birthing of six children. She could look with pride on the accomplishments of her five surviving children and their families, and she could see her legacy in the beauty of Portland's gardens. She stoically rose above the indignities of her husband's infidelities and his participation in radical causes.

Some women born in the nineteenth century developed within themselves the capacity for boldness that allowed them to become the Emma Goldmans, Marie Equis and Margaret

Sangers, championing liberal social causes in general and the causes of women in particular. Nanny Wood's privileged upbringing did not prepare her to be a rebel. Always outgoing, never shy in a social situation, she could not, however, have forced herself to stand behind a microphone and stridently exhort the masses to action. In inverse proportion to her husband's intellectualism and unorthodox behavior, she assumed a traditional, domesticated role, rarely reading a book. Although some might call her method of dealing with Wood's infidelity denial, her acceptance of the realities of her marriage required a certain measure of boldness.

Nanny's reputation as a lady remained strong during Wood's involvement with other women and extends after her death. Erskine said, "She bore her loneliness and her sorrow uncomplainingly, and still maintained the family home for us, her grown children. She always remained a favorite in Portland society. Many friends, of course, took her part, and the generation of young mothers used to call on her for the pleasure of her company, her reminiscences, witticisms and charm."[43]

Nanny's obituary in the *Oregonian* describes her as being "socially prominent in Portland for many years before the lingering illness which ended with her death."[44] In 1942, in an address to the Portland Art Association, Barbara Hartwell, who as a girl had been a frequent visitor in Nanny's home, said, "She was and will remain [Portland's] only 'grande dame.' She was completely at home in any circle and always captured it.... She was immeasurably more interesting than a thousand people who are erudite. She knew life, society, humanity; she was inescapably the center of attraction wherever she found herself; and age could not wither her nor custom stale."[45]

Fifty-three years after her death, an article in the *Oregonian* recalling the Wood family says without equivocation, "Nanny Moale Smith... commanded a position of great respect among Portland matrons."[46]

NOTES

[1] "William Mead Ladd." *The National Cyclopedia of American Biography*, vol. 24 (New York: James T. White & Company, 1934), 371.

[2] "William Sargent Ladd." *The National Cyclopedia of American Biography*, vol. 7 (New York: James T. White & Company, 1897), 32.

[3] "Henry Winslow Corbett." *Dictionary of American Biography*, vol. 4. Eds. Allen Johnson and Dumas Malone (New York: Charles Scribner's Sons, 1930), 435.

[4] "Henry Winslow Corbett." *The National Cyclopedia of American Biography*, vol. 6 (New York: James T. White & Company, 1929), 111.

[5] Fred Leeson, *Rose City Justice: A Legal History of Portland, Oregon* (Portland: Oregon Historical Society Press, 1998), 95-96.

[6] Hubert H. Hoeltje, "When Mark Twain Spoke in Portland," *Oregon Historical Quarterly* 55 (1954): 77.

[7] "Not Worried by Seattle Critics," Portland *Oregonian*, 3 July 1907: 11.

[8] "Women of the South Resent Remarks," Portland *Oregonian*, 28 December 1907: 7.

[9] "Wood Denounces Y.M.C.A. Directors," Portland *Oregonian*, 25 May 1908: 12.

[10] "Wood is Anarchist," Portland *Oregonian*, 29 November 1909: 14.

[11] William P. Buren, "Oregon's Oldest Law Firm," *Oregon State Bar Bulletin* (November 1984): 33.

[12] "Sedition Laws Invalid, C.E.S. Wood Asserts," Portland *Oregonian*, 7 June 1919: 1.

[13] E. Kimbark MacColl, *The Growth of a City; Power and Politics in Portland, Oregon, 1915 to 1950* (Portland: The Georgian Press, 1979), 144.

[14] Erskine Wood, *Life of Charles Erskine Scott Wood* (Vancouver, WA: Rose Wind Press, 1991), 104.

[15] C.E.S. Wood Papers, Huntington Library, WD Box 260 (21).

[16] Robert Hamburger, *Two Rooms: The Life of Charles Erskine Scott Wood* (Lincoln: The University of Nebraska Press, 1998), 198.

[17] Hamburger, 198.

[18] C.E.S. Wood Papers, The Huntington Library, WD Box 260 (24).

[19] Glenda Riley, "Sara Bard Field, Charles Erskine Scott Wood, and the Phenomenon of Migratory Divorce," *California History* 69 (Fall 1990): 251.

[20] *The Portland Society Annual, 1914–15* (Portland: Lawson & Company, 1914): 103.
[21] Hamburger, 218.
[22] C.E.S. Wood Papers, The Huntington Library, WD Box 243 (27).
[23] C.E.S. Wood Papers, The Huntington Library, WD Box 260 (24).
[24] Walt Curtis, "Charles Erskine Scott Wood," *Multnomah Monthly* (September 1984): 12.
[25] C.E.S. Wood Papers, The Huntington Library, WD Box 260 (32).
[26] C.E.S. Wood Papers, The Huntington Library, WD Box 260 (35).
[27] "Albert Ehrgott Accuses Colonel E. Wood Publicly," Portland *Oregonian*, 30 May 1919: 5.
[28] C.E.S. Wood Papers, The Huntington Library, WD Box 260 (47).
[29] C.E.S. Wood Papers, The Huntington Library, WD Box 261 (28).
[30] C.E.S. Wood Papers, The Huntington Library, WD Box 260 (49).
[31] C.E.S. Wood Papers, The Huntington Library, WD Box 260 (50).
[32] Erskine Wood, *Life of Charles Erskine Scott Wood* (Vancouver, WA: Rose Wind Press, 1991), 128.
[33] Wood, 132.
[34] I thank Marian Kolisch, Berwick Bruce Wood's daughter, for kind permission to quote from this letter. She has the original, and a photocopy is in the C.E.S. Wood Papers, Oregon Historical Society Library, MSS 800.
[35] C.E.S. Wood Papers, The Huntington Library, WD Box 261 (32).
[36] C.E.S. Wood Papers, The Huntington Library, WD Box 261 (13).
[37] C.E.S. Wood Papers, The Huntington Library, WD Box 261 (14).
[38] C.E.S. Wood Papers, The Huntington Library, WD Box 243 (29).
[39] Hamburger, 323.
[40] Wood, 153.
[41] Wood, 142.
[42] Eugene E. Snyder, *Portland Names and Neighborhoods: Their Historic Origins* (Portland: Binford & Mort, 1979), 231. Northwest Wood Street is named for W. G. Wood, secretary of the St. Johns Land Company. Snyder says specifically of C.E.S. Wood, "There is no street named for him."
[43] Wood, 127.
[44] "Mrs. C.E.S. Wood," Portland *Oregonian*, 19 December 1933: 9. Her obituary follows:

Mrs. C.E.S. Wood

The funeral services for Mrs. C.E.S. Wood, who was socially prominent in Portland for many years before the lingering illness which ended with her death yesterday morning, will be held at her home, 1128 Southwest Vista Avenue, Thursday. The service will be private, for only relatives and a few intimate friends.

Mrs. Wood was 78 years of age when her death occurred. She was born in Baltimore, Md., January 12, 1855, and came to Portland in the early '80's. She had been a member of the Town club.

Surviving her are four children: Erskine Wood, Berwick Bruce Wood, Mrs. David T. Honeyman, all of Portland and Mrs. G. Kirkham Smith of San Rafael, Cal.

[45] Barbara Bartlett Hartwell, *The Wood Household* (Portland: Portland Art Association, 1942), 8, 9. The quotation "Age cannot wither her, nor custom stale" comes from Shakespeare's *Antony and Cleopatra*, II, ii, 243:

> Age cannot wither her, nor custom stale
> Her infinite variety; other women cloy
> The appetites they feed, but she makes hungry
> Where most she satisfies.

[46] Karl Klooster, "The Woods: A Portland Family," *This Week* [Portland *Oregonian*] 10 August 1986: 2.

PART TWO:
Her Times

INTRODUCTION

In 1855, THE YEAR NANNY WAS BORN, Walt Whitman published the first edition of *Leaves of Grass*, transforming America's conception of poetry. Nineteen of the fifty states had not yet been admitted to the growing Union. The American Civil War would not begin for six more years, but when it did, it forever shattered the mirror in which Americans viewed themselves. In the latter half of the nineteenth century when Nanny grew up, America also came of age.

Part Two seeks to complement Nanny's life by placing her in the context of American culture when dramatic changes in society occurred. For some events—the Civil War, the emerging acculturation of the northwest United States, and the erosion of the sanctity of marriage—Nanny was a participant. In others, such as advances in medicine, art, literature, law, and politics—arenas dominated by men—Nanny and most other women of that time could only observe. In general, unless she were willing to become a firebrand after the fashion of Emma Goldman, Margaret Sanger, or Sara Bard Field, a woman in America in the late nineteenth and early twentieth centuries was closeted in a domestic world of marriage and child rearing.

Nanny's life can be illuminated by examining her ancestors and her acquaintances, especially the men, clearly exceptionally talented people, who made significant contributions to American culture.

CHAPTER EIGHT

PATRIOTS

NANNY'S MATERNAL AND PATERNAL ANCESTORS contributed abundantly to the history of the United States and especially to the Baltimore and greater Maryland area. Her mother was a Moale, one of the most distinguished old Maryland families. She was also related to the Curzon (later changed to Curson), Poultney, Seton, and Pleasants families. The extent to which these families intermarried may be seen in the names of Nanny's relatives Elizabeth Moale Poultney Pleasants and Ellin Moale Curson Poultney.

Nanny's great-great-grandfather John Moale was born in Kenton Parish, Devonshire, England, 30 October 1697. He came to America and settled on land that came to be called Moale's Point on the Patapsco River, part of present day Baltimore. Maryland's Colonial Assembly at Annapolis wanted to buy Moale's Point in 1728 to build a new town because it had navigable water on both sides of it, but John Moale refused to sell, and the new town, named after the Lords Baltimore was established the next year slightly to the northeast of Moale's Point. Later, Baltimore Town would extend to Moale's land and subsume it anyway.

He married Rachel Hammond and they had two sons, John and Richard Moale.[1] John Moale (1730–98), Nanny's great-grandfather, married Ellin North (1740–1825) the daughter of ship's captain Robert North in Baltimore in 1758. North was one of the commissioners who laid out Baltimore Town in 1729 or 1730 following the refusal of his kinsman by marriage to sell Moale's Point.[2] "Ellin" was the surname of a friend of Captain North, and the name frequently reappears in Nanny's family for several generations, occasionally transforming into "Ellen." At one point so many girls in the family were named Ellin that they became known as "red-haired Ellin," "black-haired Ellin," "freckled Ellin," and "the beautiful Ellin."[3] In 1742 Captain North built Green Spring, the oldest house in the Green Spring Valley, and it passed to his daughter Ellin, hence into the Moale family, upon his death.[4]

For years, in numerous print sources, Ellin North Moale was erroneously known as the "first white child born in Baltimore."[5] Baltimore, as an incorporated city, was eleven years old when Ellin was born in 1740 (some sources list 1741), and it is improbable that other children would not have been born there before she was. Nanny's relative Dr. J. Hall Pleasants (1873–1957), the son of Elizabeth Moale Poultney Pleasants, insisted that Ellin was merely the oldest person living in Baltimore who had also been born there when she died at age eighty-four.[6] At her death in 1825 the obituary blurred the facts and the error was perpetuated in various publications and histories of the city.

John Moale was a Whig and used his wealth and prominence to support the American cause during the Revolutionary War. In 1775 the Maryland Convention required all the counties in the state to elect Committees of Observation to carry out the orders of the Convention as they prepared to go to war with England. John Moale represented the Green Spring Valley on the Baltimore County Committee.[7] He also served as lieutenant colonel in the Baltimore Town battalion militia from May 1776 until the end of the war.[8]

Nanny's relatives the Poultneys and the Cursons were involved in scandals in the eighteenth and nineteenth centuries. Thomas Poultney (1762–1828) came to Baltimore in 1791 and established the Poultney and Thomas Company, a mercantile trade. His son Samuel Thomas Poultney (1797–1864) married

Ellin Moale Curson in 1828, daughter of Richard Curson Jr. Another son, Evan Thomas Poultney, using the considerable funds amassed by his father's business, became a private banker and later became president of the Bank of Maryland. Evan Poultney and his brothers Samuel and Philip and their brother-in-law William M. Ellicott devised a complicated scheme to increase the note circulation of the Bank of Maryland. They enticed investors with the promise of five percent interest on deposits, then moved the notes through various agencies over the United States. But in the winter of 1833, when the Union Bank of Maryland stock that Evan and his partners had purchased using Bank of Maryland money could not be sold at a profit, they disbanded. The closure of the Bank of Maryland led to the Baltimore panic of 1834. A subsequent investigation revealed that the Bank's expansion and overextended condition was because of paper without the backing of adequate reserves. Evan, Samuel, and Philip Poultney and William Ellicott were tried for fraud and mismanagement. Found guilty, they were ordered to pay almost $350,000 to depositors.[9]

Richard Curson Sr. came from a wealthy London family. He established Curson and Seton Company of New York and in the Dutch West Indies. Richard was an American patriot who had to leave New York in 1776 and relocate to Baltimore because of his vocal support of the revolutionary cause. There he established Richard Curson and Company, importing goods and wine from Italy and Spain. When the Revolutionary War began, Richard became a privateer, obtaining letters of marque and reprisal from the Continental Congress authorizing eight of his ships, although lightly armed, to attack British ships. Some people today regard privateers as ranking slightly higher than pirates in legitimacy, but the system efficiently used naval resources to obtain goods from merchantmen vessels operating in American waters. Letters in the archives of the Maryland Historical Society show that Richard Curson Sr. was a good friend of Thomas Jefferson and Benjamin Franklin during and after the revolution.

Richard Curson Jr. (1763–1808) married Elizabeth Moale,

daughter of Colonel John Moale. As mentioned above, their daughter Ellin Moale Curson, married Samuel T. Poultney. Nanny was close to her aunt Ellin Moale Curson Poultney, who lived until December 1880.

Another of Richard Sr.'s sons was Samuel Curson (1763–86) who also was tainted with scandal. Samuel Curson allegedly had fathered the illegitimate child of Betsey Burling who subsequently married John Whittell of England. Her brother Walter Burling sent letters, approaching the level of blackmail, demanding a financial settlement from Samuel. Denying any wrongdoing in the matter, Samuel refused to pay. Then Burling came from England and challenged Samuel to a duel with pistols in New York City. They fought on 21 April 1786, and Burling mortally wounded Samuel who died three days later. Evidence suggests that Samuel was killed by John Whittell using the alias of Walter Burling.[10]

Nanny's grandfather was Samuel O. Moale (1773–1857), one of John and Ellin Moale's sons. During his law school days he had a disagreement with Judge Hanson and they fought a duel with pistols, but neither was injured and they repaired the difficulty between them and became friends. Samuel O. Moale continued the family's tradition of service as a citizen-soldier. On 19 September 1808, he received an appointment as first lieutenant in the Maryland Militia, and on 24 May 1812 he served as an artillery captain, commanding the Columbian Artillery. He advanced through the ranks to become a colonel.[11]

In 1814 he participated in the defense of Baltimore against the British at Fort McHenry during the famous bombardment that inspired "The Star Spangled Banner" by Francis Scott Key, who was the grand-uncle of Wilson C. Nicholas II, husband of Nanny's aunt Augusta.[12] Recall that a cousin of C.E.S. Wood's law partner Stewart Linthicum introduced the bill in Congress making "The Star Spangled Banner" the National Anthem. As an aside, Samuel Moale's great-great-great-great granddaughter Ellin Travers Mckay was the second wife of Irving Berlin (1888–1989)[13] who wrote "God Bless America";

thus Nanny has family connections to two of America's most patriotic songs.

When he was twenty-five years old Samuel married Ann M. Howard, and with her he had three children. His daughter Ellin (by his first wife) married Samuel Hollingsworth who had been a colonel in the War of 1812, at the same time Elizabeth (Betsy) Patterson married Jerome Bonaparte. They were close friends, and Baltimoreans called their nuptials the two "brilliant" weddings of the day. During the American Revolution, Betsy Patterson Bonaparte's father William Patterson placed all his valuable possessions on two ships and sold them in France to procure arms for George Washington at a critical time in the war.[14]

One year after his first wife died, Samuel married Nanny's grandmother Ann G. White on 1 September 1828, and with her he had eight children, including Nanny's mother. Two of those children died in infancy. Nanny's mother, her siblings, and their spouses made substantial contributions to American history. Mary Susan, who married General John Gray Foster; Frances North who married General John Gibbon; Ann White, Nanny's mother, who married Dr. Berwick Bruce Smith, son of the distinguished Dr. Nathan R. Smith; Henry who became a prominent merchant in Baltimore; General Edward Moale, Nanny's "Uncle Ned"; and Augusta who married Colonel Wilson C. Nicholas II who fought with the Confederate army.

Nanny's uncle Wilson Cary Nicholas II was sympathetic to the Southern cause, despite the fact that his father was a captain in the United States Navy. The Nicholas family's roots were in Maryland and Virginia. His paternal grandfather, the first Wilson C. Nicholas, commanded Washington's Life Guard during the American Revolution and later served as a member of the Virginia House of Delegates, a United States Congressman, and governor of Virginia. His grandfather is buried at Monticello near his friend Thomas Jefferson. Before the Civil War, Nicholas graduated from Oxford College in Maryland and worked with the B&O Railroad, founded in 1827 by William Patterson, father of John Patterson who married Nicholas's aunt Mary Buchanan. John and Mary Patterson raised Wilson C. Nicholas while his parents traveled to his various duty stations as a naval officer.

When the Civil War began, citizens in the Baltimore area loyal to the South formed units with colorful names such as the Patapsco Dragoons and the Independent Grays. Nicholas became the captain of the Garrison Forest Rangers, later Company G, 1st Maryland Infantry Regiment (Confederate). On 20 April 1861, leading a small force, he seized the United States arsenal at Pikesville with its supply of small arms and gunpowder.[15] Operating in the Shenandoah Valley in June 1862 he captured Lieutenant Colonel Thomas L. Kane, commander of the First Pennsylvania Rifles.[16] The commander of his regiment, Colonel Bradley T. Johnson commended him for his bravery in his report of 7 July 1862 for stalling the advance of a Union cavalry unit.[17] When the original First Maryland Regiment disbanded and reorganized, the new commander Colonel George H. Steuart wrote to General George W. Randolph, secretary of war for the Confederacy, that Nicholas was "an officer of experience" and saying, "I earnestly recommend that he may be again appointed [as drillmaster] or some other position in the Provisional Army—first lieutenant or captain."[18]

In July 1864, at Rockville, Maryland, Nicholas's unit was attacked by a Federal cavalry regiment. He led the first squadron in a counterattack, but he was shot and captured. Held prisoner at Fort Delaware, he was on the list to be sent to the prisoner of war camp at Hilton Head, South Carolina, but he was exchanged in October of 1864. He had attained the rank of major when he was paroled in May 1865. He returned to Atamasco in the Green Spring Valley where he was a prosperous farmer of 900 acres for the rest of his life.[19] Colonel Johnson said, "He was as good a soldier and as gallant a gentleman as ever rode a horse in that war."[20] As did many Southern officers after the war, no matter what rank they had held, Wilson enjoyed the title of "Colonel" for the rest of his life.

When Nicholas worked for the B&O Railroad, Louis McLane was the president of the line and a leading figure in American politics. This Louis McLane was the father of the Louis McLane with whom Nanny and Wood stayed for several days in San Francisco on their honeymoon. Nanny had reason to be proud of this branch of her extended family. Theirs is a story of astonishing accomplishment.

The scion of this family was Allen McLane (1746–1829), a captain in the Revolutionary War with the reputation for being a fearless fighter. He was with George Washington at Valley Forge in the winter of 1777. When the British general Sir Henry Clinton ordered his troops to evacuate Philadelphia in 1778, McLane used his skills as an expert horseman to navigate the narrow city streets and round up prisoners. After the war, Washington, in gratitude for his heroism, appointed him collector of customs at Wilmington, Delaware. In the War of 1812, the old soldier took command of the defenses of Wilmington. He had fourteen children, but only three of them survived past infancy. He had two sons named Louis, the first dying as an infant.

Louis McLane Sr. (1784–1857) was appointed a midshipman in the United States Navy but left to study law. He inherited his father's unwillingness to be trifled with and fought a pistol duel with John Barratt in 1807. Both men fired two shots each and were injured but survived, resumed their friendship, and were admitted to the bar that same year.[21]

In the War of 1812 he was a volunteer and assisted in the defense of Baltimore when the British threatened the city. Following the war he occupied a number of important posts in government. First, he represented Delaware in the United States Congress. Then, in 1827, he was elected a Senator. In 1829 President Jackson appointed him minister plenipotentiary to the Court of St. James's. He returned from England to become Secretary of the Treasury in 1831, and in 1833 he became Secretary of State. Then in 1834 he became president of the railroad, moving to Baltimore. Ironically, while the Oregon boundary negotiations were pending, President Polk appointed him special minister to England, and he was instrumental in obtaining a treaty with England for the area where Nanny would reside for her adult life.[22] A United States Navy ship, the *U.S.S. Louis McLane,* was named for him as a tribute to his service to the nation.

Louis McLane married Catherine Milligan of Maryland, and their son Louis McLane Jr. (1819–1905) became a navy midshipman like his father. During the Mexican War he served with John C. Fremont in the California Battalion. He resigned from the navy in 1850 and moved to San Francisco where he took charge of the Pacific coast operations of Wells, Fargo & Company. He became president of Wells, Fargo in 1866 and moved to New York City. When he retired in 1868 he returned to San Francisco where he engaged in a number of enterprises: the Bank of California, the Pacific Insurance Company; California Dry Dock Company; Sacramento Gas Company; the Overland Stage Company. He was the owner of the California Telegraph Company and the San Francisco Gas Company. When Nanny and Wood stayed with him in San Francisco, he was the president of the Nevada Bank of San Francisco.

Louis McLane Sr.'s daughter Rebecca Wells McLane married Philip Hamilton, the youngest son of Alexander Hamilton, Secretary of the Treasury under George Washington. One of their sons, Allan McLane Hamilton, M.D., served as a sanitary inspector for the New York City Board of Health[23] and later became the leading "alienist" or psychiatrist of his day.[24] Another son, Louis McLane Hamilton, served in the Union army during the Civil War, attaining a reputation for gallantry in several battles.[25] He enlisted as a private, but Abraham Lincoln took the time to write a personal letter to the Secretary of War requesting a lieutenancy for young Hamilton.[26] Following distinguished service at Fredericksburg, Chancellorsville, Gettysburg, and Petersburg, he joined his cousin Edward Moale for Lee's surrender at Appomattox.[27]

After the war he became a captain in Custer's Seventh Cavalry. In 1868, eight years before the ill-fated Battle of Little

Bighorn, he drew the duty of remaining in charge of the rear guard of a large wagon train of supplies for the Battle of the Washita. Not wishing to be left out of the raid on Chief Black Kettle's camp, Hamilton convinced another officer to exchange duties. Custer relates what happened: "Hamilton, who rode at my side as we entered the village and whose soldierly tones I heard for the last time as he calmly cautioned his squadron, 'Now, men, keep cool, fire low, and not too rapidly,' was among the first victims of the opening charge, having been shot from his saddle by a bullet from an Indian rifle. He died instantly."[28] Custer and General Philip Sheridan served as pallbearers at his funeral.[29] Louis McLane Hamilton was not the first of his family to die in battle with Indians. His uncle George M. McLane was killed by Indians in 1861 when he was serving in New Mexico as a captain in a regiment of mounted riflemen in the United States Army.[30]

Another son of Louis McLane Sr., Robert Milligan McLane, graduated from West Point in 1837 and served about five years in the army. In 1843 he was admitted to the bar of Maryland, and in 1845 and 1846 he served in the state legislature. Then he represented Maryland in the United States Congress. President Pierce appointed him minister to China in 1852; President Buchanan appointed him minister to Mexico in 1859. In early 1861, he was one of a group of commissioners sent by the Maryland legislature to confer with President Lincoln about the unconstitutional activities of Federal troops in the state. McLane worked to ameliorate the harsh feeling on both sides, urging that Maryland not secede with the Southern states but also that Maryland not send troops into military action against the South. In 1883 he was elected governor of Maryland. He resigned that post in 1885 to become Minister to France at the request of President Grover Cleveland. He died in Paris on 16 April 1898.[31]

Second Lieutenant Robert McLane served in the army with a dignified bachelor, Joseph E. Johnston. Facing a Christmas alone in 1840, Johnston accepted McLane's offer of a visit to his family's home on Maryland's eastern shore for the holidays.

The McLane mansion, known as Bohemia, had a private dock on the Bohemia River, formal English gardens, and grand rooms for Robert's parents, Louis and Catherine (Kitty), and his four brothers and three sisters. Johnston, then thirty-three, fell in love with Robert's younger sister Lydia, eighteen years old. They corresponded and met infrequently for five years, but they could not marry because Johnston could not support her on his modest salary. When Lydia inherited a considerable sum of money from an aunt, the two married in Baltimore in 1845.[32]

In 1846 he served with Winfield Scott in Mexico and was at the battle of Molino del Rey. When the Civil War began, Johnston was serving as quartermaster general of the army, but, like Robert E. Lee, as a loyal son of Virginia he resigned to become a major general in the Confederate army. He served with distinction at Manassas, Bull Run, and Fair Oaks where C.E.S. Wood's mentor Oliver O. Howard had his right arm shot off by enemy fire.

After the war, Johnston served in Congress representing the Richmond district of Virginia. He was a pallbearer at the funeral of his old foes Ulysses S. Grant in 1885 and William T. Sherman in 1891. At Sherman's funeral, Johnston stood hatless in a cold rain, caught a cold, and died.[33]

Another son in this remarkable family, Allan McLane, married Maria Bache, the great-granddaughter of Benjamin Franklin. He became the president of the Pacific Mail Steamship Company in San Francisco.

Another daughter, Sallie Jones McLane, married Henry Tiffany, and their son Louis McLane Tiffany (1844–1916) studied medicine under Nanny's uncle Nathan R. Smith at the University of Maryland. Dr. Tiffany became a distinguished surgeon and at various times was president of the Baltimore Medical Association, the Medical and Chirurgical Faculty of Maryland, the Southern Surgical and Gynecological Association and the American Surgical Association.[34]

His close cousin with a similar and more recognizable name was Louis Comfort Tiffany (1848–1933). The famous jewelry and home accessory designer shares his family first name with Louis McLane Tiffany and Louis McLane Hamilton. In 1912, calling upon their family connection, the Moales of St. Thomas' Church in the Green Spring Valley, commissioned Louis C. Tiffany to execute a stained glass window for the church's south transept honoring the memory of nine year old Alexander Stewart whose parents had lived in the Green Spring Valley. Earlier that year, young Alexander awoke one morning to tell his mother that he had dreamed that an angel came to him and told him it would return that night to take him on a journey. That evening Alexander died without apparent cause. Designed personally by Louis C. Tiffany, the large window depicting an angel hovering above a small boy was installed by Tiffany Studios in 1914.[35]

Although Nanny's mother and her aunts did little more than marry well, their relationships with men of achievement indicate the kind of family Nanny came from and, consequently, the kind of person she was. While she knew the McLanes, the Tiffanys, and other assorted cousins, she was closest by far to her mother's siblings and their spouses.

Nanny's uncle John G. Foster (1823-74) grew up in New Hampshire and graduated fourth in his class at the United States Military Academy in 1846. He served under General Winfield Scott in Mexico with his wife's cousin Joseph E. Johnston, being severely wounded at the battle of Molino del Rey on 8 September 1847.

From 1848 to 1855 he was an assistant engineer building Fort Carroll, Maryland, at Baltimore where he met Nanny's aunt Mary Susan Moale.[36] They married on 21 January 1851, and they went to West Point when he was appointed a professor of engineering. Three years after that assignment, as an engineer officer, he was in charge of the fortifications in Charleston. His professional reports on the strengthening of Fort Moultrie and Fort Sumter form a solid factual basis for the sequence of events leading up to the firing on Fort Sumter in April 1861.[37] Part One of this volume contains an account of John Gray Foster's activities during the siege of Fort Sumter at the start of the Civil War.

In November 1861, in New York City where the Union soldiers went after departing Fort Sumter, he converted to Catholicism.[38] Nanny's mother Ann and her sister Mary had earlier converted from the family's Episcopalian roots to Catholicism, the only ones in the family to do so. With the carnage of the war now inevitable, Mary prevailed upon Foster to convert to her religion to ease her anxiety about his exposure to the lethality of the battlefield.

When Nanny, her mother, aunt, and cousin rejoined Foster in North Carolina, he had been promoted to brigadier general where he commanded 9,000 men in the Department of North Carolina.[39] During this time Nanny was an eyewitness to combat when her uncle took her on a mission aboard a steam-powered gunboat on the Neuse River. As the war progressed, Foster was promoted to major general with increasing responsibilities; as commander of the Department of the South he helped General William T. Sherman coordinate the campaign against Savannah and Charleston.[40]

He was always one of Nanny's favorite uncles, and when her aunt Mary died in 1871, she was glad to see him happily married to her friend Nannie Davis in 1872. Foster did not live long after marrying his second wife; he died in 1874.[41] Foster and Mary had one child, Nanny's Fort Sumter playmate Annie.

Annie married Henry Seton, son of Saint Elizabeth Ann Seton, the first American-born saint in the Roman Catholic Church. Henry Seton had served under Foster during the Civil War and with General Crook in the Indian wars on the plains. He died in 1904 at age sixty-six from tuberculosis.[42] His obituary in the Baltimore *Sun* says, "Mrs. Seton, who survives her husband, is connected with the most prominent families in Baltimore, being a granddaughter of Samuel Moale and related to the Pleasants, Poultney, McLane and other Baltimore families."[43]

In yet another of the coincidences pertaining to this family, Major Seton's mother, who had converted from the Episcopal religion to Roman Catholic in 1805,[44] was the founder of the American Sisters of Charity which was instrumental in staffing with nurses the Providence Hospital in Washington, DC, where Nanny's step-father, Dr. Nathan Smith Lincoln was chief surgeon.

Nanny's uncle John Gibbon, born in 1827, entered West Point in 1842 with his future brother-in-law John Foster, but Gibbon, only fifteen when he was a plebe, encountered some academic difficulty and was held back one year, graduating twentieth in a class of thirty-seven in 1847. Among his classmates were General Ambrose P. Hill and George Edward Pickett of the Confederate Army and Ambrose E. Burnside of the Union. As did Foster, Gibbon, too, saw service in Mexico, and they served together as instructors at West Point where Robert E. Lee was their commanding officer as superintendent. While assigned there he married Frances North Moale on 16 October 1855.

When the Civil War began, Gibbon served with General Irvin McDowell[45] whom Nanny met in San Francisco on her honeymoon journey with Wood to his post at Vancouver Barracks. Gibbon saw combat at Manassas Junction and at South Mountain where his troops gained the sobriquet "The Iron Brigade."[46] He saw further combat at Antietam where he was wounded in the left wrist by an artillery shell fragment, an injury that earned him a brief convalescent leave to Baltimore to see his family. Next he was at Chancellorsville, then Gettysburg where he was wounded in the left shoulder. He commanded a division at the "Bloody Angle," the farthest advance of Pickett's Charge at Gettysburg, led by his former West Point roommate, George Edward Pickett.[47]

As the Battle of Gettysburg approached, Gibbon was elevated from his brigade to command the Second Division. The Third Brigade of this division was commanded by Colonel Norman J. Hall who had been with Nanny and her uncles at Fort Sumter. Another subordinate unit of Gibbon's division was the Twentieth Massachusetts Regiment, also known as the "Harvard Regiment" because many of its officers were Harvard graduates. Early in the war this unit was commanded by Colonel William R. Lee, a cousin of Robert E. Lee. The Twentieth Massachusetts suffered many casualties at Gettysburg, including Colonel Paul Revere, grandson of the famous midnight rider, and Lieutenant Sumner Paine, great-great nephew of Thomas Paine whose *Common Sense* helped form American sentiments in favor of independence from England. Lieutenant Paine took over command of a company when Oliver Wendell Holmes, Jr., later a Supreme Court justice, was wounded at Fredericksburg and could not be present at Gettysburg.

At the surrender of the Army of Northern Virginia, Grant and Lee met at Wilmer McLean's farmhouse at Appomattox Court House on 9 April 1865. The next day Gibbon was one of three Union officers assigned the responsibility of drafting the specific terms of the surrender agreement. Gibbon's headquarters had a small printing press under the supervision of his brother-in-law, Edward Moale, serving as his Assistant Adjutant General. Gibbon and Moale composed and printed a pass to be signed by the surrendering Confederate soldiers attesting to the fact that the bearer would no longer "serve in the armies of the Confederate States, or in any military capacity whatever, against the United States of America."[48] They would carry their passes with them as a sign of their parole as they returned home.

A historically interesting document records the remarkable presence of two of Nanny's uncles at the events occurring at Appomattox Court House. They printed an order stipulating that former Confederate soldiers should have safe passage as they returned from the war by showing their paroles.

After the Civil War John Gibbon commanded soldiers against Sitting Bull and the Sioux in 1876. He and his regiment were the first to arrive at the Little Bighorn River 27 June 1876, two days after George Armstrong Custer's unit had been obliterated.[50] Also in 1876, participating in the same campaign as his niece's future husband Wood, Gibbon led his regiment in pursuit of Chief Joseph of the Nez Perce. Like Wood, Gibbon became friends with Chief Joseph after hostilities ceased.[51] In an altogether different use of federal troops, President Grover Cleveland ordered Gibbon to suppress anti-Chinese riots in Seattle in 1885. He retired in 1891 and died in Baltimore in 1896. The town of Gibbon, Nebraska, is named in his honor.

The third of Nanny's uncles to become a general in the United States Army was Edward Moale (1840–1913) who was with her and her family as John Gray Foster's civilian aide at Fort Moultrie and Fort Sumter and with John Gibbon as an assistant adjutant general at Appomattox Court House. In later years he enjoyed saying that he was at Fort Sumter when the war began and at Appomattox Court House when it ended.

HEADQUARTERS, TWENTY-FOURTH ARMY CORPS.
APPOMATTOX C.H., Va., *April 11th, 1865*

GENERAL ORDERS.
NO. 43.

By agreement between the officers appointed by Generals LEE and GRANT to carry out the stipulations of the surrender of the Army of Northern Virginia the evidence that an officer or enlisted man is a paroled prisoner of war is the fact of his possessing a printed certificate certifying to the fact, dated at Appomattox Court House, Va., April 10th, 1865, and signed by his Commanding Officer, or the Staff Officer of the same.

All guards, patrols, officers and soldiers of the United States forces will respect such certificates, allow free passage to the holders thereof, and observe in good faith the provisions of the surrender that the holders shall remain unmolested in every respect.

By Command of Major General JOHN GIBBON

EDWARD MOALE,
Lieut. Col. and A.A.G.[49]

He was appointed a first lieutenant in May 1861 and was rapidly promoted because of his heroism. He was brevetted major for his conduct at Spotsylvania,[52] and at war's end he was a lieutenant colonel. His service in the campaign for Richmond and Petersburg was exemplary.[53]

In 1863, following his participation in the Battle of Gettysburg, he married Jeannie Wilson in the Baltimore Cathedral. Their first child, Nannie, named after his favorite niece, was born two years later. His second child Edward Moale Jr. was born in Arkansas in 1866, and the third was Samuel, born in 1868. Their fourth child, John Gray Foster Moale, was born in Kansas in 1871.[54]

After the Civil War he reverted to the rank of captain in the regulars and continued to advance again through the officer ranks. He again served with his brother-in-law John Gibbon in the Sioux campaign against Crazy Horse; Gibbon's troops had not engaged the Sioux, but their imminent arrival with a substantial force prompted the Indians' hasty withdrawal from the site of the Battle of the Little Bighorn. When they arrived at the scene of Custer's last stand, they found a gruesome sight and had to bury the mutilated dead. Moale also participated in the pursuit of Chief Joseph and the Nez Perce as part of the large force in which C.E.S. Wood served. Had these two campaigns gone differently, it is possible that Nanny could have lost Gibbon, Edward Moale, and C.E.S. Wood, just as Elizabeth Custer lost five members of her family at Little Bighorn.[55]

In 1887 Moale went to the Pacific coast, commanding Benicia Barracks and the Presidio of San Francisco. He accompanied the expeditionary force out of The Presidio to the Sioux campaign of 1890 and 1891. He was promoted to the rank of colonel in 1897. During the Spanish-American War he served in campaigns in Cuba and the Philippines, and a year later he was with the China Relief Expedition in 1900. At the end of his forty years of service he was promoted to Brigadier General, the third of Nanny's uncles to attain general officer rank.

Three weeks before he died in San Francisco in 1913, Edward and Jeannie Moale returned to the Baltimore area to see their families one last time and to celebrate their golden wedding anniversary in Baltimore where they were married. His nephew George S. Nicholas, son of Wilson C. Nicholas, at Atamasco, scene of so many happy memories for Nanny, received a telegram informing him of Edward's death from pneumonia. At the time of his death Edward Moale was the best known retired officer living in San Francisco.

Nanny's cousin Edward Moale Jr. (1866–1903), Uncle Ned's second child, grew up at the various army posts where his father served, but entered the United States Naval Academy at Annapolis in 1882, graduating in 1887. He was a classmate of the famous Richmond Hobson who led a volunteer team on a dangerous mission in Cuba during the war to sink a coal ship in an attempt to block Santiago Harbor. Although unsuccessful, Hobson and his seven enlisted men received the Medal of Honor for their action.[56]

Lt. Edward Moale Jr., married in 1891 Adria Maud Semple from Seattle whose father was the last Governor of Washington Territory, known thereafter as Washington State. Lt. Moale's father was stationed in Seattle as a commander of a regiment. Following in his family's footsteps, Lt. Edward Moale Jr. saw combat. As the officer in charge of a detachment of sailors aboard the gunboat *Helena* in 1898, he fought the Spanish land and naval forces at Santiago de Cuba. From there he sailed around the Cape of Good Hope to the Philippines where his father was serving in the army. Lt. Moale's ship carried a contingent of Marines who were ordered to go ashore and attack a fortification, but when the officers in charge saw that the Marine force was too small, Moale and several of his sailors put on infantry leggings and went ashore to fight. He was part of the force that captured the Philippine rebel leader Emilio Aguinaldo.

In the Cagayan Valley swamps on Luzon in the Philippines, Moale contracted malaria in 1899. He never recovered from that illness and died in Baltimore in 1903. For his conspicuous gallantry, the navy named the *U.S.S. Moale* (DD-693) after him. The ship was launched by his daughter-in-law Mrs. Edward S. Moale in January 1944; in this ceremony she followed the actions of her mother-in-law, Mrs. Edward Moale Jr., who cut the rope and broke a bottle of wine across the bow of the torpedo gunboat *Rowan* at the Seattle shipyard, 8 April 1898.[57]

The *Moale* struck Japanese airfields in the Philippines and participated in the assault and occupation of Iwo Jima and Okinawa. As part of a screening force 100 miles north of Okinawa, one of the missions of the *Moale* was to report on incoming Japanese kamikaze formations. At war's end, the *Moale* steamed into Tokyo Bay on 16 September 1945. She was decommissioned in 1973.[58]

Edward Moale Jr.'s son, Edward Semple Moale (1892–1986) entered the United States Military Academy at West Point in the class of 1915 where he soon made friends with classmates Dwight D. Eisenhower and Omar Bradley. Edward S. Moale did not graduate; his nephew John Gray Foster Moale II says the story told in the family is that "Eddie" was caught with an "unauthorized female visitor" in his barracks room and was dismissed.[59] He served in the Merchant Marine, the New York Army National Guard (where he served on the Mexican border in a campaign against Pancho Villa), the Regular Army (where he fought with the American Expeditionary Force in France and Germany, 1917–19), the Coast Guard, and the United States Naval Reserve during World War II and the Korean War.[60] A self-described non-conformist, Eddie confessed in 1950 in a letter to his ex-classmates at West Point that he had led "a multifarious career."[61]

Uncle Ned's other son was John Gray Foster Moale, reprising the name of his brother-in-law. This name has been sustained to the present John Gray Foster Moale IV. The first John Gray Foster Moale graduated from the United States Naval Academy in 1891, but served only two years, receiving an honorable discharge in 1893. He spent the rest of his life as a civilian in San Mateo, California, where he died in 1933.

His son, John Gray Foster Moale II, eighty-two years old at this writing, was attending New Mexico Military Institute when Pearl Harbor was attacked, and as a result of that training he was commissioned as an army officer in 1942. He spent two years in the Pacific theater including the last battle of Okinawa; he served eighteen months during the Korean War. He retired as a lieutenant colonel in the Army Reserve and became a professional educator and administrator. In July 1996, at age seventy-six, as an acknowledgment of his active involvement in the community, he was selected to carry the Olympic torch in his retirement town of Melbourne, Florida.[62]

John Gray Foster Moale III, born in Pasadena, California, in 1947, was in the United States Army, 1967–69, serving part of that time in the Republic of Korea. He and his wife Jean Ann have continued the tradition by naming their son John Gray Foster Moale IV (born 1982) and revived the historic family names with their daughter Elizabeth Jean Ellin Moale (born 1989).

The patriotic Moale side of Nanny Moale Smith Wood's family held positions of leadership as officers in the Revolutionary War, the War of 1812, the Mexican War, the Civil War, the Spanish American War, World Wars I and II, and the Korean War. To date, the Moale men furnished the nation eight officers in the U.S. Army and seven to the U.S. Navy and Coast Guard.

Scandals attaching to a few uncles over deadly duels and banking fraud add spice to the family history but do not diminish the contributions of Nanny's ancestors and their descendants. No history of the city of Baltimore, state of Maryland, or the United States is complete without including the activities of the Moales, Cursons, McLanes, and Poultneys.

NOTES

[1] Luther W. Welsh, *Ancestral Colonial Families: Genealogy of the Welsh and Hyatt Families of Maryland and Their Kin* (Independence, MO: Lambert Moon Printing Company, 1928), 163.

[2] "A Portrait by Joshua Johnston," *Bulletin of the Municipal Museum of the City of Baltimore,* 11 (December 1941): 2.

[3] Mary Bourke Emory, *Colonial Families and Their Descendants* (Baltimore: Press of the Sun Printing Office, 1900), 84.

[4] Kitty Washburne, Letter to the author, 20 September 2001. Ms. Washburne is the present owner of Green Spring.

[5] Helen Cadwalader, "Today Marks Birth Date of First Child Born Here," *Baltimore Sun,* 29 April 1938: 32. "An Historical Sketch of St. Thomas' Church," an information sheet dated August 1999 states, "Ellin North, the first white child born in Baltimore City after it was incorporated in 1729, married Richard Moale and is buried in the Moale family mausoleum in the churchyard." In 1932, Frederick Philip Stieff collected recipes from the old Maryland families. Walter de Curzon Poultney's family contributed "Ellin North Plum Pudding." A note appearing before the recipe says it "was handed down from Mrs. John Moale (Ellin North) to her great-grandson the late Walter de Curzon Poultney. Ellin North, born in 1740, is generally reputed to have been the first white child born in Baltimore." See *Eat, Drink, and Be Merry in Maryland* (Baltimore: The Johns Hopkins University Press, 1998), 366–67. This is a reprint of the original 1932 edition published by G. P. Putnam's Sons.

[6] Robert G. Breen, "Disputed First Baltimore Baby," *Baltimore Sun,* 13 December 1957: 21.

[7] Dawn F. Thomas, *The Green Spring Valley: Its History and Heritage* vol. 1 (Baltimore: Maryland Historical Society, 1978), 127.

[8] Rev. Ethan Allen, *The Garrison Church* (New York: James Pott & Co., 1898), 145.

[9] Melinda K. Friend, *J. Hall Pleasants Papers,* MS 194, Manuscripts Department, Maryland Historical Society, 1991: 13-14.

[10] Friend, 6.

[11] *The Biographical Cyclopedia of Representative Men of Maryland and the District of Columbia* (Baltimore: National Biographical Publishing Company, 1879), 277.

[12] Dawn F. Thomas, *The Green Spring Valley: Its History and Heritage* vol. 1 (Baltimore: Maryland Historical Society, 1978), 134.

13 Gary Boyd Roberts, "Notable Kin," *New England Historic Genealogical Society Nexus* 4 (1987): 26.
14 Mary Bourke Emory, *Colonial Families and Their Descendants* (Baltimore: Press of the Sun Printing Office, 1900), 85.
15 Bradley T. Johnson, "Maryland" in *Confederate Military History* vol. 2 (Atlanta: Confederate Publishing Company, 1899), 23.
16 Robert N. Scott, ed. *The War of the Rebellion* Series I, Part I, vol. 12 (Washington: Government Printing Office, 1885), 817.
17 Robert N. Scott, ed. *The War of the Rebellion* Series I, Part II, vol. 11 (Washington: Government Printing Office, 1884), 621.
18 Robert N. Scott, ed. *The War of the Rebellion* Series I, Part II, vol. 19 (Washington: Government Printing Office, 1887), 665.
19 Kevin Conley Ruffner, *Maryland's Blue and Gray* (Baton Rouge: Louisiana State University Press, 1997), 319–20.
20 Bradley T. Johnson, "Maryland," in *Confederate Military History* vol. 2 (Atlanta: Confederate Publishing Company, 1899), 128.
21 John A. Munroe, *Louis McLane: Federalist and Jacksonian* (New Brunswick, NJ: Rutgers University Press, 1973), 38.
22 "Louis McLane," Biography File, Sacramento: California State Library, 1952.
23 "The Ills of Car-Drivers," *New York Times* 26 January 1879: 5.
24 John A. Munroe, *Louis McLane: Federalist and Jacksonian* (New Bruswick, NJ: Rutgers University Press, 1973), 510
25 "The Death of Captain Louis McLane Hamilton," *New York Times* 6 December 1868: 11.
26 The Angelica Schuyler Church Papers, accession number 11245, Special Collections Department, Alderman Library, University of Virginia.
27 Robert M. Utley, *Life in Custer's Cavalry* (New Haven, CT: Yale University Press, 1977), 262.
28 George A. Custer, *My Life on the Plains* Ed. Milo Milton Quaife (Lincoln: University of Nebraska Press, 1952), 345.
29 Dan L. Thrapp, *Encyclopedia of Frontier Biography* vol. 2 (Spokane, WA: The Arthur H. Clark Company, 1990), 610.
30 "Louis McLane," Biography File, Sacramento: California State Library, 1952.
31 Frank F. White Jr., *The Governors of Maryland, 1777–1970* (Annapolis: State of Maryland, 1970), 203–4.
32 Craig L. Symonds, *Joseph E. Johnston: A Civil War Biography* (New York: W. W. Norton & Company, 1992), 51.
33 "Joseph Eggleston Johnston," *The National Cyclopedia of American Biography* vol. 5 (New York: James T. White & Company, 1907), 329.

34 "Louis McLane Tiffany," *Dictionary of American Biography* Ed. Dumas Malone (New York: Charles Scribner's Sons, 1936), 535.
35 William P. Baxter, Jr., Letter to the author, 20 March 2001. The Rev. Baxter is the rector of St. Thomas' Church.
36 "John Gray Foster," *The National Cyclopedia of American Biography* (New York: James T. White & Company, 1909), 134.
37 John Gray Foster, "Recollections: Witnesses to History,'" *American History* 32 (October 1997): 58-59.
38 "John Gray Foster," *Dictionary of Catholic Biography* (Garden City, NY: Doubleday & Company, Inc., 1961), 437.
39 John G. Barrett, *The Civil War in North Carolina* (Chapel Hill: The University of North Carolina Press, 1963),128.
40 "John Gray Foster," *Webster's American Military Biographies* (Springfield, MA: G. & C. Merriam Company, 1978), 129.
41 "John Gray Foster," *Dictionary of American Biography* vol. 6. Eds. Allen Johnson & Dumas Malone (New York: Charles Scribner's Sons, 1931), 550.
42 "Major Henry Seton," *New York Times* 7 September 1904: 7.
43 "A Noted Army Officer Dead," *Baltimore Sun* 7 September 1904: 10.
44 J.B. Code, "Elizabeth Bayley Seton," *The New Catholic Encyclopedia,* vol. 13 (New York: McGraw-Hill, 1967), 136.
45 "John Gibbon," *The National Cyclopedia of American Biography,* vol. 4 (New York: James T. White & Company, 1897), 178.
46 Ezra J. Warner, *Generals in Blue: Lives of the Union Commanders* (Baton Rouge: Louisiana State University Press, 1964), 171.
47 Steven J. Wright, "This Miserable War: The Civil War Letters of General John Gibbon," *Loyal Legion Historical Journal* 45 (Winter 1989): 1.
48 James W. Wensyel, *Appomatox: The Passing of the Armies* (Shippensburg, PA: White Mane Books, 2000), 226.
49 George B. Davis, Leslie J. Perry, and Joseph W. Kirkley, *The War of the Rebellion* Series I, Part III, vol. 46 (Washington: Government Printing Office, 1894), 709–10.
50 "John Gibbon," *Webster's American Military Biographies* (Springfield, MA: G. & C. Merriam Company, 1978), 141.
51 "John Gibbon," *Dictionary of American Biography,* vol. 7 (New York: Charles Scribner's Sons, 1931), 237.
52 "Brig. Gen. Edward Moale," *New York Times* 28 September 1913: 7.
53 "Edward Moale," *Who Was Who in America* vol. 1 (Chicago: The A. N. Marquis Company, 1942), 852.
54 Robert A. Bird, Letter to the author, 28 May 2002.
55 Evan S. Connell, *Son of the Morning Star: Custer and the Little*

    Bighorn (New York: Harper & Row, 1984), 288. The five family members to die at Little Big Horn were George A. Custer, his brothers Tom and Boston, brother-in-law James Calhoun, and nephew Autie Reed.

[56] Jack Sweetman, *American Naval History* 2nd ed. (Annapolis, MD: Naval Institute Press, 1991), 107.

[57] "Successful Launching of the United States Torpedo Boat *Rowan*," *The Seattle Post-Intelligencer,* 9 April 1898: 16.

[58] John Gray Foster Moale II, Letter to the author, 3 May 2002.

[59] John Gray Foster Moale II, Telephone interview with the author, 10 June 2001.

[60] "E.S. Moale, Retired Navy Commander, Dies," [Charleston, SC] *Evening Post* 31 December 1985: 15-A.

[61] *Thirty-Five Year Book* (West Point: United States Military Academy, 1950), 66.

[62] L.A. Davis, "Residents Leap into Torch Run," *Viera Sun,* 16 June 1996, n.p.

CHAPTER NINE

PHYSICIANS

I
NEW ENGLAND

IF NANNY'S MATERNAL SIDE, the Moales, can be characterized generally as "patriots," then her paternal side, the Smiths, represent accomplishment in American medicine as the "physicians." The scion of this branch of her family was Daniel Smith (1672–1724) of the Plymouth Colony town of Rehoboth, Massachusetts. He led a stormy life worthy of Hawthorne's *The Scarlet Letter*. Daniel married Abigail Preston on 23 June 1696, and on 2 November 1696, Mary Newman, unwed daughter of Deacon Samuel Newman, gave birth to his child, Newman Smith. Daniel was required by the Court of Quarterly Sessions to pay Mary three shillings each week for the child's support. When Mary sought to change the child's name from Newman Smith to Daniel Smith, Nanny's great-great-great grandfather objected by stopping the support payments. The Court appointed a panel to hear his petition and the parties reached a settlement in the sum of £40, and the case for non-support was dismissed.

Then Daniel Smith opened a tavern in Rehoboth and became one of the town's most popular men. At various times he was moderator of town meetings, chairman of the selectmen, a member of the school board, and a member of a committee to audit the town's treasurer's accounts. He was a justice of the peace for three years. In 1722 he was accused of making counterfeit Province Bills of Public Credit, but the record is silent on the outcome of this charge.[1]

Daniel Smith's son John (born 1718), Nanny's great-great-grandfather, married twice. His first wife, with whom he had four children, died in 1755. With his second wife he had four more children, including their fourth son, Nathan, Nanny's great-grandfather, born in 1762. They moved from Rehoboth to Chester, Vermont,

Near the end of the Revolutionary War, as a teenager, Nathan Smith joined a Vermont Militia unit who kept in check a group of hostile Indians. In 1784, when he was a twenty-two-year-old farmer, an event occurred that would change the course of medical education in the new nation. Nathan assisted Dr. Josiah Goodhue of Putney, Vermont, in tying off an artery during a surgery. Nathan's intelligence impressed Dr. Goodhue under whom he became a student, learning medicine by going about the countryside treating all types of ailments. In 1787, having only the experience of apprenticeship, he began to practice medicine in Cornish, New Hampshire. In 1789 he was accepted at the Medical School of Harvard University where he received the degree of Bachelor of Medicine in 1790.

In 1796 he studied at the great medical centers of Glasgow, Edinburgh, and London.[2] Returning to the United States, he gave the first medical lectures at Dartmouth College; in 1798 he became Professor of Anatomy, Chemistry, Surgery, and Theory and Practice of Medicine. In 1801 Dartmouth awarded him the M.D. degree, and in 1811 Harvard recognized his accomplishments by converting his M.B. to an M.D.

He resigned from Dartmouth to become one of the founders of the Yale medical school in 1813. Yale proudly displays an oil portrait of Nathan Smith by Samuel F. B. Morse in the university's art gallery. In 1821 he began teaching medicine at Bowdoin College, thereby establishing the Medical School of Maine. This medical school existed for one hundred years but closed its doors in 1921. That same year he also founded the Medical School of the University of Vermont in Burlington. His astonishingly productive career as the founder of four medical colleges—Dartmouth, Yale, Maine, and Vermont—is unequalled in the history of medicine in the United States.[3]

The most famous medical doctor in the world at the turn of the last century was Sir William Osler (1849–1919). The Canada native taught and practiced at McGill University, the University of Pennsylvania, and The Johns Hopkins University where he was physician-in-chief. His *Principles and Practice of Medicine* (1892) became the standard medical text for decades following its publication. Later Osler became the Regius Professor of Medicine at Oxford University. In May 1896, while he was still at The Johns Hopkins, Osler said, "If I had typhoid fever and had a theosophic option as to a family physician I would choose Nathan Smith, nor would I care whether it was while he laboured in the flesh in the little town of Cornish, N.H., in 1798, or after he had become the distinguished Professor of Medicine in Yale."[4]

In speech after speech to medical colleagues Osler invoked the name of Nathan Smith. In his farewell address, as he departed the United States for England in 1905, Osler said, "I have had but two ambitions in the profession: first, to make of myself a good clinical physician, to be ranked with the men who have done so much for the profession of this country—to rank in the class with Nathan Smith [and nine others]. The chief desire of my life has been to become a clinician of the same stamp with these great men, whose names we all revere and who did so much good work for clinical medicine." His second desire was to build up large clinics with staffs of house physicians and assistants.[5]

Osler's tributes to Nanny's paternal great-grandfather Nathan Smith indicate the stature that he attained in the medical profession. Nathan Smith also began a "dynasty" of sorts, a legacy of medical doctors in the Smith line that extended to Nanny's father and stepfather and to the present time.

Nathan Smith had four sons, all of whom became physicians.[6] Tracing Nanny's line, his second son, Nathan Ryno Smith (1797–1859) was her grandfather with whom she and her mother lived after her father died and in whose home in Baltimore she married C.E.S. Wood. The unusual middle name Ryno came from the name of a character in the poems of "Ossian," a questionably authentic legendary Gaelic hero and bard of the third century A.D.

Nathan Ryno Smith studied at Dartmouth, then Yale where he received his M.D. degree in 1823. He began his career by practicing in Burlington, Vermont, in 1824, and became a professor of surgery and anatomy the following year. From there he went to the Jefferson Medical College in Philadelphia as chair of anatomy where he was the professor to Samuel D. Gross, the "Emperor of American Surgery," and the subject of the famous painting *The Gross Clinic* by Thomas Eakins.

In 1827, Nathan R. Smith left the Jefferson to go the University of Maryland where he taught for fifty years until he died in 1877.[7] For a brief time in 1838 he left Maryland to become chair of the practice of medicine in the department of medicine at Transylvania University in Kentucky. While the family was there, his oldest daughter Sarah Francis Smith met Elisha Warfield Theobald (1818–51) who earned his M.D. degree from Transylvania College in 1839, thus adding yet another physician to the family.

Mrs. Theobald brought her five children to live with Nathan Ryno Smith when the Civil War began; her family included her sons Samuel (1846–1930) M.D., University of Maryland in 1867, and Elisha Warfield Theobald, Jr. (1850–77), M.D., University of Maryland in 1875. Elisha Jr. became a distinguished ophthalmologist in Baltimore following study at the University of Vienna and the Royal London Ophthalmic Hospital. He discovered the efficacy of applying boric acid directly to the eye. Among his many honors, he was elected president of the American Ophthalmological Society in 1909.[8]

Nanny's paternal grandmother, Julietta Octavia Penniman Smith (1798–1883), was the daughter of Dr. Jabez Penniman and Frances Montesque Allen, widow of the famous Ethan Allen of the "Green Mountain Boys" of Vermont.[9]

II
MARYLAND

Nathan Ryno Smith's death in 1877 was front-page news in Baltimore, and his obituary in the *Sun* said, "Prof. Smith has for many years past been not only the undisputed leader of surgical art in Maryland but, in the opinion of many, the first in the United States."[10] He was particularly well known for his surgical procedures dealing with lithotomy, removal of stones. Dr. Osler praised Nathan R. Smith just as he had his father Nathan Smith. At the Boston Medical Library in 1901 he called him an "American medical classic. . . who carried away from [his] New England home a love of truth, a love of learning and above all a proper estimate of the personal character of the physician."[11]

Nathan R. Smith had four sons, and each of them became physicians also. This generation of brothers seems to have been particularly susceptible to infectious diseases. Nanny's father Berwick Bruce Smith (1826–60) was the oldest of Nathan Ryno Smith's four sons and four daughters. Berwick completed his M.D. at the University of Maryland in 1849. After contracting an infection in the dissecting room, he died at age thirty-five at the family residence at 89 Saratoga Street in March 1860; his death brought about Nanny's presence in Charleston with her uncle, Captain John Gray Foster, just before the opening shots of the Civil War. His obituary said, "The deceased was a son of the eminent Prof. N.R. Smith of this city, and inherited much of this father's talent, which added to acquired surgical and medical knowledge, opened a promising future for him had his life been spared to mature years."[12]

Berwick's brother, Nathan Ryno Smith, Jr. (1831–56) earned his M.D. from the University of Maryland in 1855, but he died just one year later. Another brother, Alan Penneman

Smith (1840–98), received his M.D. degree from the University of Maryland in 1861. He entered into private practice and became an adjunct professor of surgery at Maryland. In 1875 he was appointed a professor of surgery. A member of the board of The Johns Hopkins University, he worked with William Osler when the medical school was established.[13] Alan was the only one of Nathan Ryno Smith's sons to outlive their father.

Finally, Nathan Ryno Smith's fourth son, Walter Prescott Smith (1842–63), graduated with the M.D. degree from the University of Maryland in 1863, in the middle of the Civil War. Despite his family's New England roots, following his graduation he joined the Confederate side and left for service as an army surgeon in Virginia. Working under the grim conditions of a field hospital, he was exposed to the deadly infections rampant in the camps and died of typhoid in Danville, Virginia, in 1863.[14] Ironically, his grandfather, Nathan Smith, the founder of four medical colleges in the Northeast, had published in 1824 what was at that time the definitive work on typhoid fever.[15]

III
WASHINGTON

Nanny's widowed mother married Nathan Smith Lincoln, a grandson of Nathan Smith. After graduating from Dartmouth, Lincoln went to the University of Maryland where he studied medicine under his uncle, Dr. Nathan Ryno Smith. He graduated with the M.D. degree in 1852 and moved to Washington, D.C., in 1854. Chapter 2 mentioned his important work as surgeon-in-chief with the army hospitals in Washington during the Civil War and his association with the Providence Hospital for many years following the war. He was also president of the District of Columbia Medical Society in 1875–76. He enjoyed a reputation as an excellent surgeon and treated most of the wealthy people in the nation's capital.[16]

Because of his status in Washington, Dr. Lincoln was one of the first to attend to President James A. Garfield on 2 July 1881 when an assassin, Charles Guiteau, shot him. Medical historians now view the treatment of President Garfield as an example of gross incompetence by the doctors who treated him, but Nathan Smith Lincoln bears no responsibility for the treatment. Ten doctors rushed to the Baltimore and Potomac railroad station in Washington, including Charles Burleigh Purvis (1842–1929), an African–American doctor who was the second physician to arrive on the scene. Dr. Willard Bliss was summoned by Secretary of War Robert Todd Lincoln whose father Abraham Lincoln had been assassinated in 1865. Bliss coveted the position of being in charge of the case, and when it became apparent that no less than twenty-two doctors were in attendance offering their services, he decided to trim the team to just a few. He selected himself as physician-in-charge, Surgeon General of the army Joseph K. Barnes, army surgeon Joseph Janvier Woodward (who had performed the autopsy on President Lincoln in 1865), and Robert Reyburn. All the other doctors, including Nathan Smith Lincoln, were dismissed. [17]

They might have been miffed at the time for being removed from the case, but later they had occasion to be glad that they were not implicated in the incompetence by the medical team that almost certainly caused Garfield's death. Medical pathologists today interpret the sequence of events of treatment and the revelations of the autopsy as showing that the President died from infection because the doctors did not sterilize either themselves or their instruments as they probed and poked in an effort to find the assassin's bullet. The President suffered excruciating pain from the day of the shooting on 2 July until his death on 19 September. Charles Guiteau argued unsuccessfully at his trial that he had, in fact, shot Garfield, but it was his doctors who had killed him. The autopsy revealed that the bullet was not lodged in Garfield's liver as the medical team thought, but was ten inches away, harmlessly surrounded by tissue in Garfield's side.[18]

Dr. Allan McLane Hamilton, Nanny's cousin and grandson of Alexander Hamilton, testified for the government at Guiteau's trial as an expert on insanity and the practice of phrenology, still an accepted psychoanalytical approach. He measured Guiteau's head but saw no signs of abnormality that would justify an insanity plea.[19]

Nathan Smith Lincoln was concerned about damage to his reputation in the ensuing demand in the press for explanations about why the President had to suffer for over two months and not recover. Lincoln and three other doctors who had been part of the original team dismissed by Willard Bliss wrote a critical report of Bliss's handling of the case. Lincoln noted that his diagnosis recorded on the day of the shooting was correct as revealed by the autopsy.[20]

Dr. Lincoln's reputation remained intact, and he became the family physician to President Chester A. Arthur's family when Arthur succeeded Garfield.

Nanny's stepfather was not her only relative to treat a president of the United States. In 1849, President Zachary Taylor (1784–1850) became seriously ill on a trip through Pennsylvania. When he arrived in Erie on 25 August 1849, he was stricken with severe diarrhea and high fever. The father of Nanny's future husband C.E.S. Wood, Dr. William Maxwell Wood (1809–80), was stationed at Erie Harbor as a navy surgeon. Like Nanny's Smith relatives, Wood had received his M.D. degree at the University of Maryland in 1829. President Taylor was taken to Dr. Wood's home for treatment where he stayed for several days until he recovered. One year later, Taylor, attending a Fourth of July celebration at the Washington monument, contracted an intestinal infection complicated by heat exhaustion, and he died four days later.[21]

By appointment from President Grant, Dr. Wood became the first Surgeon-General of the United States Navy from 1869–71.[22] The *U.S.S. Wood*, commissioned in 1945 one week before the atom bomb was dropped on Hiroshima, is named for him, thus three ships of the United States Navy, the *Wood*, the *Moale*, and the *Louis McLane* were named for relatives of Nanny.

PHYSICIANS

None of Nanny's children or grandchildren became medical doctors, but her great-grandson Kirkham Berwick Wood, M.D., graduated from Albany Medical College in New York and is today an eminent spinal surgeon in St. Paul, Minnesota.

NOTES

[1] Richard LeBaron Bowen, *Early Rehoboth* (Rehoboth, MA: Privately printed, 1946), 115–16.
[2] *Ancestral Records and Portraits* vol. 2 (Baltimore: Genealogical Publishing Company, 1969), 618.
[3] Oliver S. Hayward and Constance E. Putnam, *Improve, Perfect, and Perpetuate: Dr. Nathan Smith and Early American Medical Education* (Hanover, NH: University Press of New England, 1998), 269–70.
[4] Harvey Cushing, *The Life of Sir William Osler* vol. 1 (Oxford: The Clarendon Press, 1926), 436.
[5] William Osler, "L'Envoi," in *Aequanimitas* (Philadelphia: P. Blakiston's Son & Company, Inc., 1932), 450–51.
[6] David Solon Chase Hall Smith (1795–1859), M.D. Yale 1816; Nathan Ryno Smith (1797–1877), M.D. Yale, 1820; James Morven Smith (1805–53), M.D. Yale 1828; John Derby Smith (1812–84), M.D. University of Maryland, 1846.
[7] John R. Quinan, *Medical Annals of Baltimore* (Baltimore: Press of Isaac Friedenwald, 1884), 33.
[8] "Samuel Theobald," *The Cyclopedia of American Biography* vol. 24 (New York: James T. White & Company, 1935), 74–75.
[9] *Ancestral Records and Portraits* (Baltimore: Genealogical Publishing Company, 1969), 619–20.
[10] "Death of Prof. N.R. Smith," *Baltimore Sun* 5 July 1877: 1.
[11] William Osler, "Books and Men," in *Aequanimitas* (Philadelphia: P. Blakiston's Son & Company, Inc., 1932), 214–15.
[12] "Death of a Physician," *Baltimore Sun* 21 March 1860: 1.
[13] "Alan Penneman Smith," *The National Cyclopedia of American Biography* vol. 3 (New York: James T. White & Company, 1893), 154.
[14] Details of the death of Walter Prescott Smith are contained on page 117 of a handwritten record book of family births and deaths owned by Nanny's great-grandson Kirk Johns.
[15] See Nathan Smith, *A Practical Essay on Typhus Fever* (New York:

Bless & E. White, 1824). At this time typhus and typhoid fever had not yet been distinguished; despite its title, Smith's book dealt with typhoid.

[16] "Nathan Smith Lincoln," *The National Cyclopedia of American Biography* vol. 3 (New York: James T. White & Company, 1893), 154–55.

[17] Charles A. Roos, "Physicians to the Presidents, and Their Patients: A Bibliography," *Bulletin of the Medical Library Association* 49 (1961), 335.

[18] Edward B. MacMahon and Leonard Curry, *Medical Cover-Ups in the White House* (Washington, DC: Farragut Publishing Company, 1987), 33.

[19] *The United States versus Charles J. Guiteau, Indicted for the Murder of James A. Garfield, Twentieth President of the United States.* (privately printed, 1882): 1173–74.

[20] See Smith Townshend, Charles B. Purvis, Nathan S. Lincoln, and Philip S. Wales, "President Garfield's Wound and Its Treatment, *Walsh's Retrospect* 2 (1881): 623–33.

[21] Charles A. Roos, "Physicians to the Presidents, and Their Patients: A Bibliography," *Bulletin of the Medical Library Association* 49 (1961), 315.

[22] See W. M. Kerr, "William Maxwell Wood: the First Surgeon-General of the United States Navy," *Annals of Military History* 6 (1924): 387–425.

CHAPTER TEN

PAINTERS AND SCULPTORS

Nanny's family back East made contributions in the worlds of military service and medicine, but when she and Wood settled in Portland she became part of a concerted effort to improve the quality of life in her new city. She met and entertained several American painters and sculptors whose works today are both famous and valuable. C.E.S. Wood had always had a creative inclination. He wanted to resign his West Point cadetship to become a writer, but his domineering father forbade it. He finally realized his dream and published dozens of articles and, late in life, several books of poetry and prose.

Nanny had her own creative aspect, becoming a vital force on the Portland social scene for home decoration, gardening, and cuisine, especially when she served in the important role as hostess to the various visiting artists. Amidst all these creative expressions of her talent, she also adeptly fulfilled the role of mother to five energetic children, even to the point of leaving her beloved Portland for two years to ensure Erskine's return to health. One could argue that Nanny's monuments in the form of the legacy of her children and her beautification of Portland are at least as lasting as her husband's poetry.

Portland was a large town in the 1880s, but still removed from the cultural centers of New York, Boston, Philadelphia, and Washington, DC. Wood and Nanny joined the group of civic-minded leaders whose names we have seen before in this study—Failing, Corbett, Ladd, Ayer—to bring to Portland the touring theatrical companies, art exhibits, museums, libraries, statues, architecture, and parks that would make Portland a lively center for art.

When Wood was a West Point cadet he studied art under Robert Weir (1803–89), the father of artist J. Alden Weir (1852–1919) and artist John Ferguson Weir (1841–1926), the Dean of Yale's School of Fine Arts. Robert Weir is best known for his mural *Embarkation of the Pilgrims* in the rotunda of the Capitol in Washington. Cadets received instruction in drawing because many of them became engineers who had to understand perspective and graphic design. Those who would lead soldiers on the battlefield had to be able to sketch accurate maps with avenues of approach and attack routes.

Wood was a gifted amateur in both watercolors and oils, and he became especially close to Robert Weir when he returned to West Point as General Howard's aide and post adjutant. In 1882, while Wood was studying law in New York City, through his friendship with the Impressionist artist J. Alden Weir, he fell in with a group of young artists who gathered regularly at a French restaurant in Washington Square to drink wine and talk about the future of American art. The group included Weir, Olin Warner, Childe Hassam, George de Forest Brush, and Albert Pinkham Ryder.[1] Wood found their level of discourse enchanting and far removed from the world of military manuals and carrying out orders "by-the-numbers."

In 1884, when he and Nanny settled in Portland and they began to develop close ties with the wealthiest citizens of the town, he called upon his old bohemian crowd in New York City to come west, both to enrich Portland's culture and to invigorate the creativity of these artists. His group of cronies from the East would make significant contributions to the arts in Portland.

Before their separation, Nanny and Wood entertained and sponsored several important artists who visited Portland. Some of these artists she enjoyed knowing, but others, less inhibited than she would have wished, became burdensome house guests, even as they delighted her equally unorthodox husband. Her responses to the personal contacts she made with various artists provide a glimpse at another facet of her personality.

I
OLIN L. WARNER

Olin Levi Warner (1844–96), the son of an itinerant Methodist preacher, grew up in Connecticut, New York, and Vermont. Early in his youth he discovered that he had the ability to sculpt likenesses from blocks of chalk and plaster of paris. He wanted to pursue formal art training, but his father's income prohibited it. He entered work as a telegrapher with the express purpose of putting aside sufficient funds to enable him to go to Europe to study sculpture. Interestingly, Samuel F. B. Morse who promoted the telegraph and invented Morse Code was also an accomplished artist who painted a portrait of Nanny's great-grandfather Nathan Smith for Yale University.

In 1869 Warner entered the École des Beaux-Arts where he made friends with several Americans studying there, including Augustus Saint-Gaudens. A year later, along with these friends, he enlisted in the Foreign Legion and manned the barricades in Paris during France's tumultuous transition from empire to republic.

In 1872 he returned to the United States and opened a studio in New York City. His beginnings as a sculptor were inauspicious, and for a brief time he abandoned his dream and returned to live with his parents. After receiving some lucrative commissions for busts of wealthy men and women, he became one of the five original members of the Society of American Artists (later called the American Art Association) in 1877. This group came together to escape the stuffiness of the National Academy of Design that dominated American art. Augustus Saint-Gaudens enthusiastically organized as associate members a group of thirty-eight American artists living in Paris at the time.[2] Nanny's cousin Louis C. Tiffany was the treasurer of the American Art Association, and Saint-Gaudens became the vice-president. Other original members included J. Alden Weir[3] and Albert Pinkham Ryder.[4]

Artists formed these associations because they took pleasure in spending time in each other's company, encouraging each other, collaborating on exhibitions, and consorting with other creative personalities. For example, the Cornish Art Colony in New Hampshire, which flourished from 1885 until 1907, included Brush, Weir, and Saint-Gaudens. Others in that group were well-known figures Maxfield Parrish and Mrs. Woodrow Wilson, wife of the president.

While the Woods were living at West Point, C.E.S. Wood commissioned Olin Warner to do a medallion of Nanny, but the Woods could not afford a bronze medallion, so Warner made one in plaster.[5] Later, in Portland, he would cast a bronze medallion of her.

In 1888, four years after the Woods had relocated to Portland, Wood commissioned Warner to come to Portland and execute the Skidmore Fountain, still a landmark today in the city. When Stephen G. Skidmore, a pharmacist, died in 1885, he left $5,000 to the city of Portland for a fountain. True to form, Wood, as project coordinator, paid no attention to a budget, and the final cost of the fountain was $18,000. Wood's friends Charles Sitton, Henry Failing, and Tyler Wood made up the shortfall.[6] Wood composed the inscription on the fountain, "Good citizens are the riches of a city." In 1888, the location of the Skidmore Fountain at the corner of Southwest First and Ankeny Avenues was the center of the downtown area, so the fountain brought fame both to Wood locally and to Warner on the national scene. *Scribner's Magazine* sniffed that the fountain would be better appreciated in Central Park in New York City than in its provincial location in Portland.[7]

Water flows from a large upper basin that is supported by two back-to-back caryatids, a classical Greek sculptural motif, but the clean lines and simplicity of the top and octagonal bottom basins presage Beaux-Arts style that had not yet become popular in America. The fountain is considered one of Warner's best works. Critic Charles H. Caffin said of the Skidmore Fountain, "The design is almost severely simple, yet tempered with a grace of fitness in every detail, so chaste and noble as to produce an impression of perfect repose. It has, indeed, just that suggestion of being firmly footed, of strong growth upward and of natural spread at the top, which exactly befits its architectural character, while in the contour and details it is as delicate as a lily."[8]

When Warner came to Portland to oversee the construction of the Skidmore Fountain, he stayed with the Woods. They had erected a temporary studio in a shed on their property for Warner's use. Nanny and Wood prevailed upon her Uncle John Gibbon, who was commanding the army's Department of the Pacific, to grant permission for Chief Joseph and seven other chiefs to leave their reservations and come to Portland to pose for medallions. The chiefs stayed at the garrison at Vancouver Barracks, while Warner stayed with the Woods. A few years later, in 1893, Wood published an article in *Century Magazine* describing Warner's Indian portraits.

Warner also executed medallions of the Woods' children and busts of others in Portland, notably William S. Ladd, who, as a result of a series of strokes, had become a paralytic from the waist down. Nanny recalled that Ladd came to the studio every morning in a buckboard to sit for a bust by Warner. Two men accompanied him to help him from the carriage into the studio.

The Wood children were recalcitrant sitters. They hated posing for the medallion and scattered to hide when summoned to come and pose. Nanny treasured Warner's rendition of her children all her life. Warner did make a bronze medallion of Nanny, a copy of which is owned by her grandson John Gibbon Wood; a replica of this medallion appears on Nanny's grave stone in the River View Cemetery in Portland.

The Portland Art Museum's Franklin and Dorothy Piacentini Gallery contains Warner's portrait bust of C.E.S. Wood, cast in bronze in 1888. The bust is a gift to the museum by Helen Ladd Corbett, one of Wood's mistresses.

Nanny remembered that Warner was a quiet man, short and stout, not impressive looking. She had difficulty carrying on a conversation with him because their interests were so dissimilar, but Wood and Warner enjoyed each other's company enormously. She did, however, enjoy his works, and whenever she went to New York City she made a point of going to the Metropolitan Museum of Art to see them there.

Other sculptures for which he is famous include some colossal heads and decoration panels in the Long Island Historical Society in Brooklyn; five colossal heads in the Pennsylvania Railroad Station in Philadelphia; a bronze bust of abolitionist William Lloyd Garrison; colossal heads of Michelangelo, Raphael, Titian, Velasquez, and Rembrandt for the 1893 Columbian Exposition in Chicago; and the bronze main entrance door to the Library of Congress, his last work. He died in 1896 at age fifty-two when a carriage struck him in Central Park where he was riding a bicycle.

II
ALEXANDER PHIMISTER PROCTOR

Another distinguished sculptor with whom Nanny and Wood were friends in the early days of his career was Phimister Proctor (1860–1950), a native Canadian who called himself the "sculptor in buckskin." When he was still young, his family moved to Colorado where he enjoyed camping, hunting, and all outdoor actitivities. His statues depict people and animals from the American wilderness that he observed: Indians, mustang horses, buffaloes, grizzly bears, and mountain lions. Although his background sounds rustic, he acquired sophisticated training, studying in New York and Paris. He frequently used European foundries to cast his monumental bronzes, and he exhibited in major European competitions.

In his autobiography, Proctor said that in Portland in 1914 he "did a couple of bas-relief heads for my good friend Colonel

Charles Erskine Scott Wood."[9] Proctor made plaster casts of Wood, Nanny, and Nanny's daughter Lisa while staying with the Woods. Nanny loved the plaster medallion of Lisa. This delightful little work of art becomes more endearing when one considers that Proctor's specialty was in creating larger-than-life size statues of powerful subjects.

He was a frequent visitor in the Wood household, coming to Portland as part of his tours of the northwest looking for subjects. Wood's wealthy friend William Hanley who owned vast cattle holdings in eastern Oregon was also a good friend of the Proctors. The Proctors lived at his ranch almost all of 1914, and in 1915 Proctor completed a bronze bas-relief of him. Hanley would often keep the Proctors' children on his ranch on the plains near the Harney Desert while their parents would travel to Portland and other western locations. When the Proctors did take their children with them, they, too, stayed at the Wood home, becoming so close that Proctor's daughter called them "Granddaddy and Grandmama Wood."

The Woods championed Proctor's work among the Ladds, Corbetts, Failings, and Ayers. In addition to the busts and medallions executed for these families, Proctor also produced several large sculptures for Portland and for other Oregon sites. In Portland at Southwest Park Avenue and Madison, in what is known as the cultural district, his magnificent bronze of *Rough Rider (Theodore Roosevelt)* (1922) sits atop a pedestal of California light gray Raymond granite. The statue itself is twelve feet tall, and the pedestal is over eight feet tall. Similar statues may be seen in plaster at the North Dakota State Historical Society in Bismark, and in bronze at Minot, North Dakota.

In the Piacentini Gallery of the Portland Art Museum is Proctor's *Indian on Horseback* (1898), the first bronze acquired by the museum, a gift of several prominent citizens. This three-foot tall statue won a Gold Medal at the Paris Exposition in 1900. Proctor adapts the traditional equestrian statue to a particularly American subject. On display in the outdoor courtyard of the Portland Art Museum is a two-foot by six-foot bronze bas-relief, *Lions* (c. 1905–15), a gift of Winslow B. Ayer, Nanny's friend who helped establish the public library system as well as the Portland Art Museum. The relief depicts a male lion leading two female lions through the African veldt. Inside the Portland Art Museum in the American Hall is Proctor's *Stalking Panther (Cougar)* cast in bronze sometime between 1891 and 1892. While in Paris in 1894, he slightly revised the plaster cast from which this statuette was made and produced another of the *Stalking Panther* bronzes, now in the Metropolitan Museum of Art in New York.

While he was capable of producing excellent interpretations of any animal, Proctor was especially fond of depicting the large cats. In Paris in 1898, Proctor sculpted *Standing Pumas* for Prospect Park in Brooklyn, New York. His bronze *Sentinel Lions* (1904) guard the entrance to the Frick Building in Pittsburgh, Pennsylvania. In 1910 he cast in bronze, at his own expense, four tigers, each approximately four feet high, for the 16th Street Bridge in Washington, DC. On the campus of Princeton University, flanking the front entrance of Nassau Hall may be found his *Princeton Tigers* (1909), given to the university by the class of 1879. The statue was dedicated by Woodrow Wilson who was at that time the president of Princeton University.[10]

At the University of Oregon in Eugene, his bronze statue *Pioneer* (1917–18) and *Pioneer Mother* (1934), cast in bronze at a foundry in Rome, celebrate the brave people that crossed the country to settle the northwest. A similar statue of *Pioneer Mother* is on display at the Santa Barbara Museum in California. At the Oregon State Capital in Salem is his bronze on a granite base *The Circuit Rider* (1922–23).

His monumental statues celebrate people from America's past. On 12 June 1936, President Franklin D. Roosevelt dedicated Proctor's bronze *General Robert E. Lee and Young Soldier* in Dallas, Texas. Proctor collaborated with his friend Augustus Saint-Gaudens on two equestrian statues. Saint-Gaudens executed in bronze the figure of General John Logan for Grant Park in Chicago (1894–97) and summoned Proctor back from Paris to create the horse. Saint-Gaudens acknowledged that Proctor was unequalled in creating representations of animals. They similarly collaborated on the bronze statue of William T. Sherman in the Grand Army Plaza in New York City (1892–1903).

Phimister Proctor might be the most famous sculptor you never heard of, but his magnificent works deserve wide acclaim. His works beautify important sites all over the United States, and Nanny and Wood deserve credit for promoting Proctor's additions to the cultural life of Portland.

III
ALBERT PINKHAM RYDER

Albert Pinkham ("Pinky") Ryder was born in New Bedford, Massachusetts, 19 March 1847; he died in 1917, just days after his seventieth birthday. In New York City about 1870 he studied at the National Academy of Design, then joined his friends as a founding member of the Society of American Artists. Ryder was one of the original twenty-two members and was active in the group for twenty years. Once again we see the closeness of the group to which Wood was attracted. Shortly after Wood became friends with him, Ryder traveled to Europe with Olin Warner to visit galleries and museums.

The lore that has grown up around Ryder holds that he had a vision in a field as a youth. That vision told him to throw down his brushes, grab his palette knife, and make broad, sweeping strokes of color on his canvas.[11] Like Walt Whitman, Ryder lived amid a clutter of old newspapers, magazines, and rubbish. He cared nothing for money or fame. He often did not sign his works, and he re-worked them over several years so that dating them is difficult.[12] His output was small, only about one hundred and fifty works, yet art critic E. P. Richardson said, "Ryder has come to have a great position in American art."[13]

Ryder has been called the last and greatest of the mystic

painters.[14] Characteristically, his works depict the sea, clouds, waves, boats, and trees bathed in moonlight. He used subject matter from mythology, Shakespeare, the Bible, and other literature.

Ryder did not visit Nanny and Wood in Portland, but Wood became his patron by encouraging his friends to purchase Ryder's works. The American Hall in the Portland Art Museum displays Ryder's *Mother and Child* (undated), an oil on canvas. This painting was acquired by the William Mead Ladd family as a memorial to him. The Museum also has Ryder's *The Equestrian* (undated). This oil on canvas is a picture of his friend J. Alden Weir on horseback. Ryder often visited Weir at his farm in Branchville, Connecticut. This painting was bequeathed to the Museum by Winslow B. Ayer, husband of Nanny's dear friend Daisy Ayer.

IV
CHILDE HASSAM

(Frederick) Childe Hassam (1859–1935) was born in Boston of English descent. His mother was related to Nathaniel Hawthorne. After a brief career as an engraver and illustrator for magazines such as *Scribner's, Century,* and *Harper's,* Hassam went to Paris in 1886 where he studied at the Académie Julian with Gustave-Rodolphe Boulanger and Jules-Joseph Lefebvre. In Paris he became friends with other notable American Impressionist artists: John H. Twachtman, Thomas Dewing, Willard Metcalf, Robert Reid, Edward Simmons, Edmund C. Tarbell, and Frank W. Benson.[15] Tarbell and Benson became co-directors of the School of the Museum of Fine Arts in Boston.[16]

When Hassam returned to America in 1889, he established himself in New York City and joined the Society of American Artists that had broken away from the National Academy of Design; most of the members of the Society of American Artists rejoined the National Academy later. Hassam claimed credit for founding yet another breakaway group, Ten American Painters, an affiliation of outstanding Impressionists from Boston and New York, most of whom were students together at Académie Julian. The Ten were Benson, Joseph De Camp, Dewing, Hassam, Metcalf, Reid, Simmons, Tarbell, Twachtman, and J. Alden Weir.[17]

A versatile artist, Hassam painted figures, still life, and landscapes in oil, watercolor, and pastel.[18] Impressionists painted everyday scenes, using light, color, and pattern to depict the essential while eliminating unimportant details. Often misunderstood as a foil to Realistic painting, Impressionism combines visual realism with esthetic sensitivity.[19] For example, Hassam's *Columbus Avenue, Boston, Rainy Day* (1885), his *April Showers* (1888)—a rainy day on the Champs Elysées—his *Street Scene in Winter* (1901), the first painted before his study in Paris, the second during his stay there, and the third after he returned to America, all show the muted luminosity associated with Impressionism.[20] Hassam has been hailed as the greatest of the American Impressionists, although some critics also ascribe that distinction to Mary Cassatt.[21]

Childe Hassam visited Oregon twice at Wood's request. His first trip was in 1904 and the second in 1908. Nanny recalled that he stayed with them for almost an entire year and that he was a most difficult houseguest. With gentility she described him as not very dependable. Hassam drank too much and flirted with Nanny's friends. On one occasion Wood wanted to give a dinner party for some important judges and their wives who were visiting from San Francisco. Nanny, of course, wanted the meal to be perfect for these distinguished guests. Wood begged Hassam to come home sober for the dinner, but Hassam showed up inebriated and proceeded to lavish unwanted attention on the wife of one of the judges. Nanny said, "He led us a merry dance, and sometimes I had a hard time keeping things going right in the house." According to Nanny, Hassam's drinking became so pronounced that he began to suffer from delirium tremens, the D.T.s, and Wood had to send for his brother Jim to take the artist to a lodge at

Mount Hood for detoxification. Wood corroborates Nanny's thoughts about Hassam's drinking; he wrote to their daughter Nan that "Mr. Hassam has taken advantage of the trip [to Oregon] to have an attack, and I hope to bring him back in a clear and sane condition. Poor fellow. My heart aches for one with such cravings but perhaps as was said of Villon 'Had we had a better *man* we would have had a worse *poet*.'"[22]

Wood asked Hassam to paint a mural in his library, so Hassam painted, as Nanny described it, "a lot of naked ladies bathing on the rocks at the sea." She was embarrassed by the mural and by the procession of friends of hers who came to see it once the word spread around Portland.

Despite Hassam's unrestrained behavior, his visits to Oregon resulted in forty canvases of the high desert country of Harney County where the sculptor Phimister Proctor also spent time.[23]

The first original painting to enter the Museum's collection was Hassam's *Afternoon Sky, Harney Desert* (1908), purchased by subscription with funds from six donors.[24] This painting shows the semi-arid eastern Oregon plain in the foreground in tones of yellow and gold. Low-lying hills are topped by blue sky punctuated with billowing white clouds. Hassam had not experienced a country as vast as the Harney desert, and the painting reveals his joy of being there.[25] The American Hall in the Portland Art Museum exhibits several of Hassam's oils on canvas: *New England Road* (1902); *Study for Bathers* (1902-03); and *Isles of Shoals* (1907), a gift in memory of William Maxwell Wood IV, Nanny's grandson who died in 1965 at age fifty. In 1943, ten years after Nanny's death, Wood donated several works of art to the Museum in her memory. Among those items is Hassam's *Still Life, Fruits* (1904) in the Piacentini Gallery.

Another *Still Life* (1908) in the Piacentini Gallery is a triptych with a traditional arrangement of fruit and decorative glass objects in the center panel; on the right and left panels are representations of Nanny's garden showing a thick tangle of branches and leaves. Hassam painted this triptych on the porch of Nanny's home, looking at his still life objects inside the house and Nanny's profusion of plants on the outside.

An impressive oil on canvas is Hassam's *Mount Hood* (1908), the majestic snow-capped mountain that rises dramatically to the east of Portland. Another *plein air* canvas is *On the Snake River, Oregon* (1904), painted on his first visit to the state in August and September 1904.[26] This large painting resides on one side of a wide doorway to the Piacentini Gallery. On the other side is a painting of the same size that looks like a continuation of Hassam's, but an examination reveals that this is *Snake River Plain* (1906) by C.E.S. Wood. The story behind these remarkably similar paintings is that Wood and Hassam went to eastern Oregon together in 1904 and set up their easels to paint the same vista. At some point, Hassam leaned over and painted a brushstroke directly onto Wood's canvas, perhaps to show him how to render a particular object. Wood was offended and refused to finish his painting until a couple of years later, hence the discrepancy in the dates. The owner of Hassam's painting prevailed upon Wood to complete his so that he might buy it and reunite the two representations of the same scene.

V
J. ALDEN WEIR

Julian Alden Weir (1852–1919) was six months younger than C.E.S. Wood, and the two were close friends. While Childe Hassam could be impulsive and unorthodox in his behavior, J. Alden Weir had a reputation as a gentleman, exceedingly courteous to all and especially encouraging to younger artists. When the Panama–Pacific International Exposition occurred in San Francisco in 1915, Weir traveled there to serve on the jury. Wood persuaded him to come for a visit to Portland, but he came purely on a visit to his old friend and did not paint or sketch.

Years before Weir finally came to Oregon, Wood had been

promoting his paintings among his wealthy friends. Charles E. Ladd bought *The Ice Cutters* (1895–98), and his sister Caroline Ladd Pratt bought *The Black Hat* (1900) showing a fashionable, attractive young woman whose black hat contrasts with the lacy whiteness of her blouse. Both of these paintings are now in the Portland Art Museum. There, too, *Portrait of C.E.S. Wood* (1901), a gift to the Museum of Erskine Biddle Wood, shows Wood looking dandyish in his loose silk shirt with a turquoise cravat. From his jacket breast pocket emerges a handkerchief. He wears a watch fob on his belt and a pinkie ring on his right hand. This is one of two portraits of Wood by Weir.

Another Weir painting at the Museum is *Flower Piece* (1882), an oil on canvas. Against a dark background is a composition of four different vases of flowers. The flowers and decorative objects form a pyramid with strong light entering from the upper right corner.[27] This painting was a gift of brothers Henry L., Elliot R., and Hamilton F. Corbett in memory of their mother Helen Ladd Corbett.

A special painting is *Portrait of Erskine Wood* (1899), showing Nanny's oldest son when he was a student at Harvard. Erskine's serious mien tries unsuccessfully to mask eyes that hint at merriment. Erskine came to New York City from Harvard to sit for the portrait. In all, Weir painted C.E.S. Wood, Nanny, Erskine, Lisa and Nan, with most of these pieces remaining in the hands of family today.

One other painting by Weir in the Portland Art Museum is *The Spreading Oak* (c. 1910), an oil on canvas. This is one of five works of art donated to the Museum in 1943 by Wood in honor of Nanny who had died ten years earlier. The gift included four paintings and a bronze relief. In addition to the Weir painting, others were *Self Portrait* (1847) by Gustave Courbet; *Head of a Young Girl* by an unknown Dutch artist of the seventeenth century; and *Still Life, Fruits* by Childe Hassam. The bronze is one of the medallions of Nanny by Olin Warner.[28]

In a 1902 letter to Weir, Wood reveals his envy of his friend's success and perhaps something about his relationship with Nanny: "I still insist you are the most fortunate man I know. Enough to keep the wolf from the door, a clear conscience to keep ghosts from the window. Loving and lovely children, a sympathetic wife and an occupation which is always coaxing you, not driving you."[29]

VI
GEORGE DE FOREST BRUSH

In addition to Thomas Eakins and J. Alden Weir, another distinguished student of Jean-Léon Gérôme at the École des Beaux Arts in Paris who joined the Society of American Artists was George de Forest Brush (1855–1941). Brush said of his master Gérôme that "his strong love of character is, I believe, the key to his choice of subjects, which are most frequently of semi-barbaric people, in whom individuality is more strongly pronounced than among the civilized."[30]

His father was an entrepreneur from New England who succeeded at several ventures, including a stint as a dentist in Shelbyville, Tennessee, where George was born in 1855, the same year Nanny Wood was born. But with the approach of the Civil War, the Brushes deemed it advisable to return to the North, and Brush did most of his growing up in Connecticut. In 1871 he studied at the National Academy of Design in New York City, and in 1874 he enrolled in the classes of Gérôme in Paris.

Brush had family connections with Portland other than through the Woods. His father had moved from Connecticut to Portland and made a good living in business there until his death in 1908.[31] His sister Lillie married Hugh Hume, editor of *The Portland Spectator*, a weekly journal of opinion.[32] Brush had first gone to the western territories of the United States about 1879; there he observed the Indians and gathered material for later paintings. He spent considerable time with the Crow Nation in the Dakotas and with the Mandans where he celebrated in watercolor and oil on canvas the differences between the white and Indian cultures.

Brush said, "All that Rembrandt asked of the human figure was that it might exhibit light and shade; he never looked for pretty people, but found in this aspect of things a life-work. It is not necessary that an Indian learn to spell and make changes before we see that his long locks are beautiful as he rides against the prairie winds."[33]

Among his illustrations of Indians are *Mourning Her Brave* (1883) of an Indian woman standing on a snow-clad cliff, the body of her dead husband wrapped in funeral cloth, a bird—representing his departing spirit—soaring away from him; *The Silence Broken* (1886) showing a bare chested Indian brave paddling his canoe with a rock wall as backdrop; a companion picture, *Out of the Silence* (1886), of a brave aiming an arrow at an unseen flying prey; *The Indian Hunter* (undated), showing a brave clad in loin-cloth and moccasins, carrying on his back a goose he has killed; and *The Indian and the Lily* (1887) in which a hunter carrying a slain goose on his back stoops on his way home to collect a lily floating in the water, perhaps to take to his wife along with the result of the day's hunt.

Art dealer and writer Jim Vadeboncoeur of Palo Alto, California, makes a strong case that these and other Brush portraits strongly influenced illustrator N.C. Wyeth, some of whose Indian portraits are remarkably similar in composition and subject matter.[34]

Wood persuaded his wealthy friend Henry Failing to purchase Brush's *The Sculptor and the King* (1881), an exotic, colorful painting in a regal Aztec or Mayan setting, perhaps influenced by Gérôme's *The Snake Charmer* or *The Moorish Ruth* and others showing his sense of color and composition. Wood praised *The Sculptor and the King* as a masterpiece.[35] The painting shows the interior of a spacious palace room with polished stone walls and floor. The king and the court sculptor look at the bas-relief carving of the king in the Pre-Columbian style. The king stands with his arms folded across his chest as he studies the image that will be his legacy after his death. The young sculptor, holding his mallet in his right hand and a chisel in the left, awaits the king's opinion of his work. The work suggests that a work of art can exist for its own sake as art and also as a record of its time in history. In 1888, *The Sculptor and the King* won the prestigious First Hallgarten Prize[36] and a gold medal at the Pan-American Exposition, 1901–02,[37] where Augustus Saint-Gaudens also won a gold medal for his equestrian statue of General Sherman,[38] the horse being designed and executed by Phimister Proctor. *The Sculptor and the King* is now owned by the Portland Art Museum, the bequest of Mary Forbush Failing.

In the latter half of his career Brush moved to Florence and turned his attention away from the Indian culture, creating a Neo-Renaissance style, and executing many paintings on the traditional theme of mother and child. One of the best of these, *Mother and Child*, first sold for $7000 and was later acquired for the Boston Art Museum.

* * *

All these painters and sculptors knew each other. Speaking of when he was thirty-one years old in 1891, Phimister Proctor said, "Now and then a sculptor would visit the studio and offer constructive criticism. There is a very warm place in my heart for Olin Warner, who to my mind was one of the very best American sculptors. He often dropped by and gave good advice which I was quick to take."[39] Warner encouraged Proctor as Saint-Gaudens encouraged Warner; Saint-Gaudens thought Warner's bronze *Diana* "showed a modern mastery of the nude and a charm and inspiration unequaled at that time."[40] J. Alden Weir painted oil on canvas portraits of his friends *Albert Pinkham Ryder* and *Childe Hassam* (1902–03) and *Olin Levi Warner* (1879–80). Weir would sometimes buy pictures from the unworldly Ryder, sell them, and give Ryder the profits.[41] When Wood learned that Weir was painting a portrait of Ryder he wrote to Weir, affectionately calling Ryder "that sweet-minded philosopher."[42] Olin Warner sculpted a bronze bust of *J. Alden Weir* (1880). Weir knew George de Forest Brush at both the atelier Gérôme and the École Gratuite de Dessin, better known as the Petite École.[43] When George de Forest Brush took his family to France in 1898, they stayed with the Phimister Proctors in the village of Marlotte not far from the Forest of Fontainebleau.[44] Later, in 1908, Brush visited the Proctors in Bedford, New York, for two months. While he was there, Jean Clemens, daughter of Mark Twain, drove over from Mt. Kisco to Bedford to see her friend Brush.[45]

Phimister Proctor and Augustus Saint-Gaudens collaborated on two monumental equestrian statues. George de Forest Brush visited Saint-Gaudens at the Cornish, New Hampshire, artist's colony (and lived in a teepee on the grounds) and in France. In 1898 Saint-Gaudens went to Fountainbleu to have dinner with Brush and Proctor. Later that year he would visit the Brushes at their home in Boulogne.[46] Saint-Gaudens and Olin Warner studied sculpture together at the atelier Jouffroy at the École des Beaux-Arts.[47]

Those painters and sculptors who could not personally visit Portland sent their work through Wood to wealthy buyers to embellish Portland's finest homes, museums, and galleries. Directly or indirectly, Nanny observed and was involved in this influx of art to Portland in the city's formative years.

Wood was a complex person whose law career allowed him to meet interesting and controversial people and to challenge the existing social and political order. Insofar as he was able, he gave expression to his own creativity through his writing, sketching, watercolors, and oils on canvas. Bringing painters and sculptors to Portland served a civic-minded purpose and satisfied his need to be around imaginative people.

When Wood separated from Nanny, resigned from his law practice, and went to Los Gatos with Sara Bard Field, his artistic side was set free. He never forgot his fascinating time with these artists from his days with them in New York City in 1882. He was still young enough then to be enchanted with their talk of studying under European masters, of forging a distinctive American style of art—whether Realist or Impressionist—and of their special fraternity of creative painters and sculptors.

At Los Gatos he recreated the salon society he so much enjoyed years earlier in New York City. Now able to indulge his creative side with his soul mate Sara Bard Field, he entertained artist Childe Hassam, musician Yehudi Menuhin, poet Carl Sandburg, photographer Ansel Adams (with whom Nanny's granddaughter Marian Wood Kolisch studied photography), writer and "muckraker" Lincoln Steffens, and novelist John Steinbeck.

His legacy continued in Sara's daughter Catherine Caldwell who credits him with introducing her to art on a trip to Europe. She obtained a master's degree in art history from Harvard, was curator of the San Francisco city museum, taught at the University of California, Berkeley (where her husband was a professor of literature), and became professor of Oriental Art at Mills College in Oakland, California.[48]

Had Nanny been more like Sara Bard Field or her daughter Catherine Caldwell, it is possible that Wood and Nanny's marriage might have survived. Lacking any intellectual inclinations, Nanny's life was fulfilling in itself—her children, gardening, and her friends—but unfulfilling to her marriage partner. Wood needed a partner who could complement his imaginative intellect, but Nanny could not supply that need.

NOTES

[1] Edwin Bingham and Tim Barnes, *Wood Works: The Life and Writings of Charles Erskine Scott Wood* (Corvallis: Oregon State University Press, 1997), 11.
[2] Louise Hall Tharp, *Saint-Gaudens and the Gilded Era* (Boston: Little, Brown and Company, 1969), 113.
[3] Wayne Craven, *Sculpture in America* (New York: Thomas Y. Crowell Company, 1968), 378-79.
[4] Lloyd Goodrich, *Albert P. Ryder* (New York: George Braziller, Inc., 1959), 15.
[5] Hamburger, Robert, *Two Rooms: The Life of Charles Erskine Scott Wood* (Lincoln: University of Nebraska Press, 1998), 73.
[6] E. Kimbark MacColl, *Merchants, Money and Power: the Portland Establishment, 1843-1913* (Portland, OR: The Georgian Press, 1988), 305.
[7] Carl Abbott, "Portland: Civic Culture and Civic Opportunity," *Oregon Historical Quarterly,* 102 (2001): 20-21.
[8] Charles H. Caffin, *American Masters of Sculpture* (Garden City, NY: Doubleday, Page & Company, 1913), 144.
[9] Alexander Phimister Proctor, *Sculptor in Buckskin* (Norman: University of Oklahoma Press, 1971), 163.
[10] Proctor's grandson, Phimister Proctor "Sandy" Church, directs the A. Phimister Proctor Museum in Poulsbo, Washington, near Seattle. There he keeps records of Proctor's numerous creations and their provenance. I am grateful to Phimister Church for supplying the information concerning Proctor's sculptures.
[11] Lloyd Goodrich, *Albert P. Ryder* (New York: George Braziller, Inc., 1959), 13.
[12] Barbara Groseclose, *Nineteenth-Century American Art* (New York: Oxford University Press, 2000), 139.
[13] E.P. Richardson, *Painting in America* (New York: Thomas Y. Crowell Company, 1956), 351.
[14] Daniel M. Mendelowitz, *A History of American Art* (New York: Holt, Rinehart and Winston, Inc., 1964), 440.
[15] E.P. Richardson, *Painting in America* (New York: Thomas Y. Crowell Company, 1956), 277.
[16] Susan Strickler, "The Paintings of Edmund C. Tarbell," *American Art Review* 13 (October 2001): 172.
[17] Adelson, Warren, Jay E. Cantor, and William H. Gerdts. *Childe Hassam: Impressionist* (New York: Abbeville Press, 1999), 75.
[18] "(Frederick) Childe Hassam," *The National Cyclopedia of American Biography,* vol. 10 (New York: James T. White &

Company, 1909), 374.
[19] Daniel M. Mendelowitz, *A History of American Art* (New York: Holt, Rinehart and Winston, Inc., 1964), 444.
[20] E.P. Richardson, *Painting in America* (New York: Thomas Y. Crowell Company, 1956), 304.
[21] Daniel M. Mendelowitz, *A History of American Art* (New York: Holt, Rinehart and Winston, Inc., 1964), 450.
[22] Ulrich W. Hiesinger, *Childe Hassam: American Impressionist* (New York: Prestel, 1994), 126.
[23] Sidney Warren, *Farthest Frontier: The Pacific Northwest* (Port Washington, NY: Kennikat Press, 1970), 321.
[24] Prudence F. Roberts, "Shaping a Collection: C.E.S. Wood and Portland's Early Art Scene," n.d., n.p. Former curator of American art at the Portland Art Museum, Roberts wrote an essay for a brochure to accompany an exhibition of the major American holdings of the Museum.
[25] Donelson F. Hoopes, *Childe Hassam* (New York: Watson-Guptill Publications, 1979.
[26] Adelson, Warren, Jay E. Cantor, and William H. Gerdts, *Childe Hassam: Impressionist* (New York: Abbeville Press, 1999), 237.
[27] Doreen Bolger Burke, *J. Alden Weir: An American Impressionist* (Newark: University of Delaware Press, 1983), 132.
[28] Catherine Jones, "Wood Makes Museum Gift" Portland *Oregonian* 30 May 1943: sec. 3, p. 5.
[29] Dorothy Weir Young, *The Life and Letters of J. Alden Weir* (New Haven: Yale University Press, 1960), xxviii.
[30] George de Forest Brush, "American Artists on Gérôme," *Century Magazine* 37 (February 1889): 635.
[31] Nancy Douglas Bowditch, *George de Forest Brush: Recollections of a Joyous Painter* (Peterborough, NH: Noone House, 1970), 102.
[32] Bowditch, 26.
[33] George de Forest Brush, "An Artist Among the Indians" *Century Magazine* 30 (May 1885): 54.
[34] Jim Vadeboncoeur, Letter to the author, 15 April 2002.
[35] Robert Hamburger, *Two Rooms: The Life of Charles Erskine Scott Wood* (Lincoln: University of Nebraska Press, 1998), 92.
[36] Joan B. Morgan, *George de Forest Brush, 1855–1941; Master of the American Renaissance* (New York: Berry–Hill Galleries, Inc., 1985), 21.
[37] "George de Forest Brush," *The National Cyclopedia of American Biography,* vol. 13 (New York: James T. White & Company, 1906): 578.

[38] Louise Hall Tharp, *Saint-Gaudens and the Gilded Era* (Boston: Little, Brown and Company, 1969), 317.
[39] Alexander Phimister Proctor, *Sculptor in Buckskin* (Norman: University of Oklahoma Press, 1971), 115.
[40] Augustus Saint-Gaudens. *The Reminiscences of Augustus Saint-Gaudens.* London: Andrew Melrose, 1913.
[41] Lloyd Goodrich, *Albert P. Ryder* (New York: George Braziller, Inc., 1959), 26.
[42] Doreen Bolger Burke, *J. Alden Weir: An American Impressionist* (Newark: University of Delaware Press, 1983), 246.
[43] Burke, 64–65.
[44] Nancy Douglas Bowditch, *George de Forest Brush* (Peterborough, NH: Noone House, 1970), 48.
[45] Bowditch, 101.
[46] Louise Hall Tharp, *Saint-Gaudens and the Gilded Era* (Boston: Little, Brown and Company, 1969), 287.
[47] Tharp, 32.
[48] Holly Danks, "An Affair to Remember," Portland *Oregonian* 16 January 1985: C1, C4.

APPENDIX I:

THE WOOD HOUSEHOLD

by
Barbara Bartlett Hartwell

IN 1942, ON THE FIFTIETH ANNIVERSARY of the founding of the Portland Art Museum, formerly the Portland Art Association, by C.E.S. Wood, Barbara Bartlett Hartwell, gave a talk recalling her fascination with the Wood family, especially Nanny who befriended her and taught her social graces. This uncopyrighted address was privately printed in sixty copies as a souvenir for distribution to friends and family. "The Wood Household" is reprinted here with the kind permission of the Portland Art Museum.

There were in the Portland of my girlhood a number of houses which possessed individual atmospheres. Their interiors and exteriors, the feel of their carpets beneath my feet, the smell of their dining rooms, the taste of their food, the personality of their cooks, the books, manner and subtle emanations of their owners have remained with me as vividly as the smell and color of Portland's streets in the days of hot, fat, pink Caroline Testout roses down parking strip after parking strip.

In that period of cable cars groaning up the trestle over

Goose Hollow while you looked quakingly at the earth far beneath; of swimming at Bundy's; the Portland Academy where Alta Smith monotonously took all the prizes in all the subjects; picnics at Oregon City amidst poison oak, refreshed by lemon pie and sarsaparilla; when rain pattered exquisitely on the tin roofs of Victorian balconies that jutted out from numberless arched Victorian windows; when the "Rose Parade" was an intimate thing; when everyone knew everyone else and his horse and Miss Becky Biddle was pointed out by the bystanders as that "beautiful blond—the one in Alice blue and Merry Widow hat"; when the Corbetts' coachman George drove their carriage trimmed with lupin; when the sight of Miss Carrie Flanders on horseback sitting perfectly on her side-saddle made you feel Hyde Park didn't have ALL the cards or Central Park either; when . . . but I can't go on enumerating those sights and sounds that are gone forever; there must be a final "when," with its dependent clauses, that somehow sums up the whole period and gives in a sentence the essential difference between Portland then and now. When, in short, Portland was a town in size—leisurely, wooden sidewalked, spacious gardened, concentrated—with neighbor's yard touching neighbor's yard; with a clear cut "society," a rigid set of standards, a remarkable "touch" with Europe and the Eastern coast, and an equally remarkable dimness about the several thousand miles that lay between the Pacific and Atlantic; a town with an atmosphere of New England simplicity combined with dignified opulence.

Standing out against this background were the seven houses that gave the atmosphere of which I speak, an atmosphere as different from that of San Francisco, Seattle, Spokane, as great-grandmother's potpourri jar from the best concentrated Coty "Quelques Fleurs"; the H. W. Corbetts', the Ladds', the Henry Failings', the Lewis's, the Tuckers', the Ayers',—and lastly the Woods', where the Portland Heights car, containing everyone you knew by sight, whined its way over the quivering wooden inadequacy called the Ford Bridge. Seven houses, each as different as the colors of the spectrum, but blending into each other as colors do, for Portland was charmingly intimate in those days— wasn't Mrs. Wood reported to have called Mrs. Ayer "Daisy" in someone's hearing? This story was never really verified. However, I saw with my own eyes a note on her desk beginning "My dear Daisy," but imagination boggles over anyone calling Mrs. Wood "Nanny" or Mrs. Beck "Sarah." It is a surprise to me that I know what their first names were, and only shows the amazing detail with which my mother, incomparable raconteur, regaled me with stories of an older Portland than mine, when Miss Nanny Moale Smith of Baltimore married Mr. C. E. S. Wood, lieutenant in the United States army, and came out to be ever afterward the only original Mrs. Wood. I remember calling up the house in my crude girlhood—after she had collected some daughters-in-law—and asking to speak to Mrs. C. E. S. Wood. Her own voice withered me in four words. "Mrs. Wood is sufficient," she said with extreme dryness.

And, indeed, she and it were in every way sufficient to herself and her friends and to Portland. She was of that rare race of charmers who live forever; and the Wood household, with all its inhabitants from master and mistress through its distracting five children, had a QUALITY. I do not remember the current cliché word "glamour" being used then—the dictionary says "enchantment" is included within the definition. The Woods were fascinating, and to be in their house was to me an enchantment—a glamour shed itself over everything they did.

The other six houses expressed hospitality, dignity, sumptuousness, stateliness, wealth, gracious intellectuality; the Woods' was of a different world. It was Bohemia without shabbiness; it was unconventional, but shot through with conventionality like changeable silk. Just as you expected the Woods to be married in city halls or temples to Minerva, they were married in churches. But then, the sting of being married in churches was removed by the poultice of "contracts," which the protagonists signed under the Jovian guidance of Mr. Wood, while Portland Society (and those at the weddings were Portland Society) shuddered pleasurably over such a combination of the Altar and the Grove. The "contracts" were for the purpose of dissolving at will the bond just tied, and as the married pair were invariably immensely in love, with all the warmth of personal passion and mutual family benedictions, the signing of them was an excuse for champagne and jest.

The Wood house was of the world as I have said—the world of Art, Music, Literature, and also the world of "who's who" and Society Bluebooks and the I.W.W. Except that it has never been the custom of those in the Bluebook to possess it, any more than Burke's Peerage would be the bedside solace of Lord Salisbury, such a volume at the Woods' would have found itself jostling "The Masses"—or the other way about, depending upon your viewpoint. In its rooms, dark with brocade, where rareties in glass, porcelain and metal gleamed through a kind of rich smelling gloom; where footfalls were hushed on dim handicraft from Persia; where books were smooth to the cheek in hand-tooled leather, and where there was such a plethora of precious things that the bathrooms startled unacquainted bathers with plunging horses from the Parthenon threatening them in the shower, one might meet almost anything or anybody—distinguished generals; Indian chiefs; Mr. Childe Hassam collecting his colors for an onslaught into Eastern Oregon; Phimister Proctor resting between beasts; editors; men of letters; radicals; and those among that Portland society of mansard roof whose dazzlement over such exotic persons as artists and Indians exceeded their native shyness at meeting them.

The food was fit for kings—the less stodgy royalties at least—kings with catholic tastes in oil and garlic, familiar with truffles and galentines; hams stuffed with honey; canvasbacks (shot by young Erskine, that hero of romance) lying in a bed of cress, served with wild rice and spiced huckleberry. The dining room was darkness visible, made more sombre by Spanish leather chairs. On the faint gold walls the oil paintings were mere dark brown mysteries in gilt frames highlighted by the white belly of a fish, where, if one went near enough, one discerned a dead duck, a bunch of grapes, a half a pear. About the room hung an aroma of wine and spice—the darkness only added to the spell. Even a child knew that when candles were lighted, and the company sat down about the table, toying with Lucullan items, the wit crackled and flashed as in no other dining room, led by that prince of hosts and story-tellers. The slices fell from the haunch of venison (shot by Erskine, the eldest son of the house, who was my idea of the ultimate in young manhood) and the anecdotes kept up with the slices, while Mrs. Wood, in an aura of charm, sat indifferently pecking at some milk toast. The ortolans and larks' tongues meant less than nothing to Mrs. Wood, who was given to headaches and dietetic denials.

Dear Mrs. Wood! How I wish I could make you live as you lived for me and the Portland of my day! Your enchanting face with its irregular features; the sallow complexion; the deep dark eyes; the poise of the head wrapped around and around with those masses of unbelievable hair that, released from pins, fell about your knees; your voice, which I can "do" perfectly and yet can't put on paper; your complete charm a combination of the utterly natural and the woman of the world. I see you and hear you as if I had just shut the door on Ford street. She talked with everyone, male and female, with camaraderie. She was interested in everything. She could be trundled to the opera in an applebox on wheels, keep up the liveliest interchange with the vegetable man, bandy witticisms with an ambassador, be amused and amuseable, startle men callers by whisking them into the basement to help her track a rat that had been disturbing the peace; send unsuspecting men friends on mysterious errands; scramble about the rocks at Ecola in the most remarkable conglomeration of garments; and always there hung about her an impalpable but imperishable dignity. She was and will remain our only "grande dame." She was completely at home in any circle and always captured it; darkies of course adored her. They recognized at once the "quality." She had unfailing manners—she made a party.

At the end of her life, before she was an invalid, but an old woman, I remember I had an out-of-town guest either very august and dull or very crude and brilliant (I quite forget which) but I do remember that I could struggle with neither extreme. Whom to get to relieve the situation? Mrs. Wood, of course. So we thankfully drove sixteen miles to fetch her and return her. In an age of motors she never had one. She used the Portland Heights street car for her carriage to the immense enlightenment and enlivenment of the general public. It was a privilege to be delayed in the trolley before Mrs. Wood's house, while Mrs. Wood called a few last Baltimorean commands to the maid, and prepared to carry one of her unusual bundles down the steps. But having no motor was an indirect boon to duller people who owned cars. It was a delight to fetch and carry for Mrs. Wood—one fought for the honor.

She never read books, though she carried fat volumes about with a place-mark in the first fifty pages. She was immeasurably more interesting than a thousand people who are erudite. She knew life, society, humanity; she was inescapably the center of attraction wherever she found herself; and age could not wither her nor custom stale.

I felt about Mrs. Wood as the heroine of "A London Life" did about old Mrs. Berrington; and my idea of a perfect evening was Mrs. Wood and me alone—or perhaps one other person as audience to us—in front of the fire, starting the ball by looking at the old photograph book, whose introductory picture was Mrs. Wood at the age of eighteen, under a parasol, gazing up archly into the faces of a clustered group of West Point cadets of the class of '74! And the handsomest face among them was Mr. Charles Erskine Scott Wood.

The glamour of the Wood house was far more than its extraordinary mistress. Mr. Wood was even more an extraordinary man. He should have lived in New York or Paris or San Francisco. Thank heaven he did not. He painted charmingly; he wrote poetry of color, depth, great delicacy and passion; he was a brilliant lawyer, a friend of humanity, the dearest of fathers, the kindest of hosts. He was responsible for the lambent glow of originality and daring that illumined a fairly heavy and respectable quarter of a century in a town suffering from an almost too decided New England flavor. This period was before the days when business men "painted." They bought paintings but they created nothing beyond railroads and banks.

Certainly no one else on earth, as we knew it, could defend the I.W.W. in hand-tucked shirts. No other man in the world would send, or thought of sending, his eldest son to live with Nez Perce Indians and later to Harvard. He was immensely handsome with an Olympian beard and was always being compared with Jove. In an age of circumspection and avoidance of anything "animal" in conversation or art, he hurled startling Saxonisms into frightened ears. He enjoyed sending subscriptions to "The Masses" to hide-bound conservatives, he revelled in ridicule of the Church, and he was throttled by hospitality at Mount Angel. He was generous at his own table, and liked nothing better than a party for charity at which signs like "Gamble for God's Sake" shocked and tickled the eyes of a generation brought up to regard the Deity as more than an epithet or the point of a joke. His library was filled with magnificent "unexpurgated" books, first editions, translations. At fifteen one had a guilty sense that Mr. Wood's library was "wicked." Whenever I was in there I blushed if "discovered," as they say on the stage; and I did enough extremely surreptitious reading to be unstartled by Hemingway or Dos Passos in later life.

But with all Mrs. Wood's charm and Mr. Wood's versatile brilliance, the final touch to the house, that made it unique, were the children; at a time when people—fascinating, brilliant, social people who went everywhere and did everything—had children. Whether any Wood child was, as an individual, as remarkable as Mr. and Mrs. Wood I can't say; en bande they were irresistible. They were as colorful as a painting by Van Gogh. They were utterly uninhibited before anyone ever heard the word; their personalities were allowed to ramble richly at will, however they impeded the personalities of others. They sang their prayers to the street songs of the Spanish war. "Now I lay me down to sleep; I pray the Lord my soul to keep – ta-ra-boom-de-ay." They were either so good looking or so bewitching that you forgot to notice whether they were or not. They moved in the glow of the spotlight; keeping wildcats in their backyard; going off on solitary camping trips at ages so tender it was a step from pram to the tepee; holding up traffic by riding in front of horsecars. They consorted with people with names, Roosevelts and Morgans and Crowninshields; they belonged to clubs that were mentioned in novels. The East was, so to speak, their washpot, and Europe held no terrors for them. To a shy thirteen-year-old girl looking over the wall from St. Helen's Hall, which guarded the "Word" under Mr. Wood's very beard, these princes and princesses were too heady to be spoken to; they were to me a remote cyclorama of romance seen through theatrical gauze and illuminated colored lights.

To go to Nan Wood's wedding at Trinity, and watch the sun suddenly shine through stained glass onto her silver train ... ah, Beverly of Graustark ... oh, Flavia of Zenda !! Here you were in the flesh! To sit at the Woman's Exchange on Fifth street and see Lisa Wood lunching with a beau, and holding up a coffee cup on a level with her eyes to see if they matched, (I only saw this in dumb show and don't know what ardent compliment brought forth the by-play) to SEE was a thrill; and to imagine DOING it some day! Could I possibly hold anything to my eyes, just plain watery blue eyes, and have someone look at me like that? And in the dazzling publicity of the Woman's Exchange, filled with Failings and Fashion?

As for the Wood young men, they were to me gods, who came out of the great world of Harvard and Cornell; whose lives were spent in flannels, dropping witticisms, pursuing damsels, ignoring the heartbroken, indulging in cataclysmic practical jokes, holding hands with heroines of romance like Margaret Walter (oh, those braids!), dancing with rhythmic perfection, singing songs to mandolins —"and every afternoon at four, I calls upon my manicure, and takes her for a walk." Max on horseback accompanying Margaret Montgomery, who wore the first white doeskin riding breeches in Portland; Erskine walking lissomely through the garden with a book in his hand, a sort of Byron and Robert Chambers hero in one; Berwick clowning until one wanted to DIE, just laughing like that; it was such agony! I stared at them dumbly at big weddings, from street corners, in the precious darkness of their own house—a thin white blond child to whom their mother, for inexplicable reasons, was being kind.

The casualness with which these children "took" this very house was part of their fascination. Max, who looked like a Spaniard and had so much charm that it HIT you like an electric volt, was unmoved, like his mother, by pâté and truffles, though for different reasons. He liked boiled rice, lamb chops and chocolate cake, and such was his charm that no matter how inconvenient or how many other people wanted something else, he got rice, lamb chops and chocolate cake. He visited us in Lewiston before his marriage and Mamma's Norwegian cook, who never spoke, if possible, and before she gave birth to a word swallowed in a visible, sliding, Adam's apple sort of way, made chocolate cake for six weeks. We all became very weary of its very color, and finally Mamma was firm. "Hilda, you MUST made a different sort of cake; ANY kind but NOT chocolate!" That night chocolate appeared, and before Mamma's wrath Hilda merely swallowed and said stonily, "Mr. Wood like this kind best."

When these royalties began to marry, romance for me reached its highest peak. I met Becky Biddle downtown at Meier and Frank's, selecting a dance frock shortly before her wedding. She was a creature from a fairy tale, gold, and ivory, and blue! And when I learned that my hero and heroine were going off ON A CAMPING TRIP ON THEIR HONEY-MOON, nothing except the last chapter of "The Virginian" had ever given me such a tremendous thrill.

The house on Ford street is gone now—there is no Ford street, no quivering wooden bridge, no street cars packed with familiar faces. The tangled garden where Mrs. Wood scolded the gardener to his infinite delight, and where the boys dug what they thought were truffles and ate them, being followed almost immediately by near extinction, has died of neglect and starvation. No Phoenix rose from its ashes, no family will ever take the place of that radiant and radiating circle that scandalized, delighted, entertained, bewildered Portland from the eighties to the Great War. They lived through Portland at its best when it had distinction and charm. And they were the center of it—the most distinguished and most charming.

APPENDIX II:

NANNY'S PORTLAND GARDEN

As Nanny's health began to deteriorate in 1933, she and her nurse Dean Fischer walked about her property at 254 Vista Avenue. Nanny named and described her trees, flowers, and shrubs, and Fischer recorded these in a notebook, later converting her notes into a typescript. Nanny's great-granddaughter Nancy Wood Robinson von Gimbut has the originals of these documents.

Nanny promoted the beautification of Portland ("The Rose City") with plants of all types, especially roses which thrive in the area's climate. Interestingly, Nanny did not record in detail the profusion of roses that grew in her garden. This inventory provides a valuable record of Nanny's efforts as a leading citizen of the city to set the example in beautifying her city through horticulture. The record reveals that her mind was alert and that she was able to recall complicated scientific names as well as popular names of many plants. Why did Nanny make this inventory? Because she gives precise locations and, in some cases, instructions for ensuring the continued health of the plants, the inventory poignantly implies that she wanted her family to be able to identify the plants that she loved and to care for them after her death.

I
TREES

Sequoia	In the grove
Pines	Have three
Blood Oak	In the grove
American Walnut	Near the north arbor
Rock Maple	
Pin Maple	
Japanese Maple	Have three
Birch	Two
Gums	Three
Sassafras	
Beech	Two, one of the common variety and one purple beech.
Tamarack	
Chestnut	
Judas	
Elms	A row on the Main Street side
Cedar	In the kitchen garden
Sycamore	In the north part of the garden

II
VINES

Purple Clematis
  On the south arbor.
White Clematis
  A beautiful vine on the porch. Looks like a bridal veil when in full bloom.
Jasmine
  Growing on the porch at the right hand side.
Honeysuckle
  Growing on the wall under the pantry window.

III
FLOWERS

Penstemon
>Plants grow tall and flowers are in bunches at the end of the tall stalks. Blossoms are trumpet shaped growing close together and are generally pink and white.

Anemones
>Large plants growing tall late in the summer. Leaves are somewhat like grape leaves only smoother and a darker green. Colors are pale pink or white and the petals are single.

Weigela
>It needs a soil of rich top dressing. The wild species is the most satisfactory. The shape of the petals is like cornucopia or trumpet shaped. The color is pale apricot pink and very fragrant. The garden variety is not so tall in growth and is much lighter in color.

Physostegia
>A large plant—tall and branches grow loosely. The flowers are tiny pale pink and white and grow raceme form [flowers are arranged singly along a common main axis]. Mine is growing in the south garden bed and some nearer in the bed at the north of the garden.

Phlox
>Comes in many colors, lavender, white and deep pink. The plant grows tall and straight and blossoms form thick clusters at the top. The clusters are formed of single flowers but in bunches, and they need much sun.

Stocks
>Low-growing plants with grayish white dull foliage. The small flowers form in close clusters. They come in all colors and have a very delicate fragrance.

Pelargonium
>An improved form of geraniums but more elegant, although in the same family. The leafage is similar. At the end of the stem is a cluster of lovely velvet leaflets.

Matilija Poppy
   Grows tall on single, much-leaved stock and bears one blossom on each end. The large white blossoms are like a big chrysanthemum with a bright orange center of tiny florets. They grow in a bed under the pantry window and in the bed across from the rose garden.

Snapdragons or Anterrhinum
   Covers walls and stony place. Flowers grow on a long stem, and the blossoms look like slippers. Deep crimson is the prettiest color. Pure white is also striking. Best variety is Rupestris.

Saint John's Wort
   Grows in masses in the kitchen garden. A bright yellow, single-petaled, cupped-shaped flower with center of tiny stamens.

Sweet William
   I prefer a deep crimson or peach pink in color. It is a bunch of flowers composed of many little flowers making a head and is therefore rather compact and bushy.

Wisteria
   Lavender is the most beautiful. It grows as a vine and is composed of many pea-shaped blossoms on a stem. It grows on my north arbor. The white variety grows on a wire screen fronting the library door.

Hydrangeas
   Blossoms composed of many little flowers make a large head. Hedge of pink ones on the north side of the house. I like the blue ones best.

Rhododendron
   Bushes produce rose color, lavender, and white. The white has blotches of yellow on it. Are found growing in bush form on each side of the path on way to Main Street. Don't use manure.

Scillas
   Many under the north arbor and in the bed under the wall on both sides. A pretty little blue flower, many on a stem, and comes early in the Spring.

NANNY'S PORTLAND GARDEN

Tulips
Many colors and are scattered around the garden in various spots, some going down the steps to the rose garden. Many picotees [a type of carnation having pale petals bordered by a darker color] are in the big bed on the north side of the lawn.

Small roses
The bed is in the south garden and some are new varieties this year. Several climbing roses are to be found as follows: One rich, red medium sized grows as a vine under the pantry window. One white one on the bank under the wayfaring tree. Under the right bank and one under the wall on the left side. One also grows down on the lower fence.

III
BLOSSOMING TREES AND BUSHES

Prunus Pissardii
The large red trees are near Erskine's [Nanny's son Erskine and his wife Becky lived at that time on adjoining property.] One is in the kitchen garden and one at the east end near the street.

Four Cherry trees
One by the house, and three near Erskine's.

Flowering Cherry
One double pink cherry grows near Erskine's. One cream color at the top of the steps leading down to Erskine's.

Weeping Flowering Cherry
One on each side of the path going down to Erskine's Woods.

Flowering Crabapple
At the left hand side of the steps leading down to the path. Very beautiful when in bloom.

Euonymus or Strawberry Tree
>Grows on the right hand side of the path.

Magnolia-Grandflora
>Does not bloom well and last year had only one blossom.

Japanese Magnolia
>Has smaller blossom and the petals are long and slender; bloomed well this year.

Hawthorne
>White, pink, and red. White one is near the house and the red one is in the grove. One red is also in the north part of the garden.

Exochorda
>At the end of the porch. Has lovely delicate white blossoms and blooms early in the Spring.

Bechtel Crab
>Grows in the lawn. Has lovely pink blossoms.

Japanese Flowering Prune
>Is on the west end of the lawn.

Fringe tree
>Is on the path going out to Main Street.

Koelreutaria
>Blooms late in July and has long yellow sprays of blossoms on top of the tree.

Japanese Quince hedge
>Blooms early in pink and scarlet and is a hedge on Vista Avenue and Main Street with about one half of the garden on King's Court.

Lavender
>Grows at the end of the rose garden.

Flowering Almond
>On the path at the left hand side going to Erskine's.

Abelia Grandflora
>Grows at the foot of the rose garden.

Mexican Orange
>Grows near the south arbor.

Deutsis
>Northeast corner of the south ground.

NANNY'S PORTLAND GARDEN

Weigela
  Back of the north bed.
Kerria
  Near the porch, under the hawthorne.
Double Kerria
  Down on the path under the black cherry tree.
Spirea
  On the path at the right side leading to Erskine's.
Bridal Wreath
  One in the kitchen garden and one in northwest.
Syringa
  On the path leading to Erskine's.
Forsythia
  On the right side of the path leading to Erskine's.
Daphne
  On corner of intersection of the Main Street path and the path to Erskine's.
Lilacs
  White and purple hedge. The white one grows at the Judas Tree.
Lauristinus
  Northwest bed at the north of the lawn.
Japanese Snowballs
  North bed.
Common Snowballs
  One bush in the kitchen garden and another in the northeast.
Chorcorrus
  Just below the bank on the right hand side and near the Euonymus.
Camelia
  Grow in the south arbor. Two bushes, one red and one pink. Has waxy leaf and smooth overlapping petals.
Chionodoxa
  The earliest flower in the Spring. Lovely, pale blue single flowers. Grows in grass plot at the left of path going east.

Hepatica
   Along bank under the black cherry tree. The colors are pale pink and also blue. Very hard to grow and needs a shady place.

Montbretia
   Grows on the north side of the path. Scarlet blossoms on a slender stem and has a leaf like a slender iris leaf.

Solomon Seal
   A wild flower from the wood. Long spike-like stems with a bunch of feather blossoms of pale yellow on the end.

Fuchias
   I have five pots of these. One large one that Mrs. Cookingham gave me and four smaller ones in the Chinese pots.

Double Yellow Nasturtiums
   Grows in the porch box at the south end of the porch. Very deep yellow.

Narcissus
   In the bed under the trees in the grove.

Trillums
   A wild flower from the wood. Also grows in the grove.

Jonquils
   Grow in the bed at the north of the lawn. Also in a bed near the north arbor and in the grove.

Daffodils
   Grow in the same beds as the tulips.

Fragrant Yellow Lilies
   Grow in the bed at the right hand side of the path going towards Main Street.

Delphinium
   Grow in the bed at the north of the lawn. Also below the porch.

Ageratum
   Tiny little fluffy balls of lavender growing at the end of a slender stem. Grow in the south porch box.

Lantana
   The orange and light yellow grows in the porch box and

the cream with yellow centers are in a jar on the porch. Both bloom profusely.
Lobelia
Deep blue, growing as a border in the porch box and the south end of the porch.
Galega
A good-sized plant. Leaves shaped like locust leaves grow up on each side of thin stems. The flowers are pea-shaped blossoms and grow rather loosely at the end of the stem. I pulled one apart and this is how it looked: tiny little blossoms are lavender-shaded lips back of tiny little white double globules. This plant grows in the bed at the north end of the porch.
Spanish Iris
Grows at the end of the bed on the west side of the front garden. The color is deep purple with a touch of yellow on each leaf. The flower petals turn backward. Sometimes called flag-shaped.
Madonna Lilies
White flowers. Five or more form a cluster at the end of a long stem. The stem is closely covered with dark green narrow leaves. The flower is white, tinged with deep pink on the outside and has a very heavy odor.
Yellow Day Lilies
Grow plentifully in borders. Orange in color and only last one day.
Sweet Peas
The leaf and flowers are shaped like the common garden variety. Grow well supported by stakes or fence. Need plenty of sun. Now growing on my porch in boxes supported by a fence.
Heuchera
A delicate, close-growing plant. Leaves grow close to the ground. Blossoms are many little coral-shaped, tiny, pink on the edges. Very delicate spindle stems.
Verbena
Blossoms made of many little florets. Grow massed together

in clump form. Colors are generally red, pink, and white.

Petunia

Straggly in growth is the plant. Flowers are more trumpet-shaped. Pink with white throats.

Salpiglossis

A beautiful, hardy annual. Slender on erect stems. Large funnel-shaped flower or blossoms. Dark veins on a ground from white to crimson and yellow. They are planted in the new bed.

Lobelias

Tiny blue flowers for border or mixed in on bare places. Protect in winter.

Large White Rose

Grows under the south bank by the steps.

Yellow Bankshire Rose

Climbs the wall under the pantry window.

In her final note about her profusion of plants, Nanny reminded her family that in the cellar wintering-over she has "two tubs of Rose Geranium, one Lemon Verbena, one Clevia, and about ten tubs of Agapanthii."

WORKS CITED

Abbott, Carl. "Portland: Civic Culture and Civic Opportunity." *Oregon Historical Quarterly* 102 (2001): 6–21.

Adams, Charles Francis Jr. *Notes on Railroad Accidents*. New York: G.P. Putnam's Sons, 1879.

Adelson, Warren, Jay E. Cantor, and William H. Gerdts. *Childe Hassam: Impressionist*. New York: Abbeville, Press, 1999.

"Albert Ehrgott Accuses Colonel E. Wood Publicly." [Portland] *Oregonian* 30 May 1919: 5.

Allen, Ethan. *The Garrison Church*. New York: James Pott & Company, 1898.

Ancestral Records and Portraits. vol. 2. Baltimore: Genealogical Publishing Company, 1969.

Barnes, Robert. *The Green Spring Valley: Its History and Heritage,* vol. 2. Baltimore: Maryland Historical Society, 1978.

Barrett, John G. *The Civil War in North Carolina*. Chapel Hill: University of North Carolina Press, 1963.

"Thomas Henry Barry." *The National Cyclopedia of American Biography,* vol. 21. New York: James T. White & Company, 1931.

Baxter, William P. Jr., Letter to the Author. 20 March 2001.

Beal, Merrill D. *"I Will Fight No More Forever": Chief Joseph and the Nez Perce War*. Seattle: University of Washington Press, 1963.

Beirne, Francis F. *The Amiable Baltimoreans*. New York: E.P. Dutton and Company, 1951.

Bingham, Edwin and Tim Barnes. *Wood Works: the Life and Writings of Charles Erskine Scott Wood*. Corvallis: Oregon State University Press, 1997.

The Biographical Cyclopedia of Representative Men of

Maryland and the District of Columbia. Baltimore: National Biographical Publishing Company, 1879.

Bird, Robert A. Letter to the Author. 28 May 2002.

"Charles Joseph Bonaparte," *The National Cyclopedia of American Biography*, vol. 14. New York: James T. White & Company, 1910.

Bowditch, Nancy Douglas. *George de Forest Brush: Recollections of a Joyous Painter*. Peterborough, NH: Noone House, 1970.

Bowen, Richard LeBaron. *Early Rehoboth*. Rehoboth, MA: Privately printed, 1946.

Bowman, John S., ed. *The World Almanac of the American West*. New York: Pharos Books, 1986.

Boyd, W. H. *Boyd's Business Directory*. Washington, DC: W. H. Boyd, 1879.

———. *City Directory*. Washington, DC: W. H. Boyd, 1879.

———. *Boyd's Washington and Georgetown Directory*. Washington, DC: Boyd & Waite Brothers, 1866.

Breen, Robert G. "Disputed First Baltimore Baby." *Baltimore Sun* 13 December 1957: 21.

"Brig. Gen. Edward Moale." *New York Times* 28 September 1913: 7.

"George de Forest Brush." *The National Cyclopedia of American Biography*, vol. 13. New York: James T. White & Company, 1906.

Brush, George de Forest. "American Artists on Gérôme." *Century Magazine* 37 (February 1889): 634–35.

———. "An Artist Among the Indians." *Century Magazine* 30 (May 1885): 54–57.

Buren, William P. "Oregon's Oldest Law Firm." *Oregon State Bar Bulletin* 45 (November 1984): 31–34.

Burke, Doreen Bolger. *J. Alden Weir: An American Impressionist*. Newark: University of Delaware Press, 1983.

Cadwalader, Helen. "Today Marks Birth Date of First Child Born Here." *Baltimore Sun* 29 April 1938: 32.

Caffin, Charles H. *American Masters of Sculpture*. Garden City, NY: Doubleday, Page & Company, 1913.

Caldwell, Mark. *Saranac Lake: Pioneer Health Resort*. Saranac Lake, NY: Historic Saranac Lake, 1993.

Child, Paul W. Jr. *Register of Graduates*. West Point, NY: United States Military Academy, 1990.

Child, William H. *History of the Town of Cornish, New Hampshire*, vol. 2. Concord, NH: The Rumford Press, 1911.

Clampitt, John W. "The Vigilantes of California, Idaho, and Montana." *Harper's New Monthly Magazine* 83 (August 1891): 442–51.

Code, J.B. "Elizabeth Bayley Seton." *The New Catholic Encyclopedia*, vol. 13. New York: McGraw-Hill, 1967.

Coffman, Edward M. *The Old Army: A Portrait of the American Army in Peacetime, 1784–1898*. New York: Oxford University Press, 1986.

Connell, Evan S. *Son of the Morning Star: Custer and the Little Bighorn*. New York: Harper & Row, 1984.

Conrad, Barnaby. *San Francisco*. New York: Bramhall House, 1959.

"Henry Winslow Corbett." *Dictionary of American Biography*, vol. 4. Eds. Allen Johnson and Dumas Malone. New York: Charles Scribner's Sons, 1930.

"Henry Winslow Corbett." *The National Cyclopedia of American Biography*, vol. 6. New York: James T. White & Company, 1929.

Craven, Wayne. *Sculpture in America*. New York: Thomas Y. Crowell Company, 1968.

Curtis, Walt. "Charles Erskine Scott Wood." *Multnomah Monthly* (September 1984): 8–12.

Cushing, Harvey. *The Life of Sir William Osler*. vol. 1. Oxford: The Clarendon Press, 1926.

Custer, George A. *My Life on the Plains*. Milo Milton Quaife, ed. Lincoln: University of Nebraska Press, 1952.

Danks, Holly. "An Affair to Remember." [Portland] *Oregonian* 16 January 1985: C1, C4.

Davis, George B., Leslie J. Perry, and Joseph W. Kirkley. *The War of the Rebellion* Series I, Part III, vol. 46. Washington:

Government Printing Office, 1894.

Davis, L.A. "Residents Leap into Torch Run." *Viera [Florida] Sun* 16 June 1996: n.p.

"The Death of Captain Louis McLane Hamilton." *New York Times* 6 December 1868: 11.

"Death of Mrs. Julietta Smith," *Baltimore Sun* 12 April 1883:1.

"Death of a Physician." *Baltimore Sun* 21 March 1860: 1.

"Death of Prof. N.R. Smith." *Baltimore Sun* 5 July 1877: 1.

Dobie, Charles Caldwell. *San Francisco: A Pageant*. New York: Appleton-Century Company, 1939.

Dodge, Matt. "The Vigilantes: Nebraska's Public Defenders." *Real West* 27 (October 1984): 10–15.

Doubleday, Abner. *Reminiscences of Forts Sumter and Moultrie in 1860–1861*. New York: Harper & Brothers, 1876.

Dupuy, R. Ernest, ed. *Governors Island: Its History and Development, 1637–1937*. New York: The Governors Island Club, 1937.

Eberlein, Harold Donaldson and Cortlandt Van Dyke Hubbard. *Historic Houses of Georgetown and Washington City*. Richmond, VA: The Dietz Press, 1958.

Emory, Mary Bourke. *Colonial Families and Their Descendants*. Baltimore: Press of the Sun Printing Office, 1900.

Evans, Clement A., ed. *Confederate Military History*, vol. 4. Atlanta: Confederate Publishing Company, 1899.

"Henry Failing." *The National Cyclopedia of American Biography*, vol. 34. New York: James T. White & Company, 1949.

"A Female Secessionist Flaunting Her Colors." *Harper's Weekly* 7 September 1861: 1.

"Fort Sumter." *Harper's Weekly* 26 January 1861: 53.

"John Gray Foster." *Dictionary of American Biography*, vol. 6. Allen Johnson & Dumas Malone, eds. New York: Charles Scribner's Sons, 1931.

"John Gray Foster." *Dictionary of Catholic Biography*. Garden City, NY: Doubleday & Company, Inc., 1961.

"John Gray Foster." *The National Cyclopedia of American Biography*, vol. 10. New York: James T. White & Company,

1909.

Foster, John Gray. "Recollections: Witnesses to History." *American History* 32 (October 1997): 58–59.

"John Gray Foster." *Webster's American Military Biographies.* Springfield, MA: G. & C. Merriam Company, 1978.

Frank Leslie's Illustrated Newspaper 19 January 1861: 1.

Friend, Melinda K. *J. Hall Pleasants Papers.* Manuscript 194. Baltimore: Maryland History Society, 1991.

Gard, Wayne. *Frontier Justice.* Norman: University of Oklahoma Press, 1949.

"John Gibbon." *Dictionary of American Biography*, vol. 7. New York : Charles Scribner's Sons, 1931.

"John Gibbon." *The National Cyclopedia of American Biography*, vol. 4. New York: James T. White & Company, 1897.

"John Gibbon." *Webster's American Military Biographies.* Springfield, MA: G. & C. Merriam Company, 1978.

Goodrich, Lloyd. *Albert P. Ryder.* New York: George Braziller, Inc., 1959.

"George Gould." *The National Cyclopedia of American Biography*, vol. 2. New York: James T. White & Company, 1921.

Gould, Tracy. *The Bride of the Broken Vow: A Poem in Four Parts.* Troy, NY: William H. Young & Blake, 1874.

Groseclose, Barbara. *Nineteenth-Century American Art.* New York: Oxford University Press, 2000.

Hamburger, Robert. *Two Rooms: The Life of Charles Erskine Scott Wood.* Lincoln: University of Nebraska Press, 1998.

Harper's Weekly. 10 February 1861: 6.

Hartwell, Barbara Bartlett. *The Wood Household.* Portland: Portland Art Association, 1942.

"(Frederick) Childe Hassam." *The National Cyclopedia of American Biography*, vol. 10. New York: James T. White & Company, 1909.

Hayward, Oliver S. and Constance E. Putnam. *Improve, Perfect, and Perpetuate: Dr. Nathan Smith and Early American Medical Education.* Hanover, NH: University Press of New

England, 1998.
Hendrickson, Robert. *Hamilton: 1789-1804*. New York: Mason/Charter, 1976.
———. *Sumter: The First Day of the Civil War*. New York: Promontory Press, 1990.
Hiesinger, Ulrich W. *Childe Hassam: American Impressionist*. New York: Prestel, 1994.
History of the Bench and Bar of Oregon. Portland: Historical Publishing Company, 1910.
Hoeltje, Hubert. "When Mark Twain Spoke in Portland." *Oregon Historical Quarterly* 55 (1954): 71-81.
Hoopes, Donelson F. *Childe Hassam*. New York: Watson-Guptill Publications, 1979.
"Ills of Car-Drivers." *New York Times* 26 January 1879: 5.
Johnson, Bradley T. "Maryland." in *Confederate Military History*, vol. 2. Atlanta: Confederate Publishing Company, 1899.
Jones, Catherine. "Wood Makes Museum Gift: Five Works of Art to Honor Wife." [Portland] *Oregonian* 30 May 1943: sec. 3, p. 5.
"Joseph Eggleston Johnston." *The National Cyclopedia of American Biography*, vol. 5. New York: James T. White & Company, 1907.
Kerr, W.M. "William Maxwell Wood: the First Surgeon-General of the United States Navy." *Annals of Military History* 6 (1924): 387-425.
Kipling, Rudyard. *From Sea to Sea: Letters of Travel* vol. 2. New York: Doubleday & McClure Company, 1899. 2 vols.
Klooster, Karl. "The Woods: A Portland Family." [Portland] *This Week* 10 August 1986: 2.
"William Mead Ladd." *The National Cyclopedia of American Biography*, vol. 24. New York: James T. White & Company, 1934.
"William Sargent Ladd." *The National Cyclopedia of American Biography*, vol. 7. New York: James T. White & Company, 1897.
Leeson, Fred. *Rose City Justice: A Legal History of Portland,*

Oregon. Portland: Oregon Historical Society Press, 1998.
Leon, Philip W. *Mark Twain and West Point*. Toronto: ECW Press, 1996.
"G. Gould Lincoln, 94, Political Reporter." *New York Times* 2 December 1974: 36.
"G(eorge) Gould Lincoln." *Contemporary Authors*, vol. 113. Detroit: Gale Research Company, 1985.
"Natalie S. Lincoln, Author, Is Dead." *New York Times* 1 September 1935: 18.
"Natalie Sumner Lincoln." *Who Was Who in America*, vol. 1. Chicago: The A.N. Marquis Company, 1942.
"Nathan Smith Lincoln." *The National Cyclopedia of American Biography*, vol. 3. New York: James T. White & Company, 1893.
"Sumner H. Lincoln." *Who Was Who in America*, vol. 1. Chicago: A.N. Marquis Co., 1942.
Livingston, Katherine Smith. Letter to the Author. 23 March 2002.
MacColl, E. Kimbark. *The Growth of a City; Power and Politics in Portland, Oregon, 1915 to 1950*. Portland: The Georgian Press, 1979.
———. *Merchants, Money and Power: The Portland Establishment, 1843–1913*. Portland: The Georgian Press, 1988.
MacMahon, Edward B. and Leonard Curry. *Medical Cover-Ups in the White House*. Washington, DC: Farragut Publishing Company, 1987.
"Louis McLane." Biography File. Sacramento: California State Library, 1952.
Marszalek, John F., ed. *The Diary of Miss Emma Holmes, 1861–1866*. Baton Rouge: Louisiana State University Press, 1979.
Mendelowitz, Daniel M. *A History of American Art*. New York: Holt, Rinehart and Winston, Inc., 1964.
Meredith, Roy. *Storm Over Sumter*. New York: Simon and Schuster, 1957.
"Edward Moale." *Who Was Who in America*, vol. 1. Chicago: The A.N. Marquis Company, 1942.

"E.S. Moale, Retired Navy Commander, Dies." [Charleston, SC] *Evening Post* 31 December 1985: 15-A.

Moale, John Foster Gray II. Letter to the Author. 3 May 2002.

"More Arrests at Baltimore," *Harper's Weekly* 6 July 1861: 435.

Morgan, Joan B. *George de Forest Brush, 1855–1941; Master of the American Renaissance.* New York: Berry–Hill Galleries, Inc., 1985.

Morison, Samuel Eliot and Henry Steele Commager. *The Growth of the American Republic*, vol. 1. New York: Oxford University Press, 1962.

Moses, Norton H. *Lynching and Vigilantism in the United States: An Annotated Bibliography.* Westport, CT: Greenwood Press, 1997.

"Mrs. C.E.S. Wood." [Portland] *Oregonian* 19 December 1933: 9.

"Mrs. Jeanie Gould Lincoln." *Book Review Digest*, vol. 2. Minneapolis: The H.W. Wilson Company, 1906.

Munroe, John A. *Louis McLane: Federalist and Jacksonian.* New Brunswick, NJ: Rutgers University Press, 1973.

Nacy, Michele J. *Members of the Regiment: Army Officers' Wives on the Western Frontier, 1865–1890.* Westport, CT: Greenwood Press, 2000.

Nolan, Edward W. *Northern Pacific Views: The Railroad Photography of F. Jay Haynes, 1876–1905.* Helena: Montana Historical Society Press, 1983.

"Not Worried by Seattle Critics." [Portland] *Oregonian* 3 July 1907: 11.

"A Noted Army Officer Dead." *Baltimore Sun* 7 September 1904: 10.

O'Brien, Robert. *This Is San Francisco.* New York: McGraw-Hill, 1948.

Osler, William. *Aequanimitas.* Philadelphia: P. Blakiston's Son & Company, 1932.

Pease, Jane H. and William H. Pease. *Ladies, Women, and Wenches.* Chapel Hill: University of North Carolina Press, 1990.

Portland City Directory. Portland: R.L. Polk & Company, 1885.
Portland City Directory. Portland: R.L. Polk & Company, 1886.
Portland City Directory. Portland: R.L. Polk & Company, 1891.
Portland City Directory. Portland: R.L. Polk & Company, 1896.
The Portland Society Annual, 1914-15. Portland: Lawson & Company, 1914.
"A Portrait by Joshua Johnston." *Bulletin of the Municipal Museum of the City of Baltimore* 11(December 1941): 2.
Proctor, Alexander Phimister. *Sculptor in Buckskin.* Norman: University of Oklahoma Press, 1971.
Providence Centennial Book, 1861-1961. Washington, DC: Providence Hospital, 1961.
Quinan, John R. *Medical Annals of Baltimore.* Baltimore: Press of Isaac Friedenwald, 1884.
Resch, Andreas. *Gerda Walther.* Innsbruck, Austria: Resch Verlag, 1983.
Richards, Suzanne. "Historic Wedding Gown on Display." [Portland] *Journal* 12 March 1971: sec. 2, p. 1.
Richardson, E.P. *Painting in America.* New York: Thomas Y. Crowell Company, 1956.
Riley, Glenda. "Sara Bard Field, Charles Erskine Scott Wood, and the Phenomenon of Migratory Divorce." *California History* 69 (Fall 1990): 251-59.
Roberts, Gary Boyd. "Notable Kin." *New England Historic Genealogical Society Nexus* 4 (1987): 24-28.
Roberts, Prudence F. "Shaping a Collection: C.E.S. Wood and Portland's Early Art Scene," Portland Art Museum, n.d.
Roos, Charles A. "Physicians to the Presidents, and Their Patients: A Bibliography." *Bulletin of the Medical Library Association* 49 (1961): 291-360.
Rose, Mary. "Foreword." *Days with Chief Joseph* by Erskine Wood. Vancouver: Rose Wind Press, 1991.
———. "150 Years at Vancouver Barracks: Life of an Army Wife."
The [Vancouver] Columbian 28 March 1999: D7.
"A Ruffian's Career Checked." *The New York Times* 14 January 1879: 1.

Ruffner, Kevin Conley. *Maryland's Blue and Gray*. Baton Rouge: Louisiana State University Press, 1997.

Saint-Gaudens, Augustus. *The Reminiscences of Augustus Saint-Gaudens*, vol. 2. London: Andrew Melrose, 1913.

"Sawtelle," *New York Times* 5 January 1913: 17.

"Charles Greene Sawtelle." *The National Cyclopedia of American Biography*, vol. 28. New York: James T. White & Company, 1940.

Schultz, James Willard. *My Life as an Indian: The Story of a Red Woman and a White Man in the Lodges of the Blackfeet*. New York: Doubleday, Page & Company, 1907.

Scott, Robert N., ed. *The War of the Rebellion* Series I, Part II, vol. 11. Washington: Government Printing Office, 1884.

———. *The War of the Rebellion* Series I, Part I, vol. 12. Washington: Government Printing Office, 1885.

———. *The War of the Rebellion* Series I, Part II, vol. 19. Washington: Government Printing Office, 1887.

"Sedition Laws Invalid, C.E.S. Wood Asserts." [Portland] *Oregonian* 7 June 1919: 1.

"Major Henry Seton." *New York Times* 7 September 1904: 7.

Siepel, Kevin H. *Rebel: The Life and Times of John Singleton Mosby*. New York: St. Martin's Press, 1983.

"Fred Winchester Sladen." *The National Cyclopedia of American Biography*, vol. 34. New York: James T. White & Company, 1948.

"Alan Penneman Smith." *The National Cyclopedia of American Biography*. vol. 3. New York: James T. White & Company, 1893.

Smith, Edmund Banks. *Governors Island: Its Military History Under Three Flags, 1637–1922*. New York: Valentine's Manual Inc., 1923.

Snoddy, Don D. Letter to the Author, 2 January 2001.

———. Letter to the Author, 9 January 2001.

Snyder, Eugene E. *Portland Names and Neighborhoods: Their Historic Origins*. Portland: Binford & Mort, 1979.

Stout, Sally Reed. *St. Helen's Hall: The First Century, 1869–1969*. Portland: St. Helen's Hall, 1969.

Strickler, Susan. "The Paintings of Edmund C. Tarbell." *American Art Review* 13 (October 2001): 172–81, 223.
"Successful Launching of the United States Torpedo Boat *Rowan*." *The Seattle Post-Intelligencer* 9 April 1898: 16.
Swanberg, W.A. *First Blood: The Story of Fort Sumter.* New York: Charles Scribner's Sons, 1957.
Sweetman, Jack. *American Naval History*, 2nd ed. Annapolis, MD: Naval Institute Press, 1991.
Symonds, Craig L. *Joseph E. Johnston: A Civil War Biography.* New York: W.W. Norton & Company, 1992.
Tharp, Louise Hall. *Saint-Gaudens and the Gilded Era.* Boston: Little, Brown and Company, 1969.
"Samuel Theobald." *The Cyclopedia of American Biography.* vol. 24. New York: James T. White & Company, 1935.
Thirty-Five Year Book. West Point: United States Military Academy, 1950.
Thomas, Dawn. *The Green Spring Valley: Its History and Heritage*, vol. 1 Baltimore: Maryland Historical Society, 1978.
Thomas, Gordon and Max Morgan Witts. *The San Francisco Earthquake.* New York: Stein and Day, 1971.
Thompson, Courtenay. "After 104 Years, Family's Gift Fulfills Chief Joseph's Request." [Portland] *Oregonian* 27 July 1997: C1, C5.
Thrapp, Dan L. *Encyclopedia of Frontier Biography*, vol. 2. Spokane, WA: The Arthur H. Clark Company, 1990.
"Louis McLane Tiffany." *Dictionary of American Biography.* Dumas Malone, ed. New York: Charles Scribner's Sons, 1936.
Toole, Gasper Loren II. *Ninety Years in Aiken County.* Charleston, SC: Walker, Evans, and Cogswell, 1958.
Townshend, Smith, Charles B. Purvis, Nathan S. Lincoln, and Philip S. Wales. "President Garfield's Wound and Its Treatment." *Walsh's Retrospect* 2 (1881): 623-33.
Trudeau, Edward Livingston. *An Autobiography.* Garden City, NY: Doubleday Page & Company, 1916.
"Edward Livingston Trudeau." *The National Cyclopedia of*

American Biography, vol. 13. New York: James T. White & Company, 1906.

Twain, Mark. *[Date, 1601.] Conversation as it was by the Social Fireside, in the Time of the Tudors.* Franklin J. Meine, ed. Mattituck, NY: Amereon House, 1938.

Utley, Robert M. *Frontier Regulars: The United States Army and the Indian, 1866–1891.* New York: MacMillan Publishing Co., Inc., 1973.

———. *Life in Custer's Cavalry.* New Haven, CT: Yale University Press, 1977.

Vadeboncoeur, Jim. Letter to the Author. 15 April 2002.

Van Dyke, John C. "George de Forest Brush's *Mother and Child.*" *Century Magazine* 51 (April 1886): 954–55.

Warner, Ezra J. *Generals in Blue: Lives of the Union Commanders.* Baton Rouge: Louisiana State University Press, 1964.

"Olin Levi Warner." *The National Cyclopedia of American Biography,* vol. 8 New York: James T. White & Company, 1924.

Warren, Sidney. *Farthest Frontier: The Pacific Northwest.* Port Washington, NY: Kennikat Press, 1970.

Washburne, Kitty. Letter to the Author. 20 September 2001.

Wecter, Dixon. *Mark Twain in Three Moods.* San Marino, CA: Friends of the Huntington Library, 1948.

Welsh, Luther W. *Ancestral Colonial Families: Genealogy of the Welsh and Hyatt Families of Maryland and Their Kin.* Independence, MO: Lambert Moon Printing Company, 1928.

Wensyel, James W. *Appomatox: the Passing of the Armies.* Shippensburg, PA: White Mane Books, 2000.

White, Frank F. Jr. *The Governors of Maryland, 1777–1970.* Annapolis: State of Maryland, 1970.

Winther, Oscar Osburn. *The Great Northwest: A History.* New York: Alfred A. Knopf, 1948.

Wilcox, Arthur M. and Warren Ripley. *The Civil War at Charleston.* Charleston, SC: The Post and Courier, 2000.

"Women of the South Resent Remarks." [Portland] *Oregonian*

28 December 1907: 7.
Wood, Charles Erskine Scott. "The Surrender of Chief Joseph." *Harper's Weekly* 17 November 1877: 905–6.
Wood, Erskine. *Days with Chief Joseph.* Vancouver, WA: Rose Wind Press, 1991.
———. *Life of Charles Erskine Scott Wood.* Vancouver, WA: Rose Wind Press, 1991.
"Wood Denounces Y.M.C.A. Directors." [Portland] *Oregonian* 25 May 1908: 12.
"Wood Is Anarchist." [Portland] *Oregonian* 29 November 1909: 14.
Wright, Steven J. "This Miserable War: The Civil War Letters of General John Gibbon." *Loyal Legion Historical Journal* 45 (Winter 1989): 1, 5–6.
Young, Dorothy Weir. *The Life and Letters of J. Alden Weir.* New Haven: Yale University Press, 1960.

INDEX

Adams, Ansel, 211
Adirondack Mountains, 118–19
Aiken, S.C, 26–27
Alaska, 60–61, 134
American Art Association, 195
Anderson, Robert, 4, 5, 6
Appomattox Court House, 172–73
Atamasco. *See* Green Spring Valley
Ayer, Daisy, 105, 137, 202, 216
Ayer, Winslow B., 105, 216; creates public library system in Portland, 106; donates Proctor bas-relief, 200; donates Ryder painting, 202

Baltimore and Ohio Railroad Company, 71, 163, 164
Bank of Maryland, 161
Barnett, Charles Ridgly, 105
Barry, Thomas J., 120
Beauregard, Pierre G. T., 72
Beck, Kathryn ("Kitty") Seaman, 105, 129, 134, 135, 137, 145; commits suicide, 146
Berlin, Ellin Travers Mckay, 162
Berlin, Irving, 162
Boise Barracks, Idaho, 96, 97
Bonaparte, Jerome, 45–46
Bonaparte, Jerome, Jr., 46
Bowdoin College, 25, 184
Bradley, Omar, 176

Brush, George de Forest, 194, 207–9. Works: *The Indian Hunter*, 208; *The Indian and the Lily*, 208; *Mother and Child*, 209; *Mourning Her Brave*, 208; *Out of the Silence*, 208; *The Sculptor and the King*, 208; *The Silence Broken*, 208
Burke, Frances, 135
Burnside, Ambrose E., 171

Caldwell, Catherine ("Kay") Ehrgott, 137, 139–140, 144, 211
Catholicism, 171; Wood's objection to, 54–55, 139
Central Pacific Railroad, 63
Charleston, 3, 4; meeting of National Democratic Party in, 5
Chief Joseph. *See* Joseph, Chief
Citadel, The, 11
Clemens, Samuel L. *See* Twain, Mark
Cleveland, Grover, 167, 173
Colorado Springs, 114
Columbia University, 94, 96
Corbett, Helen Ladd, 108, 117, 125, 129, 134, 141–42, 198, 206
Corbett, Henry J., 130
Corbett, Henry W., 130, 148, 216
Curzon, Elizabeth Moale, 73, 161

Curson, Ellin Moale, 161; marries Samuel T. Poultney, 162
Curson, Richard, Sr., 161; serves as privateer, 161
Curson, Samuel, 162; dies in duel, 162
Curzon (Curson), Richard, Jr., 73, 161; marries Elizabeth Moale, 161
Custer, George A., 18, 62, 166–67

Darrow, Clarence: introduces Wood and Sara Field, 134
Dartmouth College, 25, 184
Davis, Jefferson C., 4, 61
Doubleday, Abner, 4, 12, 18

École des Beaux-Arts, 195, 207, 210
Edgerton, Wright Prescott, 52, 58
Ehrgott, Albert, 134; blames Wood for son's death, 140–41
Ehrgott, Albert, Jr., 139; death of, 140
Ehrgott, Sara Bard Field. *See* Field, Sarah
Eisenhower, Dwight D., 176
Ellicott, William M., 161
Emmanuel Protestant Episcopal Church, 58
Equi, Marie D., 133, 149
Espionage Law, 133

Failing, Henry, 103, 148, 216; purchases Brush painting, 209
Failing, Mary Forbush, 209
Field, Sara Bard, 134, 210, 211; attempts suicide, 143; death of, 149; miscarries Wood's child, 135; moves with Wood to Los Gatos, 143; obtains migratory divorce, 136–37
Fort Bidwell, Calif., 43, 50
Fort Canby, Wash. Terr., 104, 105
Fort Moultrie, S.C., 3, 4, 5, 6, 21, 169
Fort Snelling, Minn., 58, 61, 63, 67
Fort Stevens, Oreg., 104
Fort Sumter, S.C., 4, 5, 6, 21, 169
Foster, John Gray (uncle), 3, 12, 14, 18–21, 30, 33, 37, 39, 42, 55, 61, 163, 169, 171; converts to Catholicism, 170; marries Nannie Davis, 31
Foster, Mary (aunt), 3, 13, 17, 19, 163; death of, 30
Foster, Nannie Davis (cousin), 31, 42–43, 170
Franklin, Benjamin, 161, 168
Fremont, John C. 71, 166

Garfield, James A., 189–90
Geary, William Logan, 106
Gibbon, Fanny (cousin), 13, 16, 33, 58
Gibbon, Frances North Moale (aunt), 171
Gibbon, John (uncle), 12, 39, 55, 58, 61, 105, 171, 172; at Appomattox Court House, 172–73; and Chief Joseph, 172; and Custer, 172; marries Frances North Moale, 163
"God Bless America" (Berlin), 162

INDEX

Goldman, Emma, 132, 149
Gould, George, 48
Gould, Sarah McCoun, 42–43, 47–50
Gould, Tracy, 43–44, 48
Grant, Ulysses S., 37, 75, 168
Green Spring Valley, Md., 13, 34–37, 43, 46, 52, 53, 57, 160, 169; and the Civil War, 164
Guiteau, Charles, 189

Hall, Adelia, 14
Hall, Norman J., 7, 171
Hamilton Alexander, 46, 166
Hamilton, Allan McLane, 166, 190
Hamilton, Louis McLane, 166; death of, 167
Hamilton, Philip, 166
Hamilton, Rebecca Wells McLane, 166
Hanley, William, 135, 199
Hartwell, Barbara B., 150
Hassam, F. Childe, 96, 194, 202–7, 218; and alcohol, 204; visits Portland, 203. Works: *Afternoon Sky, Harney Desert*, 204; *April Showers*, 203; *Columbus Avenue, Boston, Rainy Day*, 203; *Isles of Shoals*, 204; *Mount Hood*, 204; *New England Road*, 204; *On the Snake River, Oregon*, 205; *Still Life*, 204; *Still Life, Fruits*, 204; *Street Scene in Winter*, 203; *Study for Bathers*, 204
Hayes, Rutherford B., 75
Hill, Ambrose P., 171
Holmes, Oliver Wendell, Jr., 172

Honeyman, Nan Wood, 88, 101, 105, 111–12, 134, 142, 144, 147; birth at West Point, 94; wedding of, 222
Howard, Oliver Otis, 61, 72, 74, 77, 81, 89, 97, 107, 120, 168, 194
Hume, Lillie Brush, 207
Hume, Hugh: *The Portland Spectator*, 207

Jackson, Andrew, 70, 165
Jefferson, Thomas, 161, 163
Jefferson Medical College, 186
Johns Hopkins University, 60, 185, 188
Johnston, Joseph E. 167, 169; death of, 168; marries Lydia McLane, 168
Joseph, Chief, 62, 85, 97, 172; and Erskine Wood, 109–11; visits Nanny's home, 107–8

Kellogg, John Harvey, 118
Key, Francis Scott, 104, 162
Kipling, Rudyard: praises Portland, 102
Klecan, Janina, 137, 138, 146; commits suicide, 143; performs abortion on Sara Field, 138
Kolisch, Marian Wood (granddaughter), 211

Ladd, Caroline Pratt, 206
Ladd, Charles E., 206
Ladd, William S., 130, 148, 197, 197
Lanier, Mary Smith, 14
Latrobe, Benjamin Henry, 45
Lazard Freres, 136, 138
Lee, George Washington Custis, 76

Lee, Robert E., 13, 168, 171
Lee, Samuel P., 13
Lee, William R., 172
Lewis, Cicero H., 103
Lewis, Emma, 104
Lincoln, Abraham, 5, 13, 15, 26–28, 30, 166, 167, 189
Lincoln, Ann Moale Smith (mother), 3, 4, 8, 17, 19, 163; illness and death of, 27–28
Lincoln, George Gould, 95
Lincoln, Gracia Eliza, 25
Lincoln, Increase Sumner, 25
Lincoln, Jeanie Gould, 42, 47–51, 55, 68, 94, 95, 96
Lincoln, Natalie Sumner, 95–96
Lincoln, Nathan Smith (stepfather), 25, 26, 37, 42, 44–45, 47–50, 53, 55, 57, 59, 68, 94, 95, 171, 188; and President Arthur, 190; and President Garfield, 189
Lincoln, Robert Todd, 89, 189
Lincoln, Sumner H., 25
Linthicum, Abner, 104
Linthicum, J. Charles, 104
Linthicum, Marie Louise, 104, 106
Linthicum, Stewart B., 104, 105, 106, 162
Livingston, Katherine S. (granddaughter), 110, 147
Lynching, 65–66

Marshall, George C., 58
Maryland Club, 67
Maryland, University of, 60, 186, 190
McClellan, George, 19
McDowell, Irvin, 72, 171
McLane, Allen, 165; serves with Washington, 165
McLane, Louis, Sr., 70, 165; fights duel, 165; marries Catherine Milligan, 166
McLane, Louis, Jr., 69, 70, 165; and the Nevada Bank of San Francisco, 71; serves in Mexico, 166; and the Wells Fargo Bank, 71
McLane, Robert Milligan, 167
Menuhin, Yehudi, 211
Merrill, Elijah, 104
Mexican War, 18, 166, 169
Mexico City, 114, 168
Miles, Nelson A., 89, 97, 120
Moale, Ann G. White (grandmother), 12, 13, 14, 17, 163
Moale, Edward (uncle), 3, 7, 12, 13, 15, 16, 72, 163, 166; at Appomattox Court House, 173; commands The Presidio, 174; and Custer, 174; death of, 175; at Fort Moultrie, 3–6; at Fort Sumter, 6–12; marries Jeannie Wilson, 174; pursues Crazy Horse, 174
Moale, Edward, Jr., 175; marries Adria Maud Semple, 175
Moale, Edward Semple, 176; dismissed from West Point, 176
Moale, Elizabeth Jean Ellin, 177
Moale, Ellin North (great-grandmother), 160
Moale, Henry, 163
Moale, Jean Ann, 177
Moale, John (great-great-grand-father), 159
Moale, John, Jr. (great-grand-

INDEX

father), 159; marries Ellin North, 159
Moale, John Gray Foster, 176
Moale, John Gray Foster II, 177
Moale, John Gray Foster III, 177
Moale, John Gray Foster IV, 177
Moale, Samuel Howard, 36, 73
Moale, Samuel O. (grandfather), 162; fights duel, 162; serves in militia, 162
Momaday, N. Scott, 111
Montgomery, Ellen Moale (aunt), 14
Morse, Samuel F.B., 184, 195

Napoleon I, 45–46
National Academy of Design, 201, 202, 207
New Bern, N.C.: battle of, 18–19
Nez Perce Indians, 61, 172
Nicholas, Augusta Moale (aunt), 12, 34, 45
Nicholas, George S., 175
Nicholas, Wilson C. II (uncle), 12, 45–46, 175; serves in the Confederacy, 163–64
Nordrach (Germany), 119–23
North, Robert, 159
Northern Pacific Railroad, 63

Oregon Historical Society, 59, 107
Oregon State University, 10
Oregon, University of, 200
Osler, William, 188; praises Nathan Smith, 185; praises Nathan R. Smith, 187

Paine, Sumner, 172

Paine, Thomas, 172
Palace Hotel (San Francisco), 70
Patterson, Carlile Pollock, 45
Patterson, Daniel Todd, 45
Patterson Elizabeth ("Betsy"), 45–46, 163. *See also* Bonaparte, Jerome
Patterson, Elizabeth ("Eliza"), 45, 50, 69
Patterson, Hallie, 45–46, 50
Patterson, John, 45, 163
Patterson, William, 45, 16
Penniman, Jabez, 186
Pickett, George Edward, 171
Pierce, Franklin, 167
Pleasants, Elizabeth Moale Poultney, 159
Pleasants, J. Hall, 160
Pleasants, Richard Hall, 30
Plymouth Colony, 183
Polk, James K., 165–66
Portland, Oreg., 60, 74, 98, 101–50
Portland Art Museum, 108, 149, 150, 197, 199, 215
Portland Garden Club, 111
Poultney, Ellin Moale Curzon, 73, 159
Poultney, Elizabeth Moale, 30
Poultney, Evan Thomas, 161
Poultney, Philip, 161
Poultney, Samuel Thomas, 73, 160, 162; marries Ellin Moale Curson, 161
Poultney, Thomas, 160
Poultney, Walter de Curzon, 73
Pratt, Frederick B., 130
Presidio, The, 72, 174
Proctor, Alexander Phimister, 198–201, 209, 218. Works: *The Circuit Rider*, 200; *General Robert E. Lee and*

Young Soldier, 200; Indian on Horseback, 199; Lions, 200; Pioneer, 200; Pioneer Mother, 200; Princeton Tigers, 200; Rough Rider (Theodore Roosevelt), 199; Sentinel Lions, 200; Stalking Panther (Cougar), 200; Standing Pumas, 200
Providence Hospital (Washington, D.C.), 26

Ramp, Floyd, 133
Randolph, Alfred Macgill, 58
Rehoboth, Mass., 183
Revere, Paul III, 172
Revolutionary War, 6, 160, 163, 184
Roman Catholic Church. See Catholicism
Ryder, Albert Pinkham, 96, 194, 196, 201–2. Works: *The Equestrian*, 202; *Mother and Child*, 202

Saint-Gaudens, Augustus, 195–96, 200–201, 209
St. Helen's Hall School, 112
St. Thomas' Episcopal Church, 34, 35, 58; and Louis Comfort Tiffany, 169
San Francisco, 68–70, 138, 139, 141
Sanger, Margaret, 132–33, 149–50
Sawtelle, Alice, 76, 81
Sawtelle, Charles Greene, 76, 81
Scott, John White, 13
Scott, Winfield, 11, 168, 169
Seton, Annie Foster (cousin), 3, 4, 17, 19, 31, 117, 170
Seton, Elizabeth Ann: first American-born saint, 170–71
Seton, William Henry, 117
Sheridan, Philip, 167
Sherman, William Tecumseh, 89, 168, 170, 201
Skidmore Fountain (Warner), 107, 196, 197
Sladen, Fred W., 78
Sladen, Joseph Alton, 78, 81
Smith, Alan Penneman (uncle), 60, 188
Smith, Berwick Bruce (father), 3, 13, 25, 57, 60, 163; death of, 187
Smith, Daniel (great-great grandfather), 183–84
Smith, Eliza ("Lisa") Bryson Wood (daughter), 106, 111–12, 123, 134, 144, 147, 148, 222
Smith, Emily (aunt), 60
Smith, Julietta Octavia Penniman (grandmother), 12, 57, 86
Smith, Nathan (great-grandfather), 25; apprentices with Dr. Goodhue, 184; becomes professor of medicine at Yale, 185; joins Vermont militia, 184; practices medi-cine in Cornish, N.H., 184; receives M.B. degree from Harvard, 184; studies abroad, 184
Smith, Nathan R. (grandfather), 12, 13, 57, 163, 168; becomes professor at Jefferson Medical College, 186; becomes professor at University of Maryland, 186; death of, 187; studies at Dartmouth, 186; studies at Yale, 186

INDEX

Smith, Nathan R., Jr. (uncle), 187
Smith, Walter (uncle), 12; death of, 188
Society of American Artists, 195, 201, 202
Star of the West, 11–12, 20
"Star Spangled Banner" (Key), 104, 162
Steffens, Lincoln, 211
Steinbeck, John, 211
Stuart, J.E.B., 76
Sullivan's Island, S.C., 5
Symons, Thomas William, 77, 104

Taylor, Charles H., 60, 62
Taylor, Zachary, 190
Ten American Painters, 203
Theobald, Elisha Warfield, Sr. (uncle), 14, 186
Theobald, Elisha Warfield, Jr. (cousin), 186
Theobald, Samuel (cousin), 119, 186
Theobald, Sarah Francis Smith (aunt), 14, 186
Tiffany, Henry, 168; marries Sallie Jones McLane, 168
Tiffany, Louis Comfort (cousin), 168–69, 195
Tiffany, Louis McLane (cousin), 168
Tilton, Charles E., 130
Trudeau, Edward Livingston, 118–19
Twain, Mark, 88–94, 210; visits Portland, 131
Twichell, Joseph, 88, 91–92

Union Bank of Maryland, 161
Union Pacific Railroad, 63–64
United Daughters of the Confederacy, 132

Vancouver, Wash., 148
Vancouver Barracks, Wash., 58, 60, 63, 72, 73–81, 86, 87, 89, 97, 101, 171
Vermont, University of, 25, 185

Walther, Gerda, 123–25; arrested by Gestapo, 124; corresponds with Wood, 124
Walther, Otto, 121–24
Warner, Olin, 107, 108, 194, 195–98. Works: *Diana*, 209; *J. Alden Weir*, 209; *The Skidmore Fountain*, 107, 196–97
Washington, George, 163, 165
Washington, University of, 131
Weir, J. Alden, 96, 137, 194, 202, 205–7. Works: *Albert Pinkham Ryder*, 209; *The Black Hat*, 206; *Childe Hassam*, 209; *Flower Piece*, 206; *The Ice Cutters*, 206; *Olin Levi Warner*, 209; *Portrait of C.E.S. Wood*, 206; *Portrait of Erskine Wood*, 206; *The Spreading Oak*, 206
Weir, Robert, 194
West Point, 33, 37–42, 78, 81, 85–98, 149, 171, 176
Willamette Valley & Cascade Mountain Wagon Road Land Grant, 136, 139
Williams, Wood & Linthicum law firm, 104
Wilson, Holt, 106, 114
Wood, Berwick Bruce (son), 106, 144, 148, 223; and World War One, 140

Wood, Charles Erskine Scott (husband), 33, 34; angers religious leaders, 131; angers United Daughters of the Confederacy, 132; begins affair with Frances Burke, 135; begins affair with Janina Klecan, 137; begins affair with Sara Field, 135; begins law career, 101; and civic projects, 102; death of, 149; declares himself an anarchist, 132; defends Floyd Ramp, 134; defends Margaret Sanger, 132–33; defends Marie Equi, 133; entertains famous visitors, 149; marries Sara Field, 148–49; opposes Roman Catholicism, 54–55, 58; resigns army commission, 98; and the Wagon Road Land Grant, 136, 139

Wood, Erskine (son), 101, 105, 144, 150, 221, 223; stays with Chief Joseph, 109–11, 112; prolonged illness of, 117–25; and World War One, 140

Wood, Hannah (sister-in-law), 94

Wood, James M. (brother-in-law), 137, 148

Wood, John Gibbon (grandson), 107

Wood, Katherine Gordon (daughter), 113

Wood, Kirkham Berwick (great-grandson), 191

Wood, Mary C. (great-granddaughter), 110

Wood, Nanny Moale Smith: accompanies Erskine to Germany, 120–25; and Alexander Phimister Proctor, 198–201; arrives at Vancouver Barracks, 74–81; death of her mother, 27; entertains Chief Joseph, 107–8; entertains Childe Hassam, 202–5; entertains Mark Twain, 88–91; entertains Olin L. Warner, 195–99; at Fort Sumter, 3–12; honeymoon of, 60–67; introduces Foster to Nannie Davis, 31; lives at West Point, 85–98; marries Wood, 57; meets Wood, 34; meets Tracy Gould, 43; in Mexico City, 114–16; moves to Portland, 101; moves to Washington, D.C., 25–26; at New Bern, 17–21; and Portland garden, 225–34; as Portland's grande dame, 215–24; in San Francisco, 67–74; visits West Point, 39; witnesses a lynching, 65–67

Wood, Peter Bryson (brother-in-law), 96, 117

Wood, Rebecca ("Becky") Biddle (daughter-in-law), 37, 144, 145, 216, 223; praises Nanny, 142

Wood, Roberta ("Berta") (sister-in-law), 94

Wood, William Maxwell (father-in-law), 34, 53; treats President Taylor, 190

Wood, William Maxwell III (son), 101, 105, 123, 137, 148, 223; death of, 143; and scarlet fever, 113

Wood, William Maxwell IV (grandson), 204

INDEX

Woodhull, Alfred A., 69; pronounces Nanny pregnant, 74
Worth, Charles, 59
World War One, 140
Wounded Knee, Battle of, 62

Yale University, 25, 184

ABOUT THE AUTHOR

PHILIP W. LEON is a professor of American literature at The Citadel where he has taught for twenty-eight years. A graduate of Wake Forest University, he holds the Ph.D. in English from Vanderbilt University. He has published books on William Styron, the Pulitzer Prize-winning novelist; Walt Whitman; Mark Twain; and on a hazing scandal that occurred at West Point at the turn of the century. He presented the results of his research on Nanny Wood's great-grandfather, Dr. Nathan Smith, at the Royal College of Physicians, Edinburgh, Scotland.

www.ingramcontent.com/pod-product-compliance
Lightning Source LLC
Chambersburg PA
CBHW060557230426
43670CB00011B/1855